## Critical Acclaim for other books in the How It Works Series

### *How Networks Work*

"Succinctly described and beautifully illustrated..."

**—Eric Cohe ... al**

### *How to Use Your Computer*

"Every so often a wonderful book appears...This is one."
"...a truly beautiful book comes along that you want to show to anyone you can. Lisa Biow neither insults your intelligence nor assumes that information about computers is hard to grasp. Her explanations are clear and the book is fun to read. And the pictures...are beautiful."

**—Barbara Berger, Pasco Area Computer Users Group Newsletter**

"Lisa Biow...has obviously taken great pains to understand what new users go through. It gives the essential explanations and a little more, leaving further research to the reader. However, it is more than enough to get users started."

**—Madhulika Dayal, *PC WEEK Asia***

### *PC/Computing How Computers Work*

"As an enjoyable way to learn what makes your system tick, nothing comes close to *How Computers Work*. Browse through it for an entertaining and informative diversion, or work your way through from cover to cover for a thorough orientation. And when you're finished, don't hide it away on some remote shelf—leave it out on your coffee table where everyone can enjoy this beautiful book."

**—Alfred Poor, *PC Magazine***

"A 'real' book, and quite a handsome one...The artwork, by Mr. Timothy Edward Downs, is striking and informative, and the text by Mr. White, executive editor of *[PC/Computing]*, is very lucid."

**—L.R. Shannon, *New York Times***

"Read *[PC/Computing] How Computers Work* to learn about the inner workings of the IBM and PC-compatible."

**—Ronald Rosenberg, *Boston Globe***

"...a magnificently seamless integration of text and graphics that makes the complicated physics of the personal computer seem as obvious as gravity. When a book really pleases you—and this one does—there's a tendency to gush, so let's put it this way: I haven't seen any better explanations written (including my own) of how a PC works and why."

**—Larry Blasko, The Associated Press**

"If you're curious but fear computerese might get in the way, this book's the answer...it's an accessible, informative introduction that spreads everything out for logical inspection.

To make everything even clearer, White introduces the explanatory diagrams with a few concise, lucid paragraphs of text. Readers will come away knowing not only what everything looks like but also what it does."

**—Stephanie Zvirin, *Booklist***

"...the text in *How Computers Work* is remarkably free of jargon and distractions. Readers are left with a basic impression of how a particular component woks; they're not overloaded with information they may never use or remember...For most PC users, the brief introduction to the subject of disk caching in *How Computers Work* is all they need to understand the basics behind the technology. This is a boon to readers who may have been totally stumped by a more technical description of the process, and who may have avoided the more indepth article. Whether you're new to computers or want a refresher course in the latest technology, *How Computers Work* offers a solid and colorful introduction."

**—Gordon McComb, Copley News Service**

"Computer users at all levels will enjoy and profit from this book."

**—Don Mills, *Computing Now!***

"From mouse to CD-ROM, the treatment manages to convey 'how it works' without being simplistic or overly complex. A very good overview for those curious about how computers make their magic."

**—Reference & Research Book News**

# *How to Use*
# WINDOWS

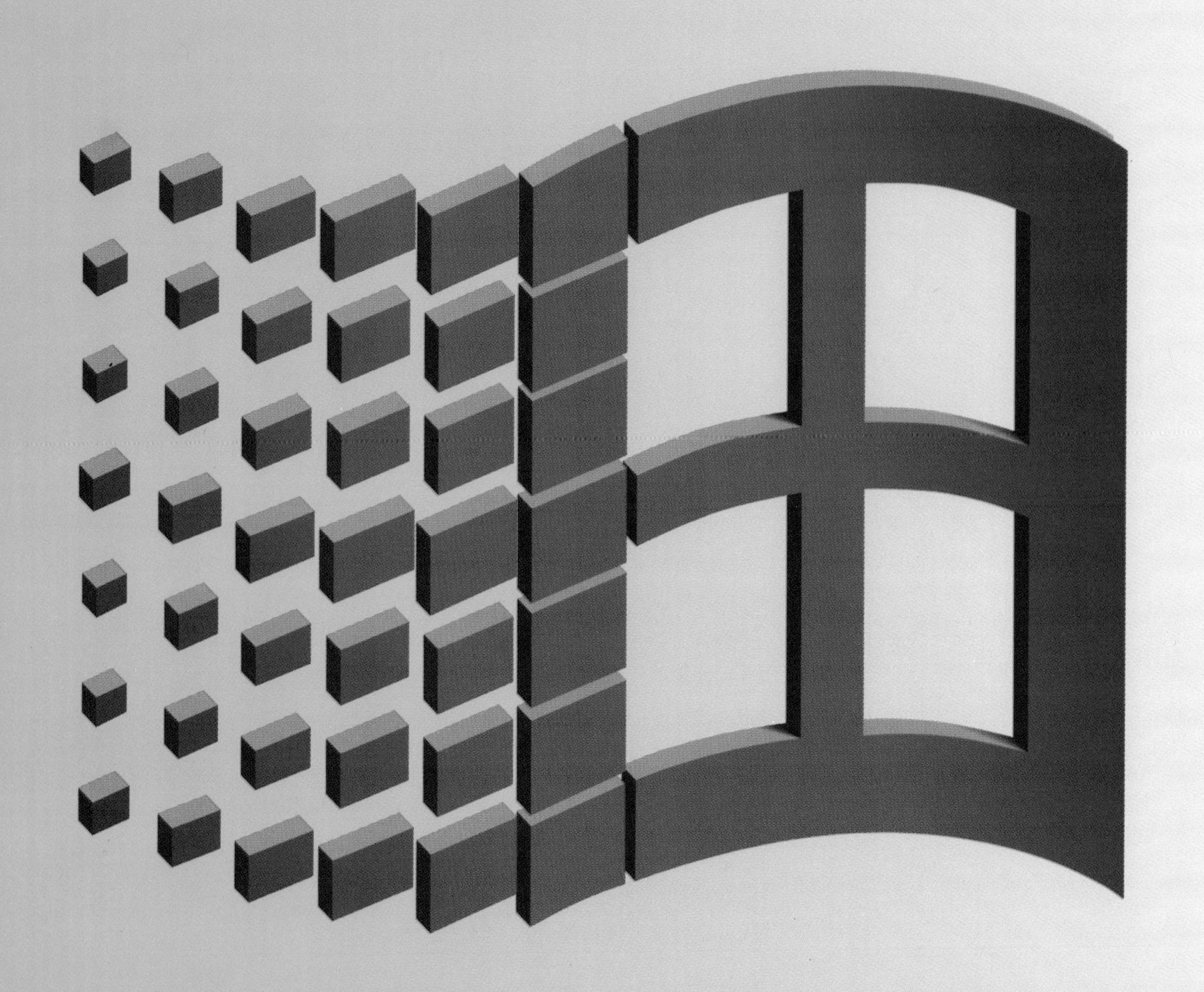

# *How to Use* WINDOWS

DOUGLAS HERGERT

Illustrated by
CHERIE PLUMLEE

**Ziff-Davis Press**
**Emeryville, California**

| | |
|---|---|
| Copy Editor | Lyn Cordell |
| Technical Reviewer | Dale Lewallen |
| Project Coordinator | Kim Haglund |
| Proofreader | Cort Day |
| Cover Illustration | Cherie Plumlee Computer Graphics & Illustration |
| Cover Design | Carrie English |
| Book Design | Dennis Gallagher/Visual Strategies, San Francisco |
| Screen Graphics Editor | Cat Haglund |
| Technical Illustration | Cherie Plumlee Computer Graphics & Illustration |
| Word Processing | Howard Blechman |
| Page Layout | Tony Jonick |
| Indexer | Valerie Haynes Perry |

Ziff-Davis Press books are produced on a Macintosh computer system with the following applications: FrameMaker®, Microsoft® Word, QuarkXPress®, Adobe Illustrator®, Adobe Photoshop®, Adobe Streamline™, MacLink® *Plus*, Aldus® FreeHand™, Collage Plus™.

Ziff-Davis Press
5903 Christie Avenue
Emeryville, CA 94608
1-800-688-0448

Copyright © 1994 by Douglas Hergert. All rights reserved.
PART OF A CONTINUING SERIES

Ziff-Davis Press and ZD Press are trademarks of Ziff Communications Company.

All other product names and services identified throughout this book are trademarks or registered trademarks of their respective companies. They are used throughout this book in editorial fashion only and for the benefit of such companies. No such uses, or the use of any trade name, is intended to convey endorsement or other affiliation with the book.

No part of this publication may be reproduced in any form, or stored in a database or retrieval system, or transmitted or distributed in any form by any means, electronic, mechanical photocopying, recording, or otherwise, without the prior written permission of Ziff-Davis Press, except as permitted by the Copyright Act of 1976, and except that program listings may be entered, stored, and executed in a computer system.

THE INFORMATION AND MATERIAL CONTAINED IN THIS BOOK ARE PROVIDED "AS IS," WITHOUT WARRANTY OF ANY KIND, EXPRESS OR IMPLIED, INCLUDING WITHOUT LIMITATION ANY WARRANTY CONCERNING THE ACCURACY, ADEQUACY, OR COMPLETENESS OF SUCH INFORMATION OR MATERIAL OR THE RESULTS TO BE OBTAINED FROM USING SUCH INFORMATION OR MATERIAL. NEITHER ZIFF-DAVIS PRESS NOR THE AUTHOR SHALL BE RESPONSIBLE FOR ANY CLAIMS ATTRIBUTABLE TO ERRORS, OMISSIONS, OR OTHER INACCURACIES IN THE INFORMATION OR MATERIAL CONTAINED IN THIS BOOK, AND IN NO EVENT SHALL ZIFF-DAVIS PRESS OR THE AUTHOR BE LIABLE FOR DIRECT, INDIRECT, SPECIAL, INCIDENTAL, OR CONSEQUENTIAL DAMAGES ARISING OUT OF THE USE OF SUCH INFORMATION OR MATERIAL.

ISBN 1-56276-190-0

Manufactured in the United States of America
10 9 8 7 6 5

# TABLE OF CONTENTS

# ACKNOWLEDGMENTS

My thanks go to Cynthia Hudson and her team of publishing wizards at Ziff-Davis Press, and to Claudette Moore of Moore Literary Agency.

# INTRODUCTION

In all kinds of work places—offices, homes, schools, labs, and even spots as unlikely as lakeside resorts, airports, and coffee shops—Microsoft Windows has redefined the way people use their personal computers and laptops. Thanks to Windows, ordinary computer users are learning to work more efficiently and reliably than ever before. Even people who can't quite remember what GUI means (graphical user interface) are beginning to recognize the familiar visual tools of the Windows desktop. These tools are the basis for a more human and genial approach to personal computing—an approach that people everywhere have taken up with enthusiasm.

*How to Use Windows* is an illustrated tutorial, introducing Windows 3.1. If you're a newcomer to the system, this book will help you explore the software resources that Windows provides. In the first several chapters you'll master the basics—icons, menus, dialog boxes, group windows, and system applications. Then you'll learn how to use Windows programs to accomplish specific jobs on your computer—produce documents, keep records, design graphics, manage schedules, perform calculations, and more. Along the way, you'll actually *see* what Windows does and how it works. And because this book uses a *hands-on* approach, you'll learn by performing each step and task on your own computer.

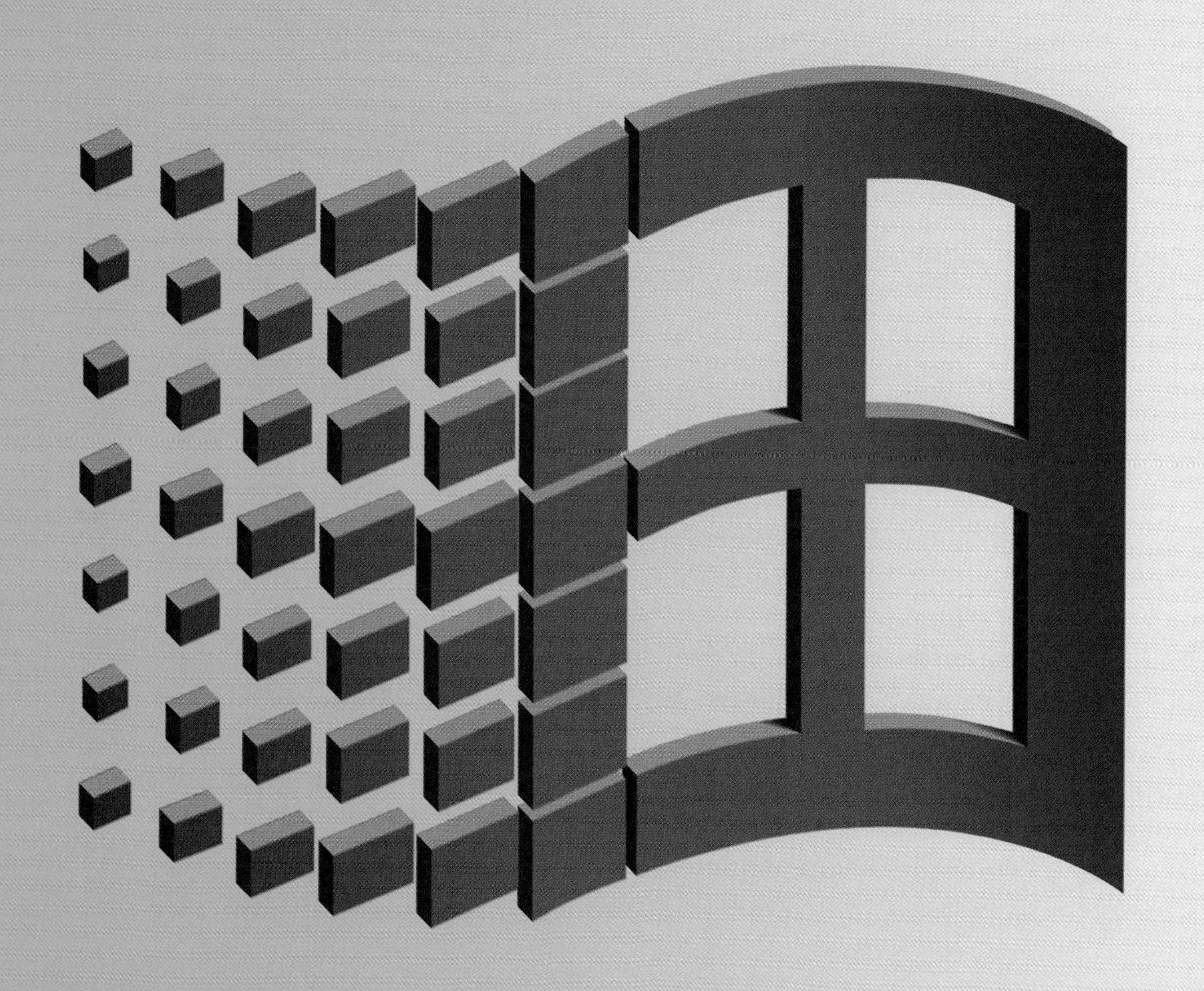

CHAPTER 1

# Getting Started with Windows

There are many reasons for running Windows on a personal computer. Some people do so simply because their favorite application—a word processing program, a database manager, or even a game—won't work without it. Other people run Windows to take advantage of a particular feature the software itself supplies—for instance, the File Manager, or the Paintbrush program that comes with the Windows package. Still others like Windows because it allows them to coordinate all their computer work in a single software environment—an environment that supplies a common set of simple mouse and keyboard operations as well as convenient ways to exchange information among programs.

You'll start out with your own particular reasons—and you may find yourself amplifying those reasons over time. But no matter what you plan to use Windows for, there are certain basic features and skills that you need to master when you first begin: You have to become familiar with the way Windows organizes your display screen. You must become proficient at using the mouse and keyboard with Windows. And because Windows offers a large variety of resources, you must learn how to make your way around the program and choose the features you want to work with. In this first chapter, you'll begin developing these important skills.

# How to Start Windows

When Windows takes control of your computer, the screen becomes a visual desktop for your work. This desktop contains icons and windows depicting the activities available to you. An icon is a small picture representing a program you can work with. A window is a framed rectangle that encloses your work in a particular program. Often, an icon represents a window that is not currently open. Like the surface of a real desk, the Windows desktop can be rearranged in many useful ways. The center of operations in Windows is the Program Manager. When you first start Windows, you may have to spend a few seconds finding your place in the Program Manager before you start your work.

## TIP SHEET

- **Some systems are set up to display a program called MS-DOS Shell instead of the DOS prompt when you turn on the computer. To start Windows directly from the DOS Shell, press Alt and then the F key on your keyboard to view the Shell's File menu. Then press R to choose the Run command. In the resulting Run box, type** win **and press Enter.**
- **If you want to work with a particular application program such as a word processor or a spreadsheet, you can start both Windows and the application in a single step. For example, suppose you want to start Microsoft Word for Windows along with Windows. At the DOS prompt, type** win winword**.**

**1** Turn on your computer and look for the DOS prompt on the screen. The prompt may appear simply as C>, which tells you that DOS is ready to start programs stored on drive C. An underscore character flashes on and off just after the prompt, marking the place where any command you type from the keyboard will be displayed.

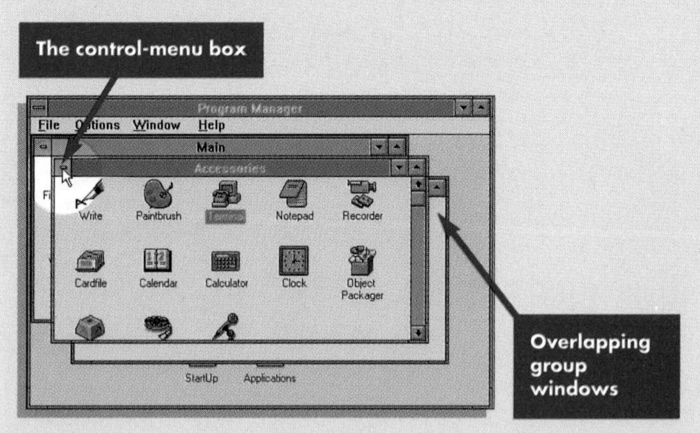


**5** Conversely, the Program Manager may start out as a jumble of several open group windows, possibly overlapping. In this case, you should next try closing all the groups but Main. At the upper-left corner of each group window is a small box called the *control-menu box*. To close a group, move the mouse pointer to this box and double-click the left mouse button. Do this for each open group except Main.

**2** Type **win** from the keyboard and then press the Enter key. A box appears briefly on the screen, telling you that Microsoft Windows is starting. Then the Windows desktop takes over your screen. If the desktop looks approximately like the large screen shown below, you can skip steps 3, 4, and 5. You are ready to begin working in Windows.

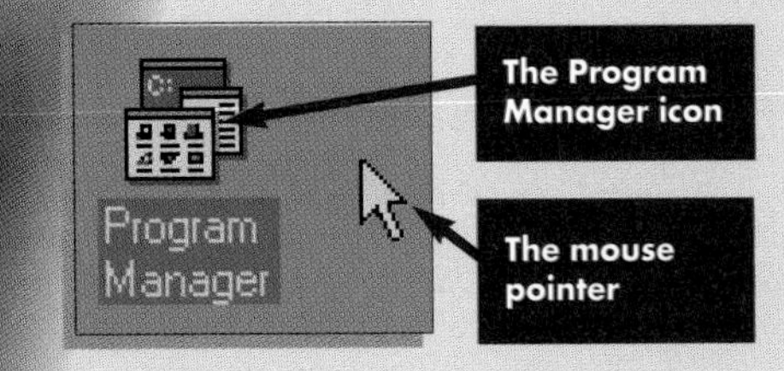


**3** If the screen is empty except for the Program Manager icon at the lower-left corner of the desktop, your next step is to open the Program Manager window. To do so, use your mouse to position the mouse pointer directly over the icon, and then *double-click* the left mouse button—that is, click the button twice in quick succession. (The *pointer* is a white arrow that moves around the screen when you move the mouse. Turn the page for more information about using a mouse in Windows.)

**4** The Program Manager contains special icons that represent *groups* of programs. If all you see inside the Program Manager window is a collection of group icons, you should open one of the groups next. Find the group icon labeled "Main." Move the mouse until the pointer is directly over the Main icon, and then double-click the left mouse button.

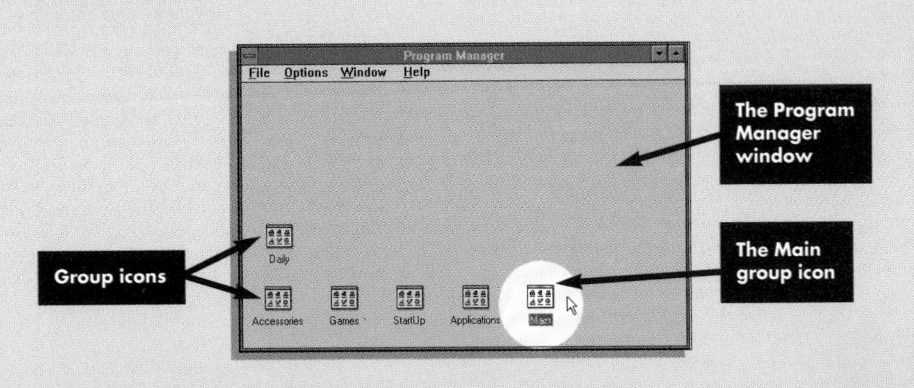

# How to Use the Mouse

The mouse is indispensable in Windows. Using the mouse that's attached to your computer, you can get things done quickly, efficiently, and intuitively. Initially, the mouse pointer is a white arrow pointing toward the upper-left area of your screen, but it sometimes changes shape as you move to different parts of the Windows environment. By moving the pointer to a particular position on the desktop, you can make an item the object of a mouse action. You'll quickly learn to perform several basic mouse actions such as moving, pointing, clicking, double-clicking, and dragging.

**TIP SHEET**

- **Although some Windows programs define specific operations for the right mouse button, you perform most mouse actions by clicking the left button.**
- **If you prefer to use the mouse with your left hand, Windows allows you to reverse the normal roles of the left and right mouse buttons. This switch can be a boon to left-handed people. For details, see "How to Change the Mouse Settings" in Chapter 5.**
- **If you prefer, you can use the keyboard to choose menu commands. To pull down a menu, press the Alt key to activate the menu bar and then press the key corresponding to the underlined letter in the menu name. For example, press Alt and then H to pull down the Help menu. To choose a command from the menu, press the underlined letter in the command name.**

**1** To *move* the mouse pointer to a new position on the Windows desktop, roll the mouse over a flat surface. The pointer moves in the same direction as the mouse.

**7** To *choose* a menu command, pull down a menu and then click the name of the command. In response, Windows carries out the command you have chosen.

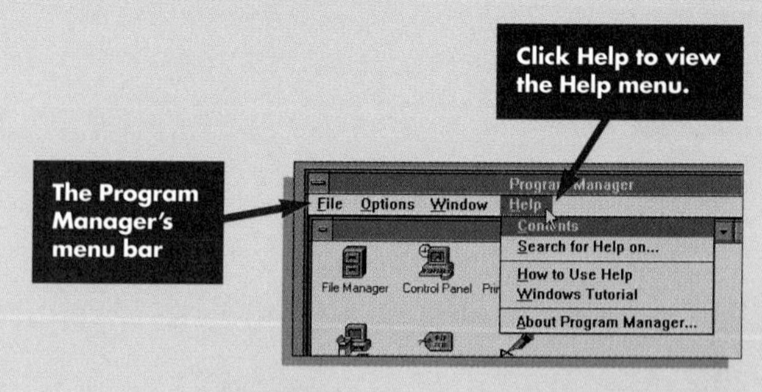


**6** To *pull down* a menu in Windows, use the mouse to click the menu's name in the menu bar.

**2** To *point* to an object on the desktop, position the mouse pointer directly over the item.

**3** To *click* an object on the desktop, position the mouse pointer over the object and then press and release the left mouse button. (A *click* is one quick press of the button.)

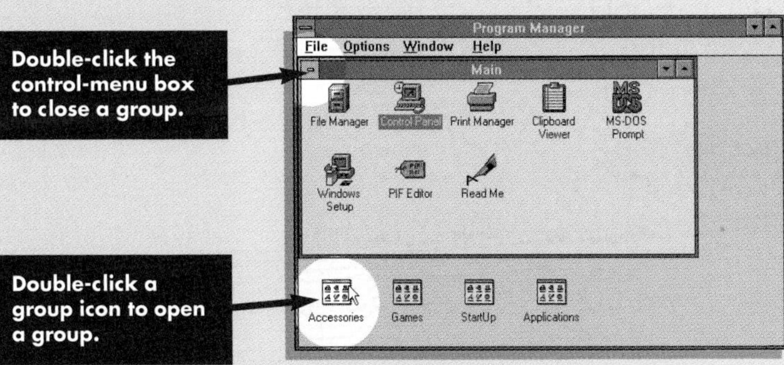


**4** To *double-click* an object, move the mouse pointer over the item and then press the left mouse button twice in quick succession.

**5** To *drag* an object, point to the item and hold down the left mouse button. Then move the mouse; as you do so, an image of the object moves on the Windows desktop. Finally, release the mouse button to settle the object in its new location.

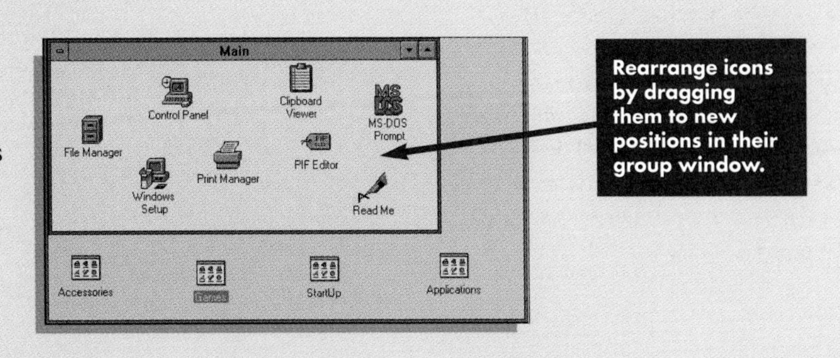

# How to Resize and Move Individual Windows

Windows allows you to arrange your desktop in any way you want. You can use your mouse to change the size of a window or to move a window to a new position. For example, suppose you are working with several windows on the desktop at once; you might want to position one window just above another, or view the contents of three windows side by side. Using the mouse to drag your windows, you accomplish these arrangements in seconds.

## TIP SHEET

- **If you decrease the size of some windows—such as group windows in the Program Manager—you may suddenly see vertical and horizontal scroll bars that were not previously part of the window. These bars indicate that the window is no longer large enough to display its entire contents at once. You can use the scroll bars to view other parts of the window's contents: Click any of the four arrow buttons to scroll through the contents in small increments, or use the mouse to drag the *scroll box* up and down the vertical scroll bar or across the horizontal scroll bar.**
- **It is possible to resize or move a window using the keyboard. Press the Alt key and then the spacebar to pull down the *control menu* for the active window. Press M to choose the Move command, or S to choose the Size command. Use the Up, Down, Right, and Left Arrow keys and press Enter to complete the operation.**

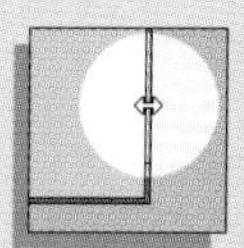

**Point to the right or left side of a window's frame if you want to change the width of the window.**

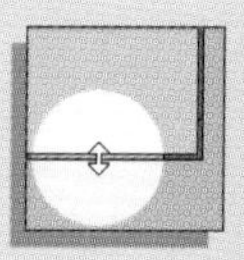

**Point to the top or bottom of a window's frame if you want to change the window's height.**

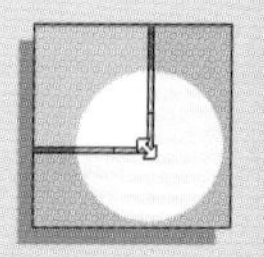

**Point to any corner of the window's frame if you want to change two dimensions at once.**

1. To change the size of a window, begin by positioning the mouse pointer over any part of the window's frame. The pointer changes to a two-headed arrow—pointing horizontally, vertically, or diagonally, depending on where you place the pointer on the frame.

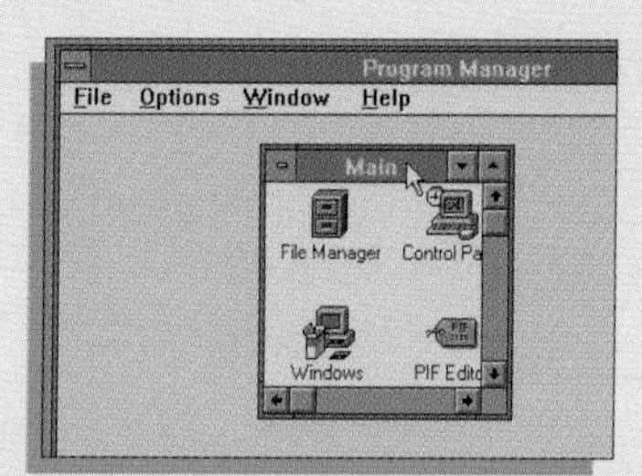


6. Release the mouse button to settle the window in its new position.

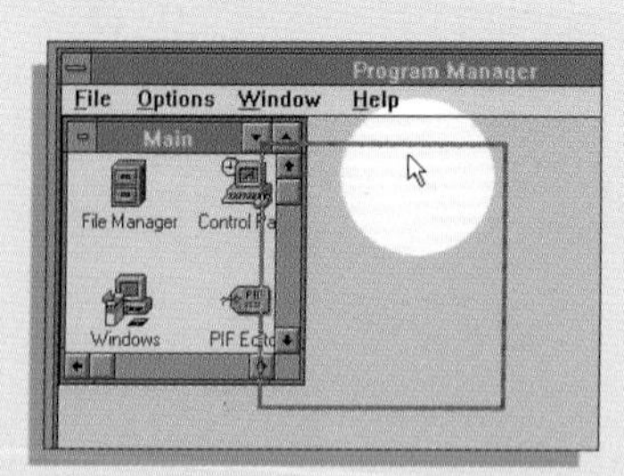


5. Hold down the left mouse button and drag the window to a new location. As you drag, an outline shows the window's new place on the desktop.

**2** Hold down the left mouse button and drag the window's frame in the appropriate direction—toward the inside of the window to decrease its size, or in the opposite direction to increase its size. As you drag, you'll see an outline of the window's new size.

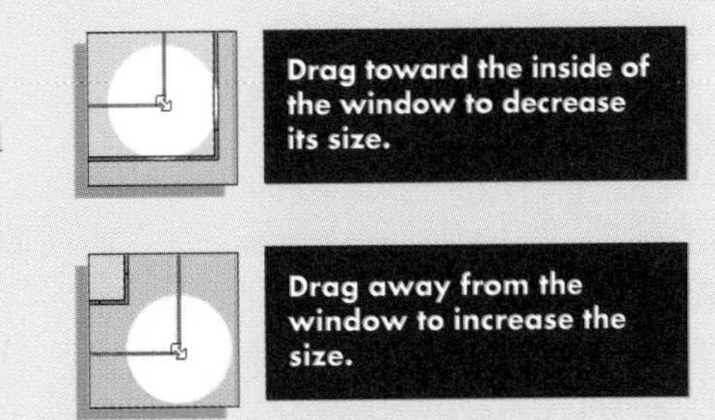


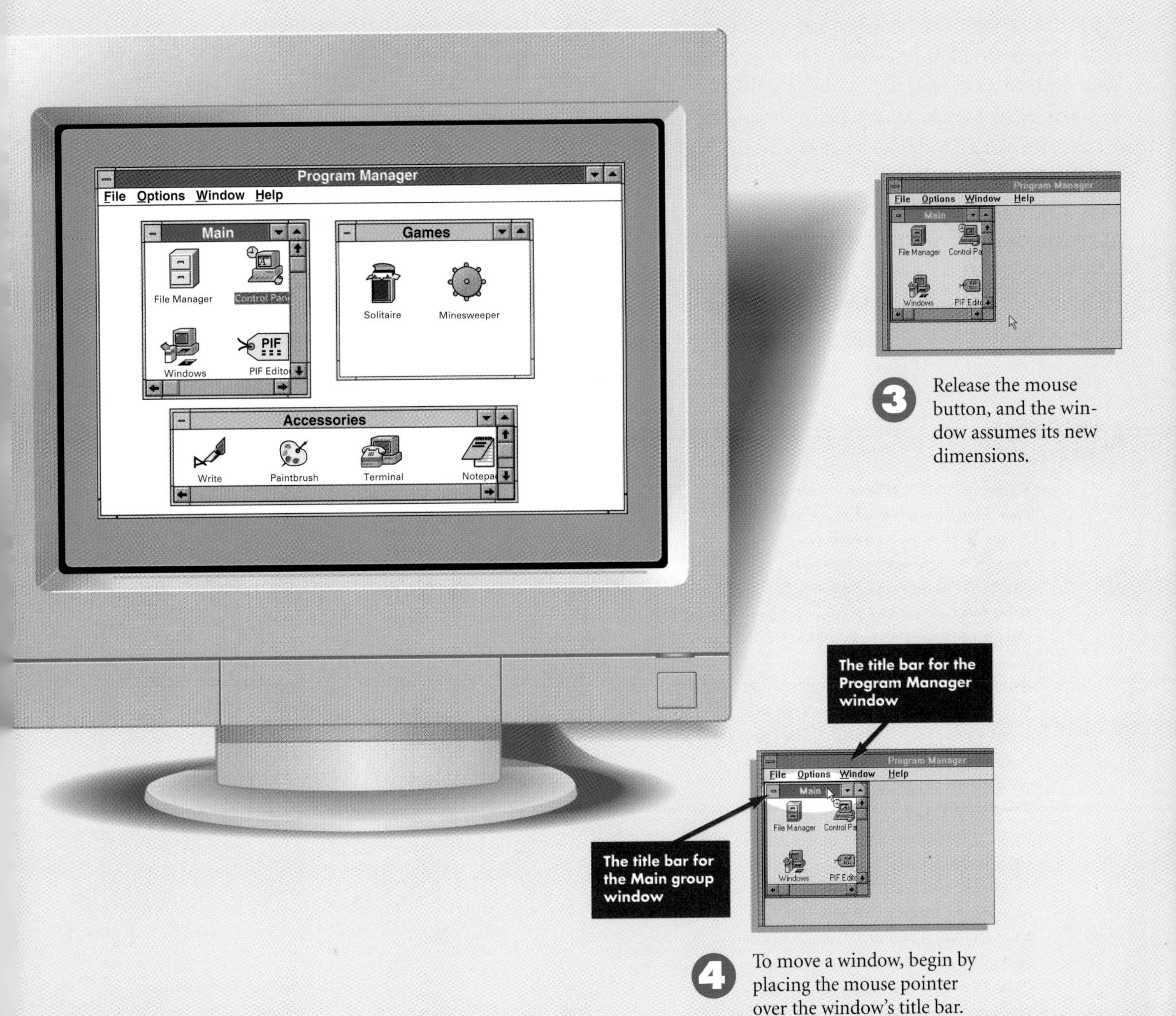


**3** Release the mouse button, and the window assumes its new dimensions.

**4** To move a window, begin by placing the mouse pointer over the window's title bar.

# How to Arrange Individual Windows

In addition to resizing and moving, there are several other ways to change individual windows on the desktop. At the upper-right corner of a window you'll find some special buttons that you can click to achieve specific effects. The *minimize* button transforms a window into an icon on the desktop. The *maximize* button increases the window's size to cover the available desktop area. The *restore* button reduces a maximized window to its previous dimensions. All these buttons are available on the Program Manager window and on each group window within the Program Manager.

**1** To minimize a window, click the window's minimize button.

**2** To change an icon on the desktop back into a window, double-click the icon.

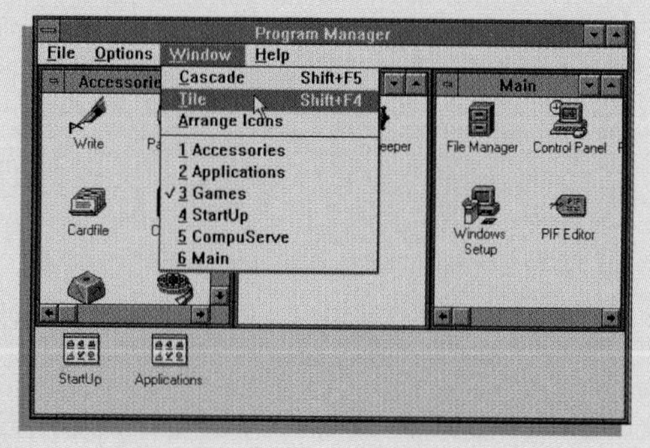


**6** To view group windows side-by-side within the Program Manager window, begin by opening all the group windows that you want to see. Then pull down the Window menu and choose the Tile command.

- By default, Windows remembers any changes that you make in the appearance of the Program Manager window. The next time you start Windows, the desktop retains its new appearance. If you *don't* want this to happen—that is, if you want to maintain the original appearance of the Program Manager—pull down the Options menu and choose the Save Settings on Exit command to *uncheck* it.
- There is an important distinction between the icons inside a group window and icons on the desktop. In a group window, an icon represents a program that is available for you to start. On the desktop, an icon represents a program that you have started but temporarily minimized while you do other work.

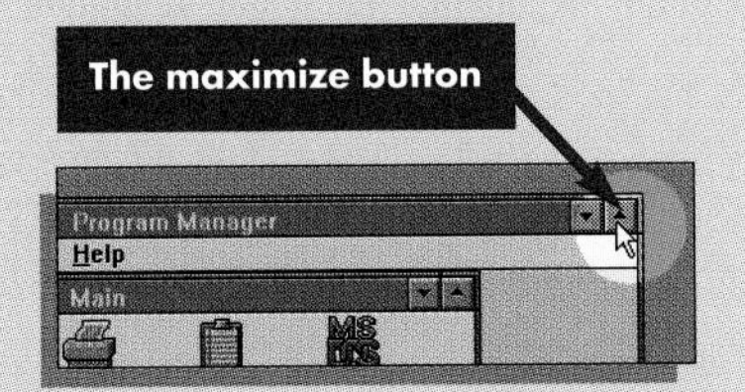


3 To maximize a window, click the window's maximize button. When a window is maximized, the maximize button is replaced by the restore button.

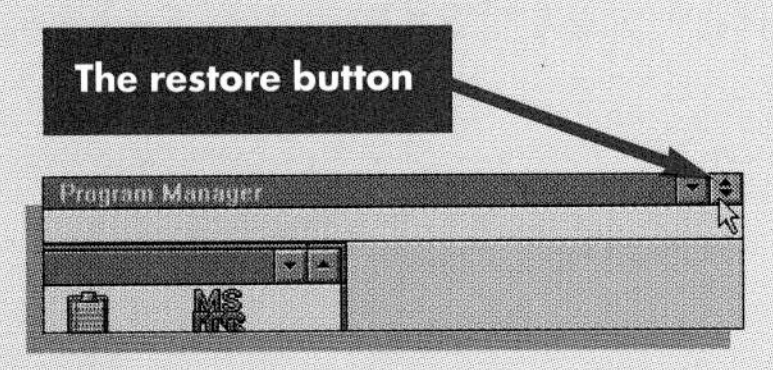


4 To restore a maximized window to its previous size, click the window's restore button.

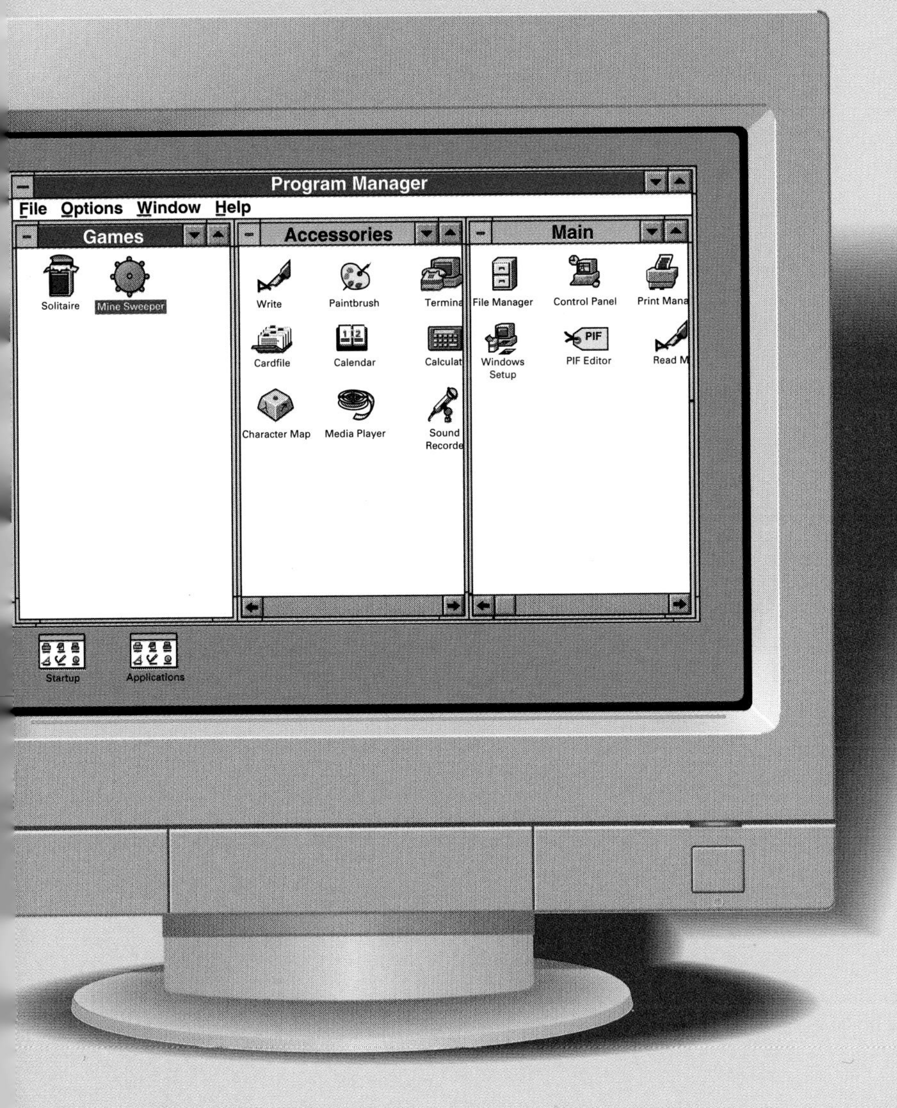


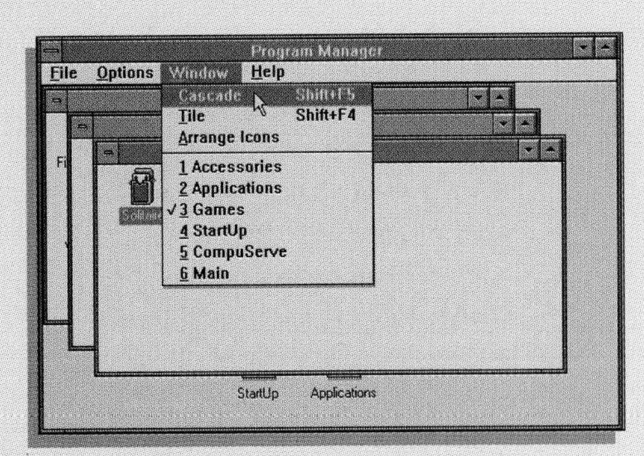


5 To view group windows in an overlapping arrangement—where one window appears in front of another—begin by opening all the groups that you want to see. Then pull down the Window menu and choose the Cascade command.

# How to Quit Windows

As long as Windows is running on your computer, the Program Manager is present on the desktop, either as an open window or as an icon. When you close the Program Manager, you also quit Windows and return to DOS. Before the exit takes place, a message box appears on the desktop telling you that you are about to end your current Windows session. This message box also gives you a chance to change your mind and remain in Windows.

**TIP SHEET**

- **There are several other ways to quit Windows. One quick technique is to double-click the control-menu box at the upper-left corner of the Program Manager window. A keyboard technique is to hold down the Alt key and then press the F4 function key. Finally, if the Program Manager is represented as an icon on the desktop (instead of an open window), you can click the icon once to view the control menu and then click the Close command.**
- **If you are running an application—such as a word processing program or spreadsheet program in Windows—you do not have to close the program before quitting Windows. If there are unsaved documents in any open application programs, Windows displays message boxes on the screen that give you the option of saving your work before exiting. You'll learn more about using applications in Windows later in this book.**

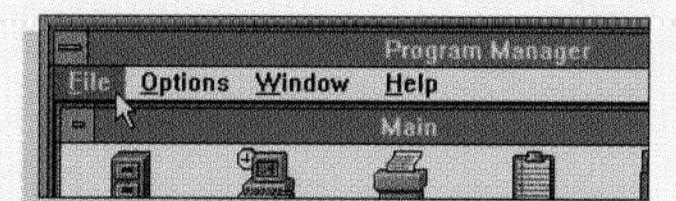


1. Move the mouse pointer to the File menu in the Program Manager's menu bar, and click the left mouse button to pull down the menu.

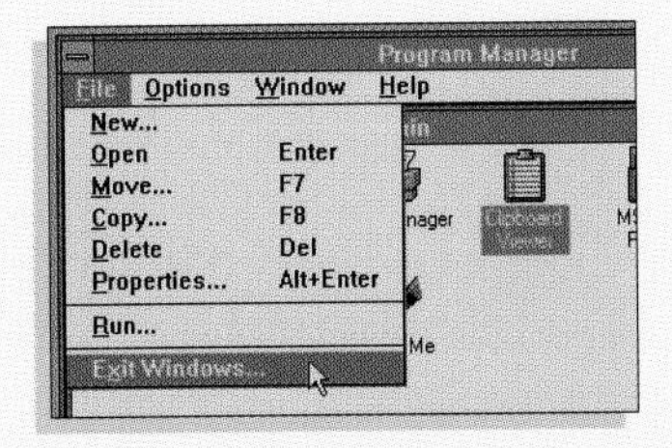


2 On the File menu, click the Exit Windows command. A box named Exit Windows immediately appears on the desktop. The box contains the message "This will end your Windows session." Beneath the message are two buttons, one labeled OK and the other labeled Cancel.

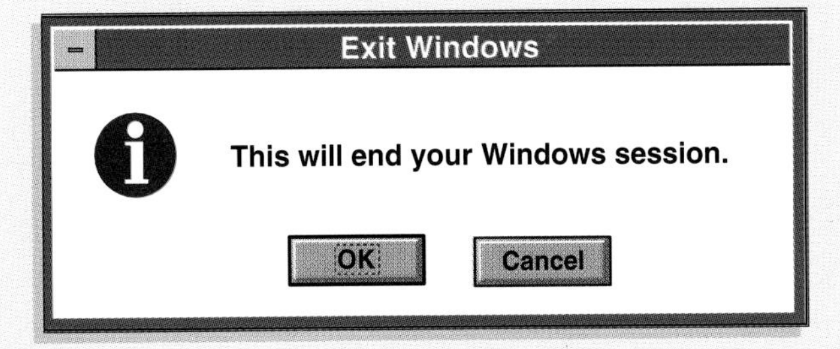


3 If you're sure you want to complete the exit, move the mouse pointer to the OK button in the message box, and click the left mouse button. (If you change your mind and decide not to exit Windows, click the Cancel button instead of the OK button.)

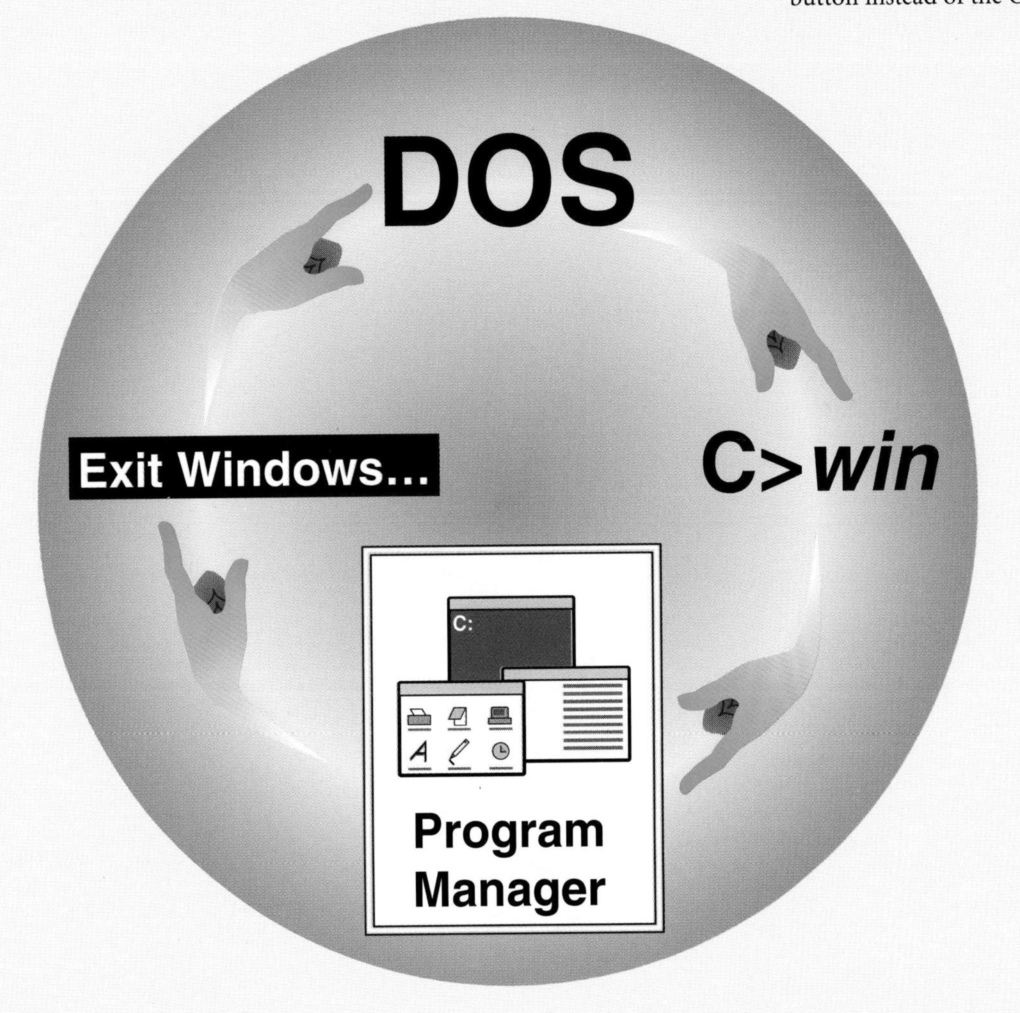

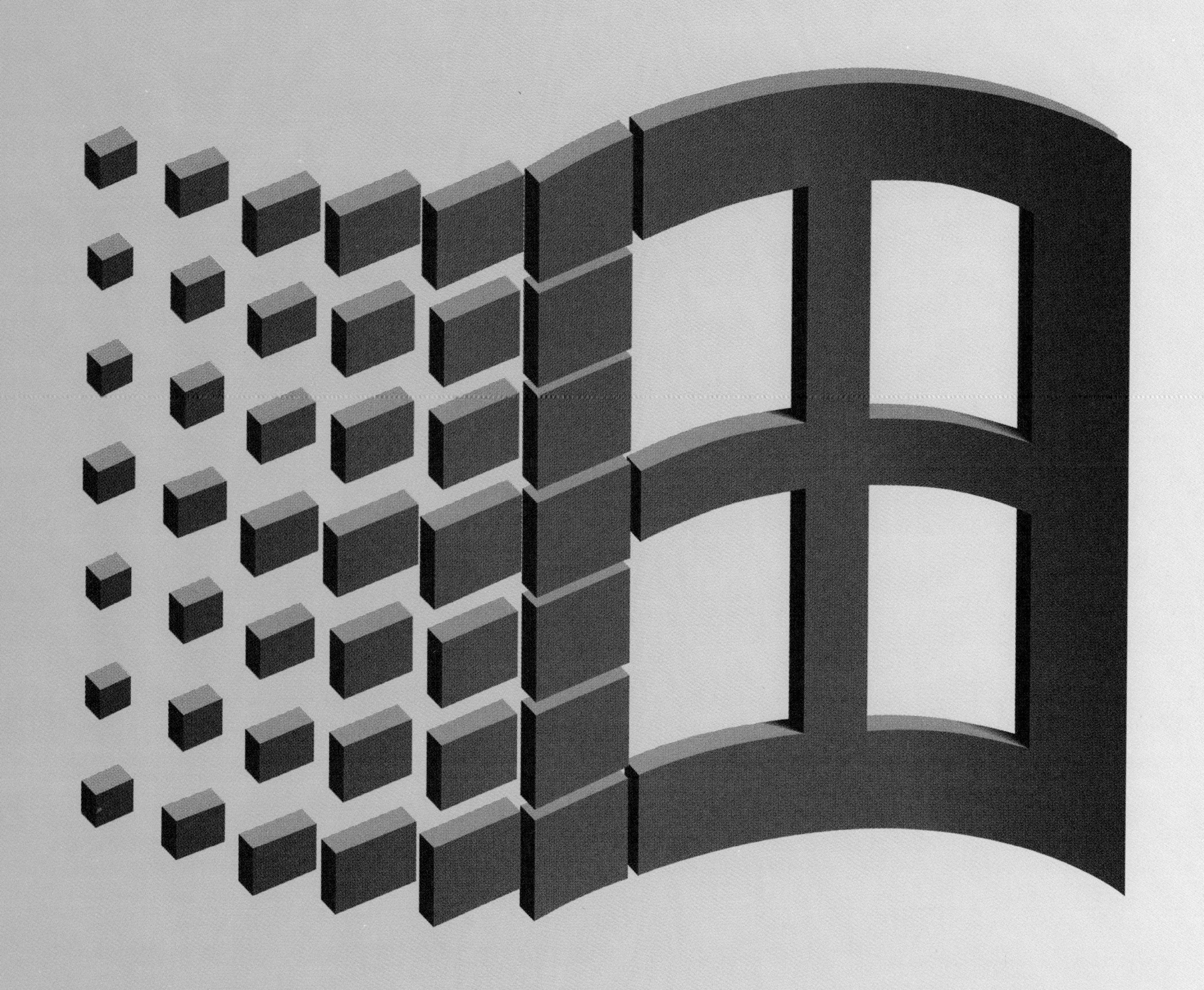

## CHAPTER 2

# The Program Manager

The Program Manager gives you a visual overview of the tools available in Windows. Applications are divided into groups in the Program Manager window. Inside each group is a collection of icons representing a particular set of programs. You're always free to display groups in any way you want. By rearranging the group windows, you can lend prominence to the programs you use frequently and temporarily hide those you seldom use.

When you're ready to start a program, the Program Manager makes the process quick and easy: You simply open the group that contains the program's icon and then use the mouse or keyboard to select the program. Even if one or more programs are already running, you can always return to the Program Manager window to start others. No matter what you're currently doing in Windows, you'll return to the Program Manager frequently to coordinate your work.

The Program Manager also gives you easy access to a useful on-line help system for Windows. When you have a question about the steps of a procedure in Windows, you can open a relevant topic in the Help window.

In this chapter you'll expand your understanding of the Program Manager window and the resources it provides. You'll learn how to organize your work effectively, start programs instantly, and get help whenever you need it.

# How to Use Groups in the Program Manager Window

Within each group window is an assortment of distinct icons that represent the programs you can run in Windows; these are sometimes known as program-item icons. The Program Manager starts out with five groups: Main, Accessories, Games, StartUp, and Applications. In the following steps you'll explore the contents of the Program Manager groups. If you find a different set of groups than described here, take this opportunity to examine whatever groups you have.

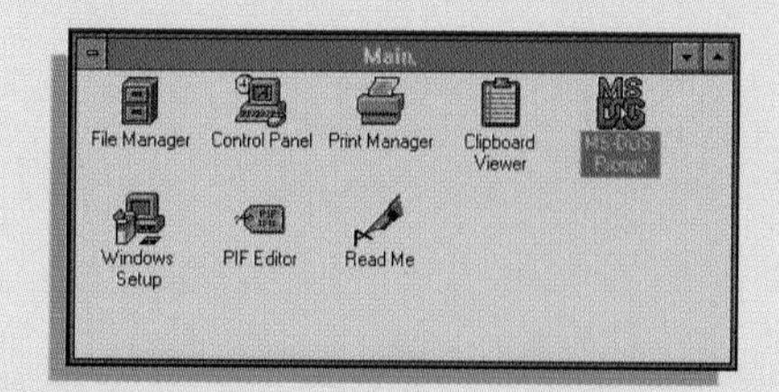


**1** First take a look at the Main group. If it is not open, move the mouse pointer to the Main icon and double-click the left mouse button. The Main group contains icons representing programs known as Windows *system applications.* Among them are File Manager, a program that simplifies tasks related to disks, directories, and files (see Chapter 6); Control Panel, which you use to change the way Windows looks and behaves (see Chapter 5); Print Manager, the program that handles printing operations for most Windows applications (see Chapter 9); and Clipboard Viewer, a temporary storage area for information that you copy or move from one place to another in Windows programs (see Chapter 8).

## TIP SHEET

- **The terms *program* and *application* are synonymous. Both refer to software tools that are designed to help you do specific kinds of work in Windows.**
- **In some groups you may find icons that represent documents rather than programs. A *document* is a file that has been created within a particular application. When you double-click a document icon, Windows first opens the appropriate application and then opens the document file itself.**
- **The Program Manager's Window menu contains a numbered list of all the groups contained in your installation of Windows. If you prefer to use the keyboard to switch to a particular group, press Alt and then W to open the Windows menu; then press the number corresponding to the group you want to open.**

**6** Now use the mouse skills you learned in Chapter 1 to rearrange the open groups in the Program Manager window. Resize each window and move it to a convenient location so you can see all the groups at once. The central graphic on this page shows one possible arrangement.

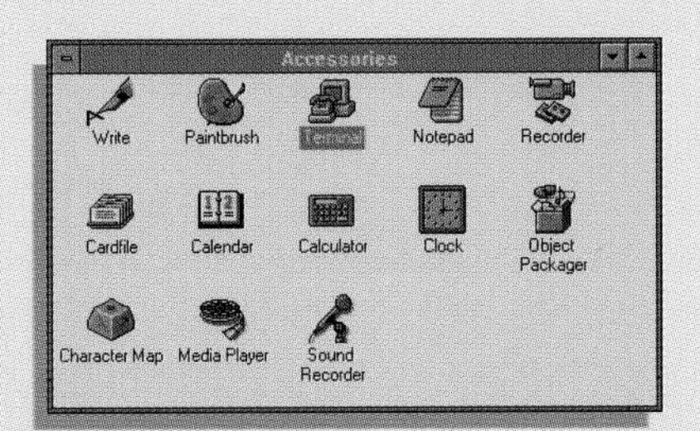


2 Move the mouse pointer to the Accessories group icon and double-click the left mouse button. This group contains icons for a variety of useful applications that are packaged with Windows, including Write, a simple word processor (see Chapter 7); Cardfile, a data file manager (see Chapter 10); Paintbrush, a drawing program (see Chapter 11); and Calendar, an appointment calendar (see Chapter 12).

3 Double-click the Games group icon. The two games included with Windows are Solitaire and Minesweeper. Both of these elegantly designed programs are worthy diversions for occasional breaks from your work.

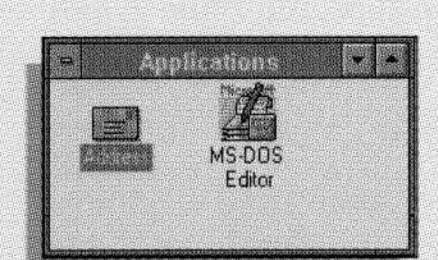


4 Double-click the Applications group icon. This group contains icons for programs that were on your hard disk when Windows was installed on your computer. (Your Applications group will probably contain different icons than those shown here.)

5 Double-click the StartUp group icon. This group window will probably be empty. You can use this group to specify programs that you want to start automatically at the beginning of each Windows session. You'll learn to set up an automatic application in Chapter 4.

# How to Start a Program

Once you're familiar with the resources Windows has to offer, you're ready to begin experimenting with individual programs. Starting, or *running*, a program takes only a few seconds. Windows automatically opens an additional application window on the desktop for each program you start. The active window on the desktop is the program you are working on at any given moment.

Many programs in the Program Manager require some explanation before you can expect to work with them productively. But a few are nearly self-explanatory.

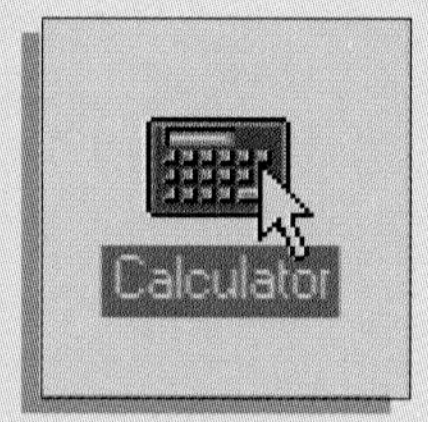


2 Within the group window, find the icon for the program you want to run. Move the mouse pointer to the icon, and double-click the left mouse button to start the program.

1 Find the group containing the icon for the program you want to run. If the group window is closed, position the mouse pointer over the group icon and double-click the left mouse button to open the window.

**TIP SHEET**

- **If you prefer, you can use the keyboard to open a group and start a program. Press Alt and then W to open the Window menu in the Program Manager's menu bar. To open a group window, press the number key corresponding to the group in the Window list. Inside the group, you select a program icon by pressing the left, right, up, or down arrow key on your keyboard. When the name of the program you want to start is highlighted, press the Enter key to run it.**
- **Windows allows you to run multiple programs at once. Each running program is represented either by an icon on the desktop or by an open application window. Chapter 4 shows you how to switch quickly from one running program to another.**

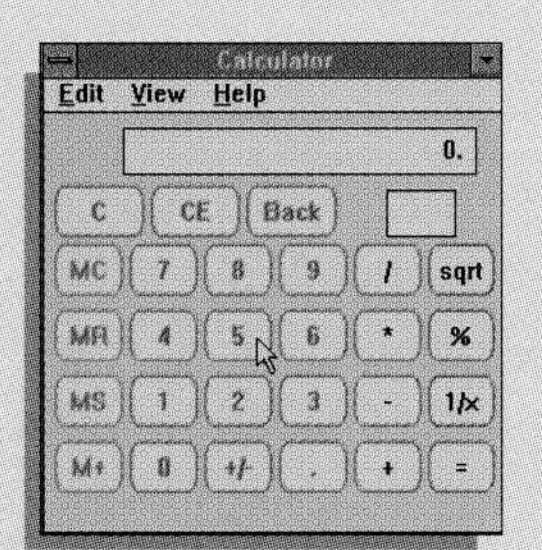


**3** The application window for the program opens on the desktop. You can now begin working with the program in whatever ways it is designed to be used. In this example, the Calculator window contains buttons that look like those of an ordinary hand-held calculator. By clicking these buttons with the mouse, you can perform any kind of arithmetic calculation. (Chapter 13 describes the Calculator program in more detail.)

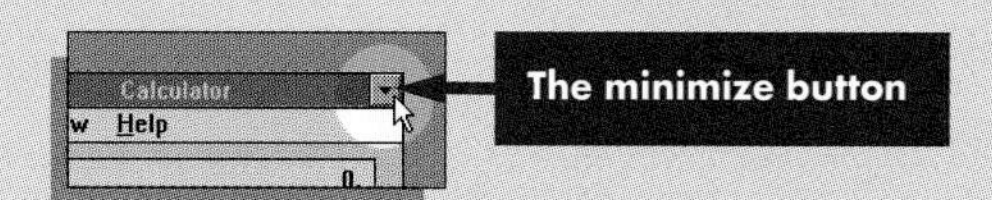


**4** If you want to put your current work aside temporarily so you can focus on some other activity, click the minimize button at the upper-right corner of the application window. Once the program is reduced to an icon on the desktop, you can start other programs by repeating steps 1, 2, and 3.

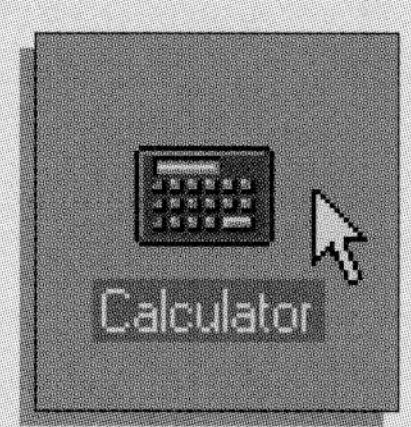


**5** When you are ready to return to your work in a minimized application, double-click the program's icon on the desktop. The application window reopens, displaying any work in progress just as you left it. For example, if you were in the middle of computing a result in the Calculator program, you could now continue exactly where you left off.

The control-menu box

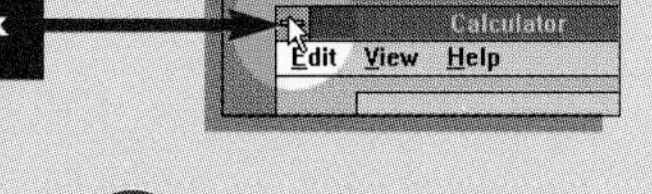


**6** When you complete your work, quit the application. Most applications contain an Exit command in their File menu, but the Calculator program is atypical in this respect; to quit the program, you must double-click the control-menu box at the upper-left corner of the application window.

# How to Get Help

The Program Manager provides a cross-referenced system of on-line help that you can turn to whenever you have a question about a particular feature or procedure in Windows. *On-line* means that the answers to your questions appear directly on the desktop in specially designed Help windows. Information is organized by individual topics. The system's cross-referencing feature allows you to move from one topic to another with just a click of the mouse.

There are a number of convenient ways to open a Help window, depending on what you're doing when you decide you need help. A good place to start is the Help menu on the Program Manager's menu bar; it provides several entries into the help system.

## TIP SHEET

- **The keyboard shortcut for opening a Help window is the F1 function key. This key provides *context-sensitive* help. For example, if you are choosing a menu command, F1 brings up a help topic that describes the command; otherwise, F1 opens the Contents list.**
- **To get help about the help system itself, press F1 when the Program Manager Help window is open. Alternatively, choose the How to Use Help command from the Program Manager's Help menu.**
- **To print a copy of the current help topic, click File on the menu bar of the Help window, and then click the Print Topic command.**
- **Each major Windows application provides its own help system designed to assist you with the operations of the program.**

1. Click Help on the Program Manager's menu bar to pull down the Help menu. Each command in this menu takes you to a particular part of the help system. For an overview of the system, click the Contents command. A window named Program Manager Help opens on the desktop, displaying a list of general help topics that you can go to next. (This window is shown as the central graphic on these pages.)

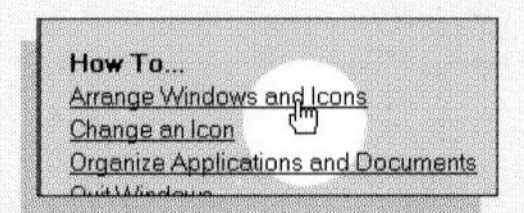


2. Move the mouse pointer to any underlined topic in the Contents list. The mouse pointer changes to a pointing hand. To "jump" to the underlined topic, click the left mouse button. The topic you've selected immediately appears in the Help window. Within this new topic you may see additional underlined cross-references. You can click any one of these to go to yet another related topic.

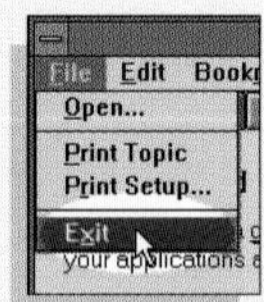

7. To close the Help window, click File on the window's menu bar, and then click Exit on the menu list.

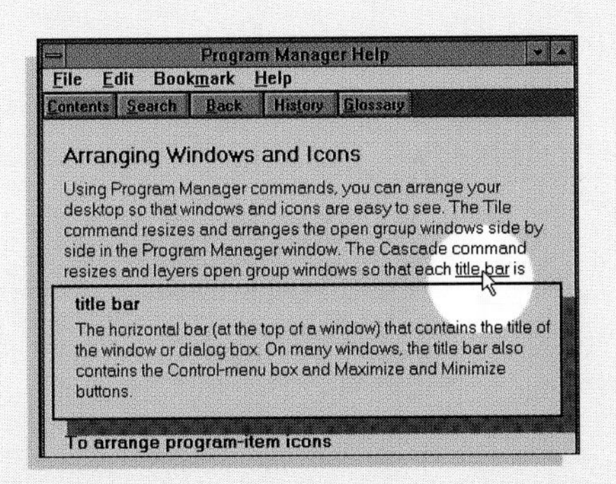


3 In some topics you'll find special vocabulary terms that are marked with dotted underlining. To see the definition of a term, click this kind of cross-reference with the mouse. The definition appears in a *pop-up* window. (To close the pop-up window, click anywhere on the desktop.)

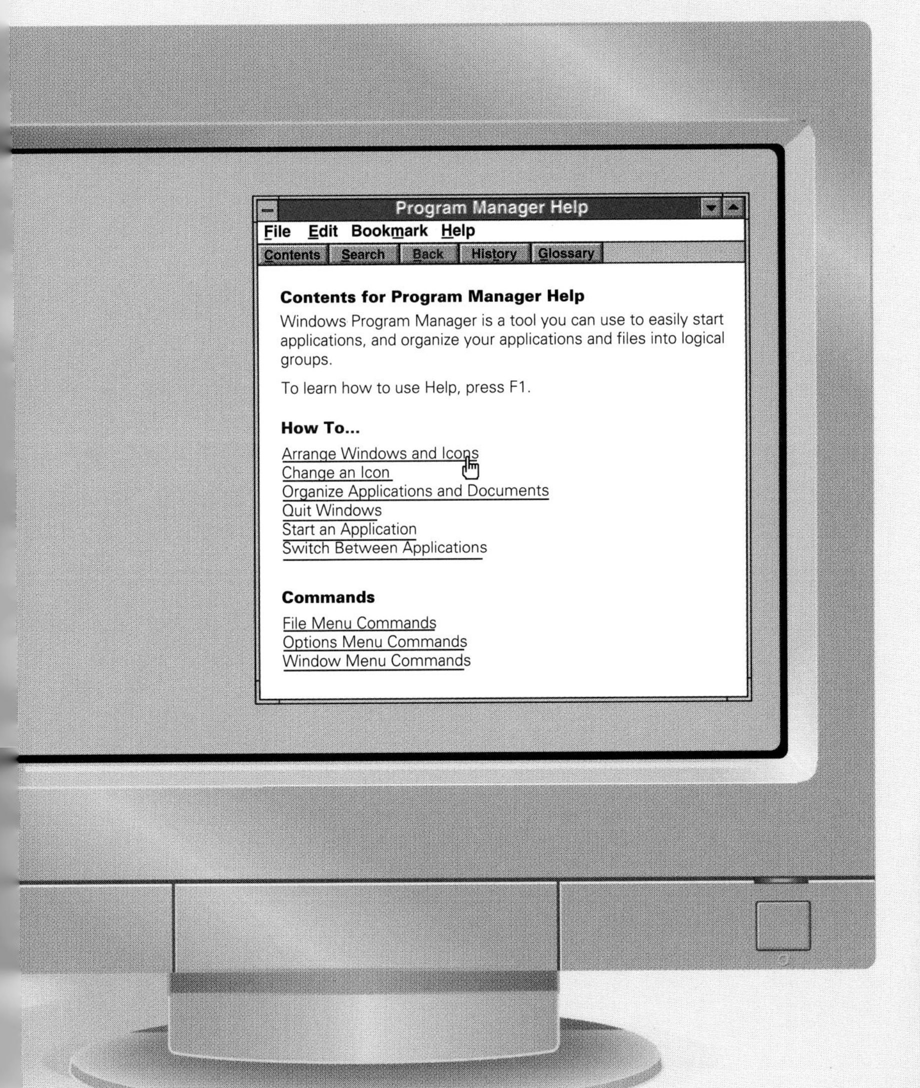

4 To search for another topic while the Help window is still open, click the Search button beneath the window's menu bar. A window named Search appears on the desktop.

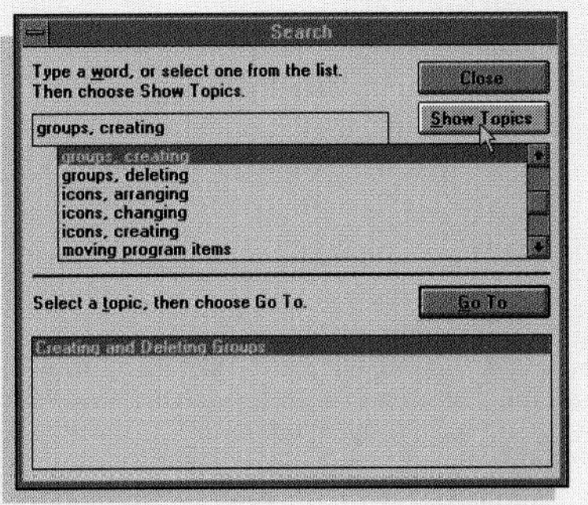


5 In the box at the top of the Search window, type the word or words you want to search for; then click the Show Topics button. A list of related topics appears in the box at the bottom of the Search window.

Click a topic and then click the Go To button to see the information you're looking for.

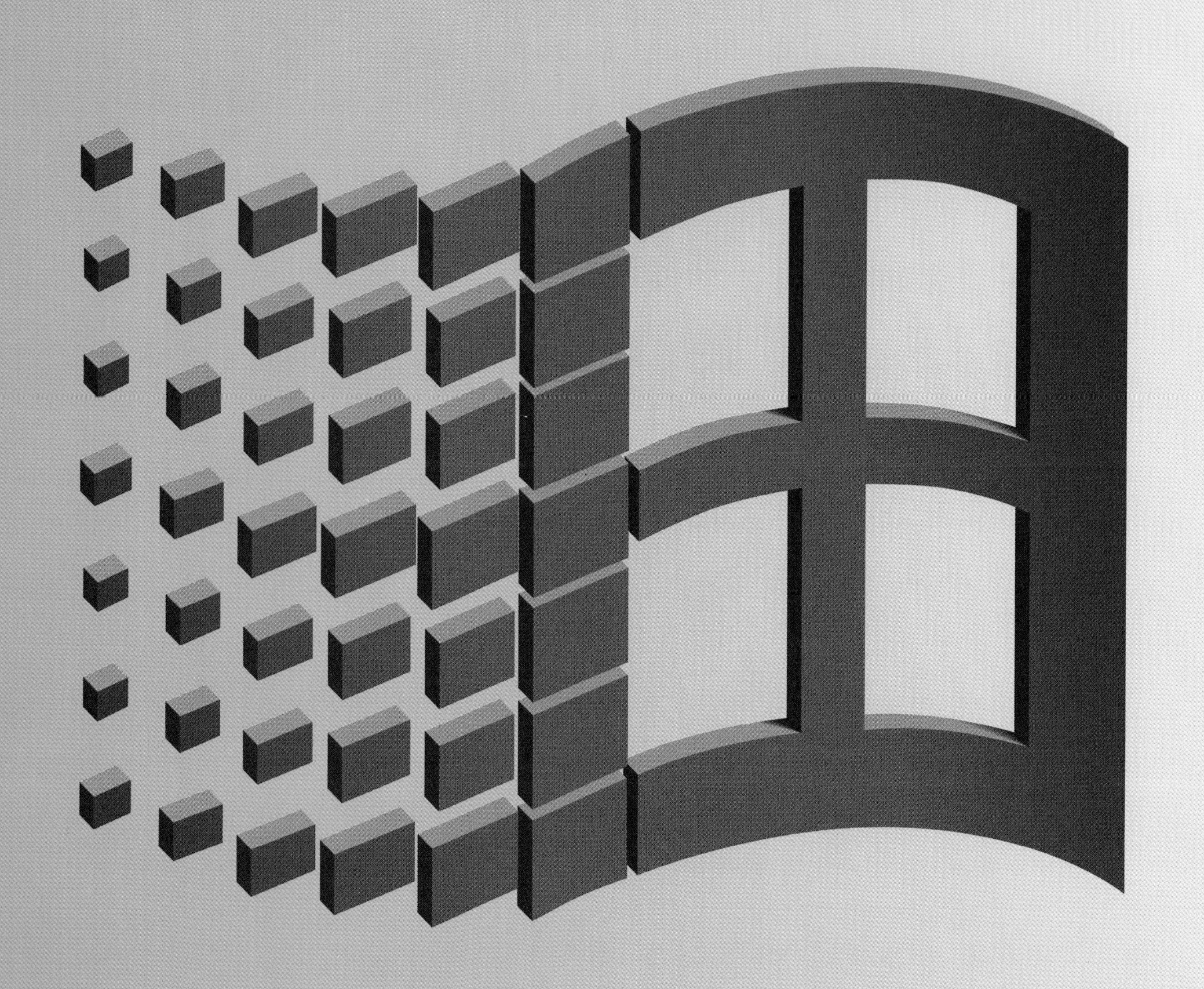

# CHAPTER 3

# Running Programs

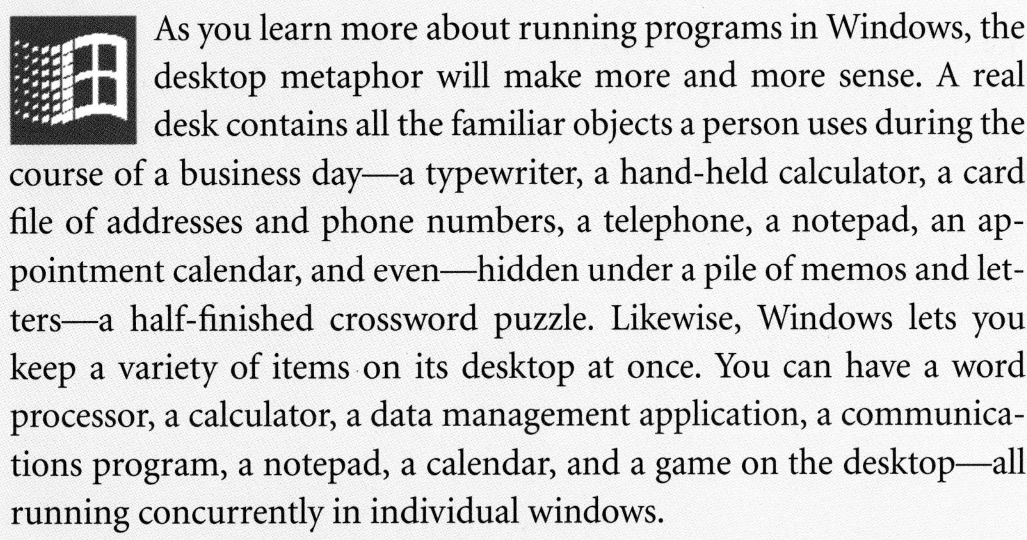

As you learn more about running programs in Windows, the desktop metaphor will make more and more sense. A real desk contains all the familiar objects a person uses during the course of a business day—a typewriter, a hand-held calculator, a card file of addresses and phone numbers, a telephone, a notepad, an appointment calendar, and even—hidden under a pile of memos and letters—a half-finished crossword puzzle. Likewise, Windows lets you keep a variety of items on its desktop at once. You can have a word processor, a calculator, a data management application, a communications program, a notepad, a calendar, and a game on the desktop—all running concurrently in individual windows.

This is one of the most important advantages of using Windows. Rather than using your computer inefficiently for one program at a time, you can place all your work in front of you at once. Each program on the desktop appears either as an icon or as an open application window. The active application is the one you are currently working on, but you can easily switch to any other program whenever you want.

In this chapter you'll practice working with multiple programs on the desktop and learn to use a variety of smooth techniques for switching among them. You'll also examine ways to arrange application windows on the desktop. Finally, you'll look at an important general tool used in most major Windows applications—the dialog box.

# How to Run Several Programs at Once

When you have multiple programs open on the desktop, you can use familiar mouse techniques to make your way from one of them to another. For example, if the active application window is taking up the entire screen, you simply click the window's minimize button to reduce the program to an icon. Then you can double-click another program icon to open a different application window. Here you'll practice opening and working with multiple applications. For the moment, it doesn't really matter which programs you start; just select a variety so you can see how the desktop looks with several activities going on at once.

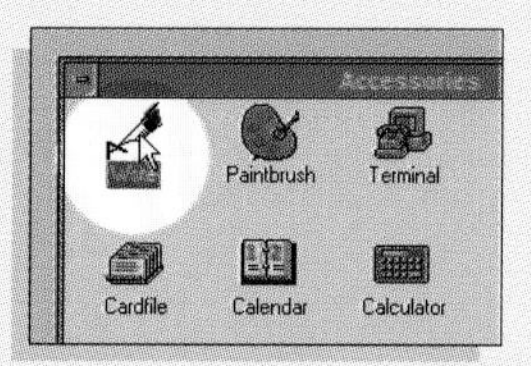


1. In the Program Manager window, select the group that contains a program you want to start. (Double-click the group icon if the group window is not open.) Inside the group window, double-click the program's icon. An application window for the program you've selected opens onto the desktop.

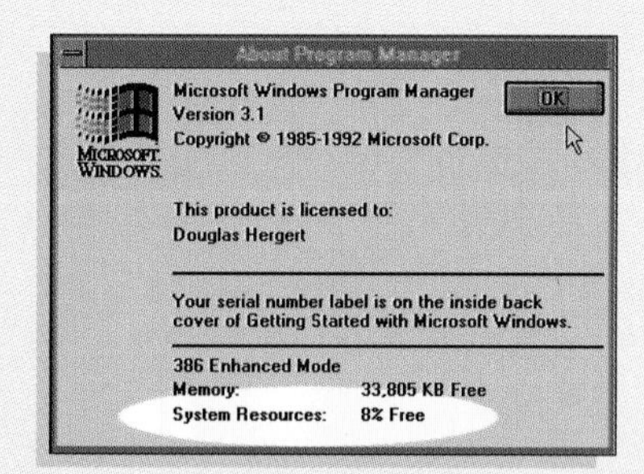


5. If you run too many programs at once, Windows may become sluggish. To check the status of your system, activate the Program Manager window and pull down the Help menu; then choose the About Program Manager command. In the resulting box, the System Resources line shows a percentage indicating the resources remaining. If this value is low (for example, less than 10 percent), you may not be able to start additional programs without closing one or more of those you're currently running.

## TIP SHEET

- If you try to run an additional program and Windows determines that your system does not have enough memory, a box named Application Execution Error appears on the screen. The box contains this message: "Insufficient memory to run this application. Quit one or more Windows applications and then try again." To carry out these instructions, close any programs that are not central to your current activities, and then try starting the new program.
- You don't necessarily have to minimize the active window to switch to another application. To read about another convenient switching technique, turn the page.
- To learn a technique for arranging open windows on the desktop, see "How to Display Windows in Cascade or Tile Arrangement" later in this chapter.

**2** If the Program Manager is now hidden behind the active application, reduce the application to an icon by clicking its minimize button. If you then find that the Program Manager window itself is minimized, double-click its icon.

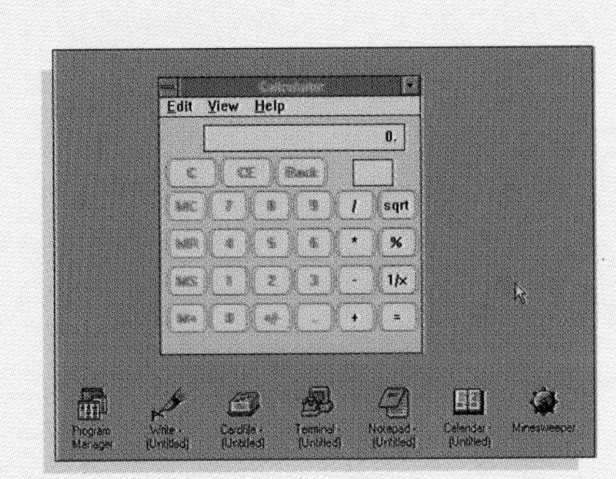


**3** Repeat steps 1 and 2 for each additional program you want to start. If your desktop begins to look crowded, you can conveniently minimize all the windows except the one you're working in.

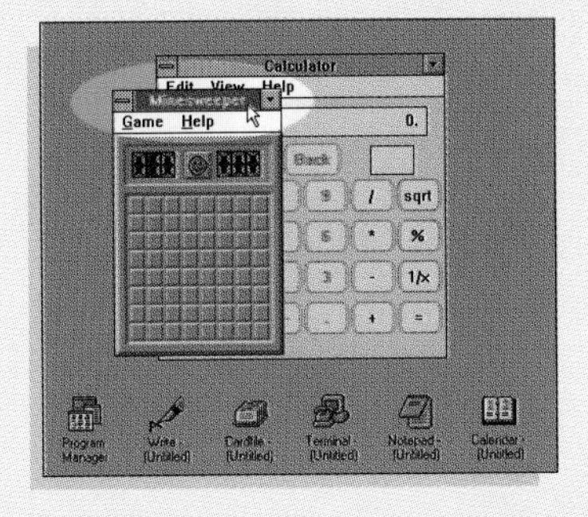


**4** To activate a program that is visible as an open application window on the desktop, move the mouse pointer anywhere inside the window and click the left mouse button. To activate a program that appears as an icon on the desktop, double-click the icon. Either way, the newly activated application window comes to the front of your work on the desktop.

# How to Switch between Applications

When you're running a major Windows application such as a word processor, you'll typically want to maximize the active application window, so you have as much space as possible for your current work. If you want to switch to another application, you can always use the familiar mouse actions of clicking the minimize button and then activating the program you want. But Windows also provides a keyboard technique for switching from one program to another. This two-key shortcut is always available, no matter where you are on the desktop.

## TIP SHEET

- **When you use the Alt+Tab shortcut to switch to a new program, the program you select is restored to its previous size and position on the desktop. If the application was maximized last time it was active, its window will be maximized again.**
- **If you are in the middle of using this technique and you suddenly decide that you don't want to switch programs after all, press the Esc key once and then release the Alt key. The box disappears from the middle of the screen, and the current application remains active.**
- **If you prefer to select from a list of all the applications that are currently running on the desktop, you can open a special window called the Task List.** **To read about the Task List, turn the page.**

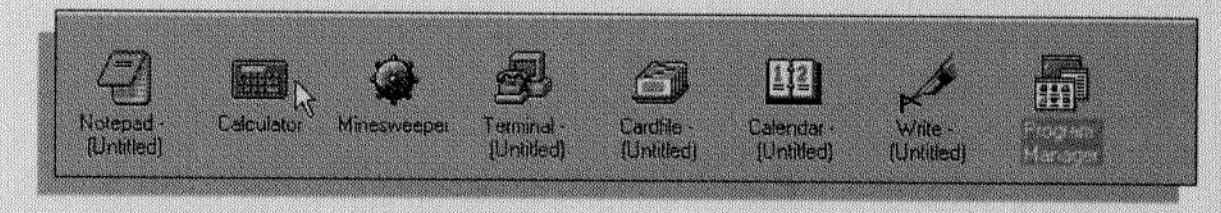


**1** Start the applications that you plan to use during the current session with Windows. Optionally, click the maximize button on the active application to expand your work over the entire screen.

**2** To switch to another application, hold down the Alt key and then press the Tab key once. (Don't release the Alt key yet.)

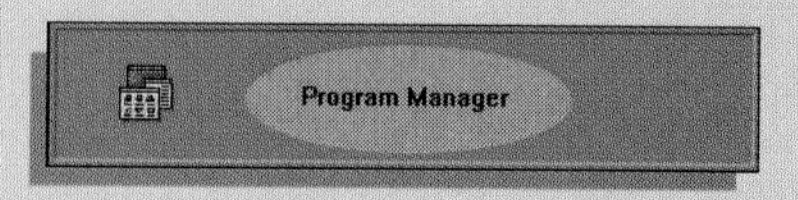


**5** To switch to the Program Manager window, hold down the Alt key and strike Tab until the box displays Program Manager. Then release the Alt key.

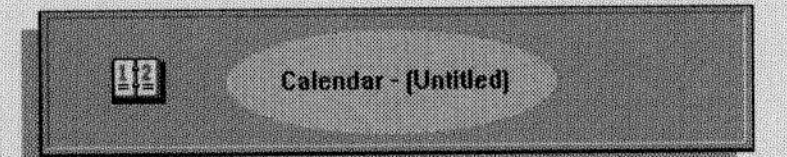


**3** A box appears in the middle of the screen, displaying the name and icon of another program that is running on the desktop. If this is the program you want to switch to, release the Alt key now. In response, Windows activates the selected program and moves its application window to the front of the desktop.

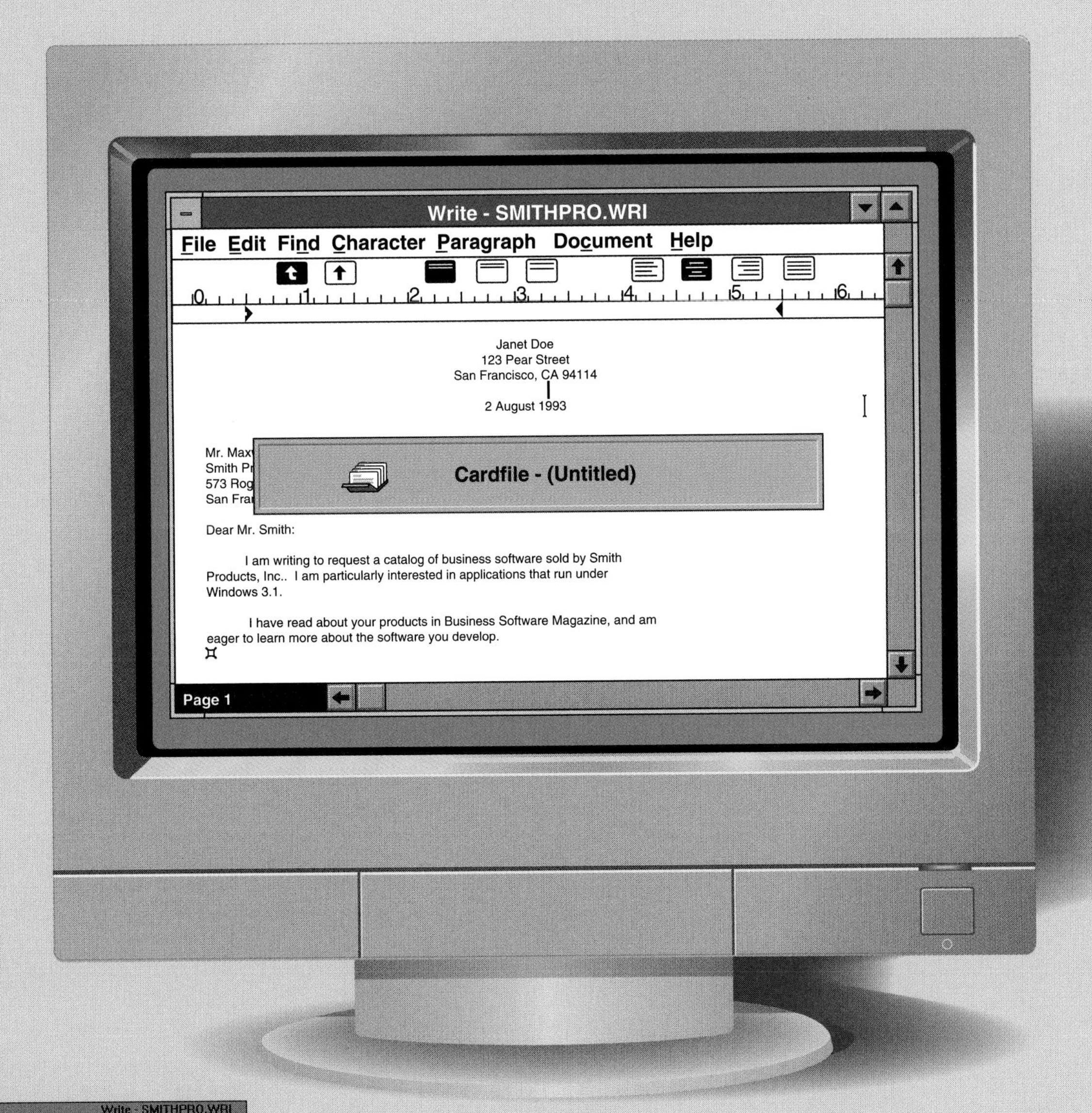


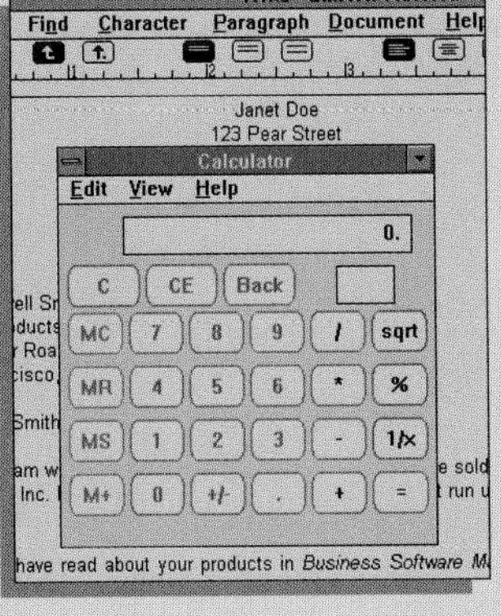


**4** If the box in the middle of the screen does not show the program you want to switch to, strike the Tab key repeatedly without releasing Alt. Each time you press Tab, the box displays the name of another application that is currently running on the desktop. When you see the name of the program you want to activate, release the Alt key. The program you've selected becomes the active application.

# How to Use the Task List

The Task List is designed to help you manage applications on the desktop. As shown in the central graphic on these pages, the Task List box contains a list of all the applications that are currently running on the desktop. Beneath the list is a collection of buttons you can click to perform specific operations. In the following steps you'll learn to use the Task List to switch from one running application to another.

## TIP SHEET

- **Instead of clicking the Switch To button after you select an application from the Task List, you can simply double-click the name of the application on the list.**
- **Here is another convenient way to open the Task List: Move the mouse pointer to any position on the *background* of the desktop—that is, to an area where no window or icon is displayed. Then double-click the left mouse button. (Of course, this technique is not available if the active application is maximized, because no part of the desktop background is visible.)**
- **If you change your mind about switching to a new application, you can close the Task List in either of two ways: Position the mouse pointer over the Cancel button and click the left mouse button; or simply press the Esc key on the keyboard.**
- **You can also use the Task List for arranging windows or icons on the desktop. Turn the page for details.**

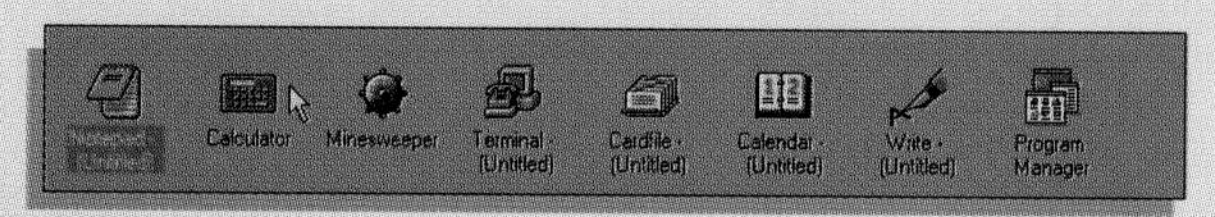


**1** Start any combination of applications. Select the program you want to work with first. (If necessary, double-click the program's icon on the desktop to open the application window.) Then click the maximize button to expand your work over the entire screen.

**2** To open the Task List, hold down the Ctrl key and then press Esc.

**5** To switch to the Program Manager window, press Ctrl+Esc to open the Task List box. Then click the Program Manager entry in the Task List. Click the Switch To button to carry out the switch.

3. In the list of tasks, position the mouse pointer over the name of the program you want to switch to, and then click the left mouse button. (If necessary, click the up- or down-arrow button on the vertical scroll bar to examine parts of the list that are not in view.)

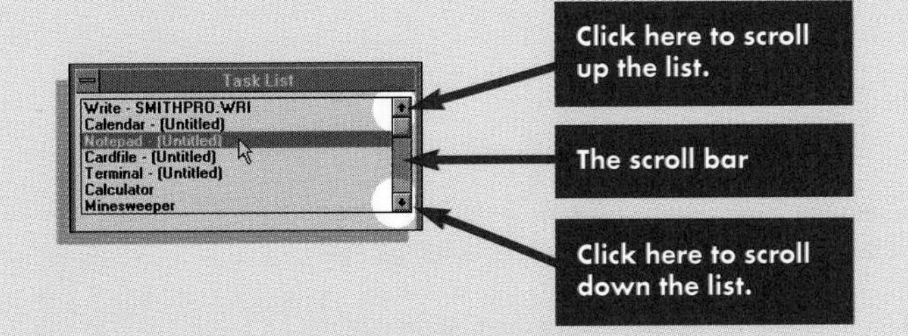


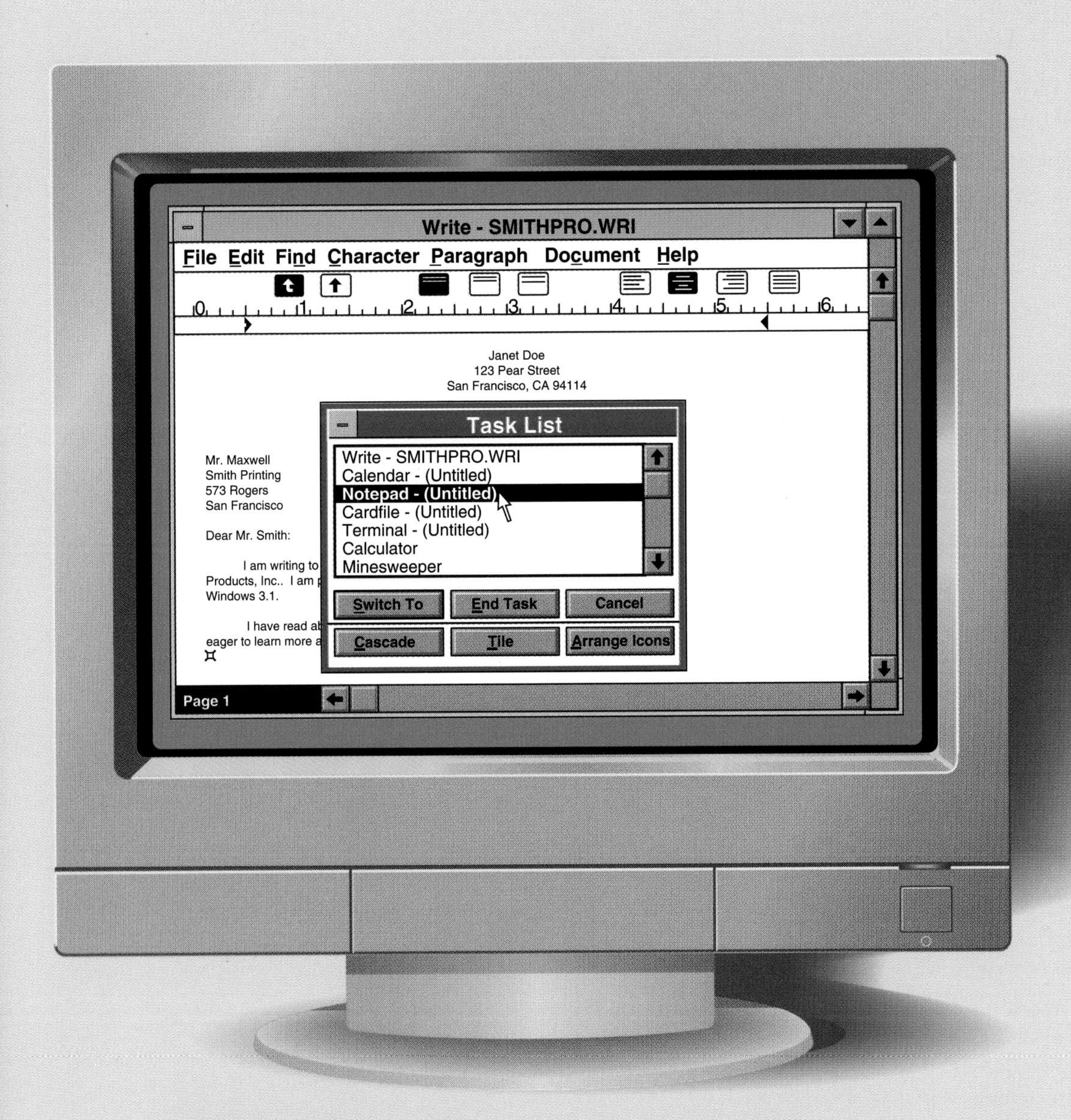

4. Position the mouse pointer over the Switch To button, and then click the left mouse button. The program you selected in the Task List becomes the active application.

# How to Display Windows in Cascade or Tile Arrangement

In addition to its use as a switching tool, the Task List gives you two quick ways to rearrange open application windows. In the *cascade* arrangement, windows are "stacked" one on top of another. Because the windows overlap, only the front window is fully visible in this arrangement; the others are identified by their title bars. In the *tile* arrangement, windows are automatically resized so they can appear side-by-side in a grid. The more windows you include, the smaller each window must be. Normally, there is no overlapping in tile arrangement.

Once you open the Task List, these two arrangements are just a mouse-click away.

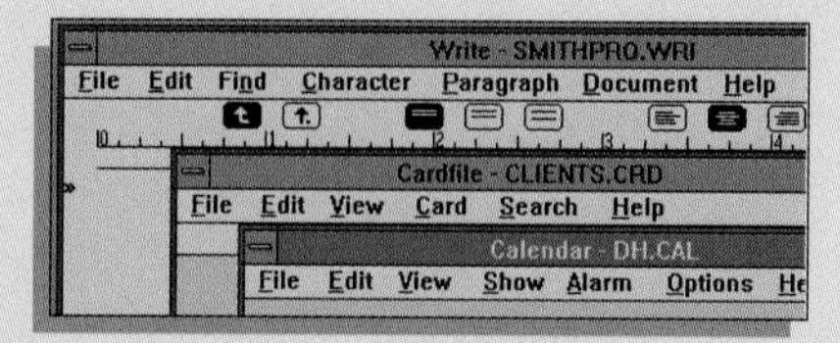


**1** Start the programs you want to work with and open all the application windows you want to include in a cascade or tile arrangement. (Applications that you don't want to include should be reduced to icons on the desktop.)

**5** In the Task List box, move the mouse pointer to the Tile button and click the left mouse button. In response, Windows displays all open windows in a tile arrangement, as shown in the central graphic on these pages.

**TIP SHEET**

- **The cascade and tile arrangements are also available for group windows inside the Program Manager window. See "How to Arrange Individual Windows" in Chapter 1 for details.**
- **You can also use the Task List to rearrange all the icons on the desktop. To do so, open the Task List and click the Arrange Icons button with the mouse. In response, Windows aligns all icons in one or more evenly-spaced rows at the bottom of the desktop.**

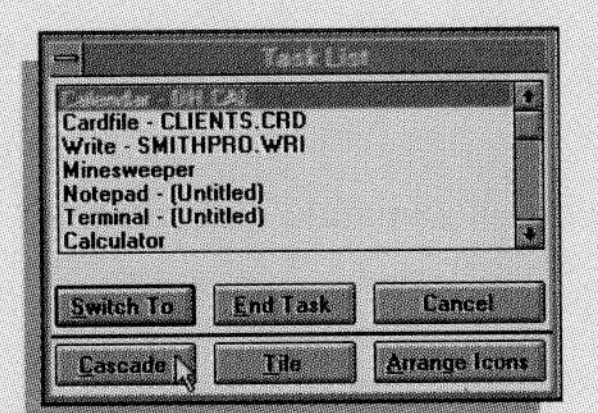

**2** Move the mouse pointer onto the desktop background—to any position where there is neither a window nor an icon. Then double-click the left mouse button to open the Task List. (If no desktop background is visible, hold down the Ctrl key and then press Esc to open the Task List.)

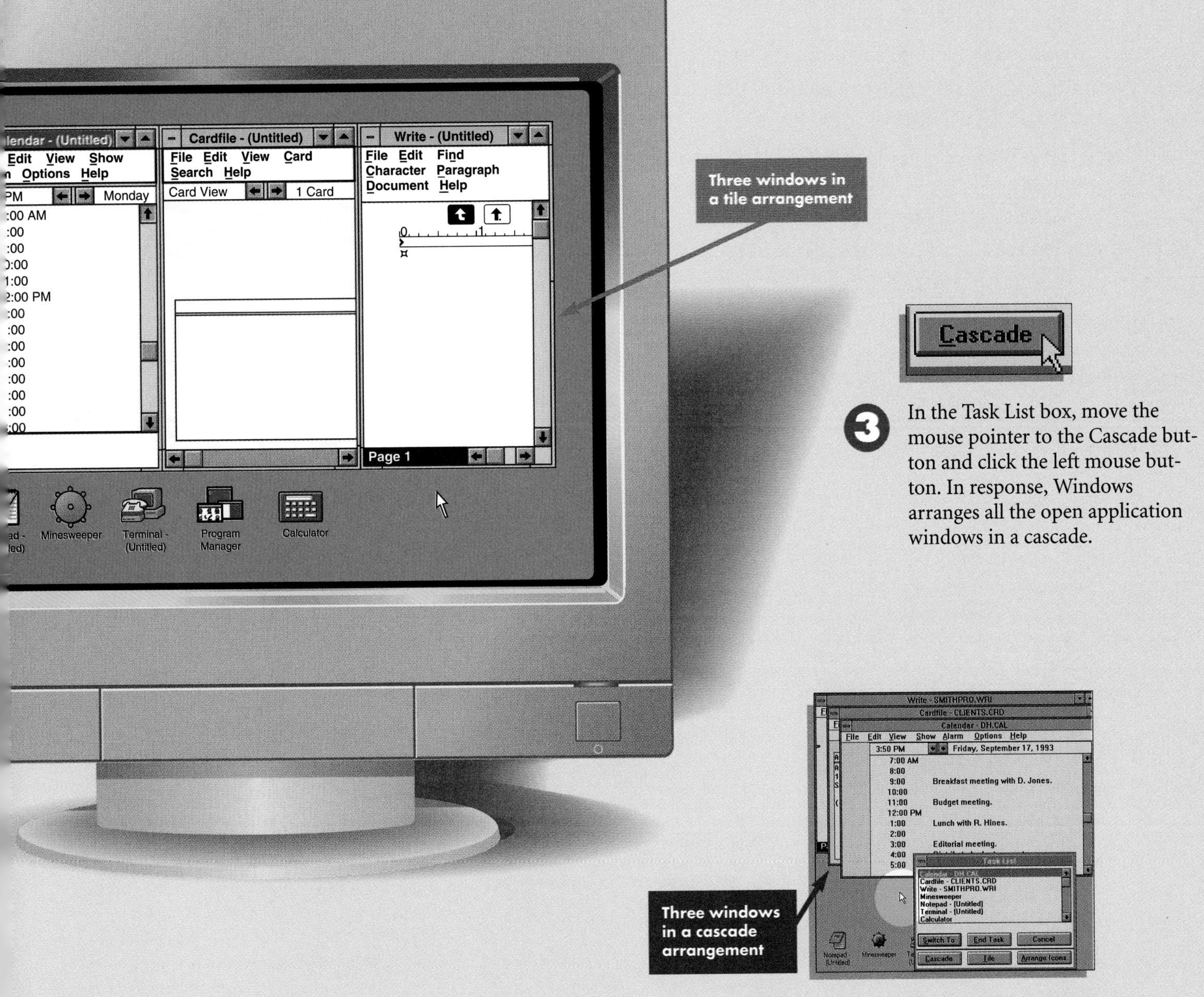


**3** In the Task List box, move the mouse pointer to the Cascade button and click the left mouse button. In response, Windows arranges all the open application windows in a cascade.

**4** Double-click anywhere on the desktop background (or press Ctrl+Esc) to open the Task List again.

# How to Use Dialog Boxes

A *dialog box* is a framed group of options from which you can make selections. A dialog box appears on the desktop when a program needs specific information from you. Dialog boxes often result when you select a menu command. You can tell when a dialog box is going to appear by looking at the command; if it's followed by an ellipsis, a dialog box will result. Dialog boxes contain several types of options that you'll quickly learn to recognize. You select an option by clicking it with the mouse, or by pressing the Tab key repeatedly until the option you want is selected.

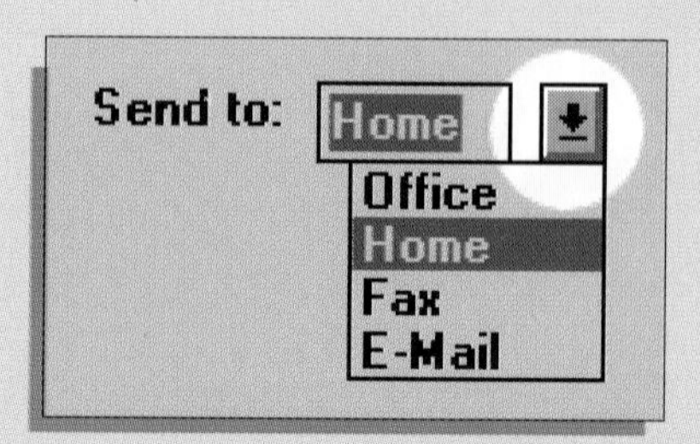


**2** To view the options in a drop-down list, click the arrow button that appears just to the right of the box. To make a selection, click any item in the list. Your selection is copied to the box above the list.

**1** To make an entry in a text box, select the box and type information directly from the keyboard. When a text box is selected, a flashing vertical *insertion point* shows you where text will appear when you start typing. When positioned over a text box, the mouse pointer takes the shape of an I-beam. In a text box that already contains information, you can click the I-beam at a location where you want to insert or edit text.

## TIP SHEET

- **You can select many dialog box options from the keyboard. To do so, hold down the Alt key and then press the underlined letter in the option's caption. For example, to choose the Right option from a group of option buttons, press Alt+R.**
- **In a dialog box that contains several command buttons, the *default* button has a heavier black border than the others. Often, the OK button is the default. To select the default, you can simply press Enter.**
- **You can usually select the Cancel button in a dialog box by pressing Esc.**
- **Although most dialog boxes have a fixed size, you can move a box to any location on the desktop. To do so, simply drag the box by its title bar.**

**6** To choose a command button, position the mouse pointer over the option and click the left mouse button. In response, the application immediately carries out the action the command button represents. Clicking the OK button is the usual way to confirm your selections in a dialog box. To close a dialog box without performing any action, click the Cancel button.

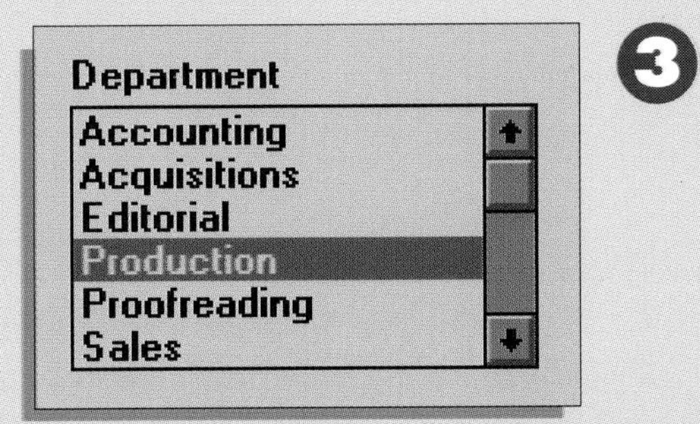


**3** To make a selection from a list box, click any item in the list with the mouse. In response, Windows hightlights your selection. A vertical scroll bar at the right side of the list box indicates that there are more entries in the list than can be displayed in the box. Click the up- or down-arrow on the scroll bar to view another part of the list.

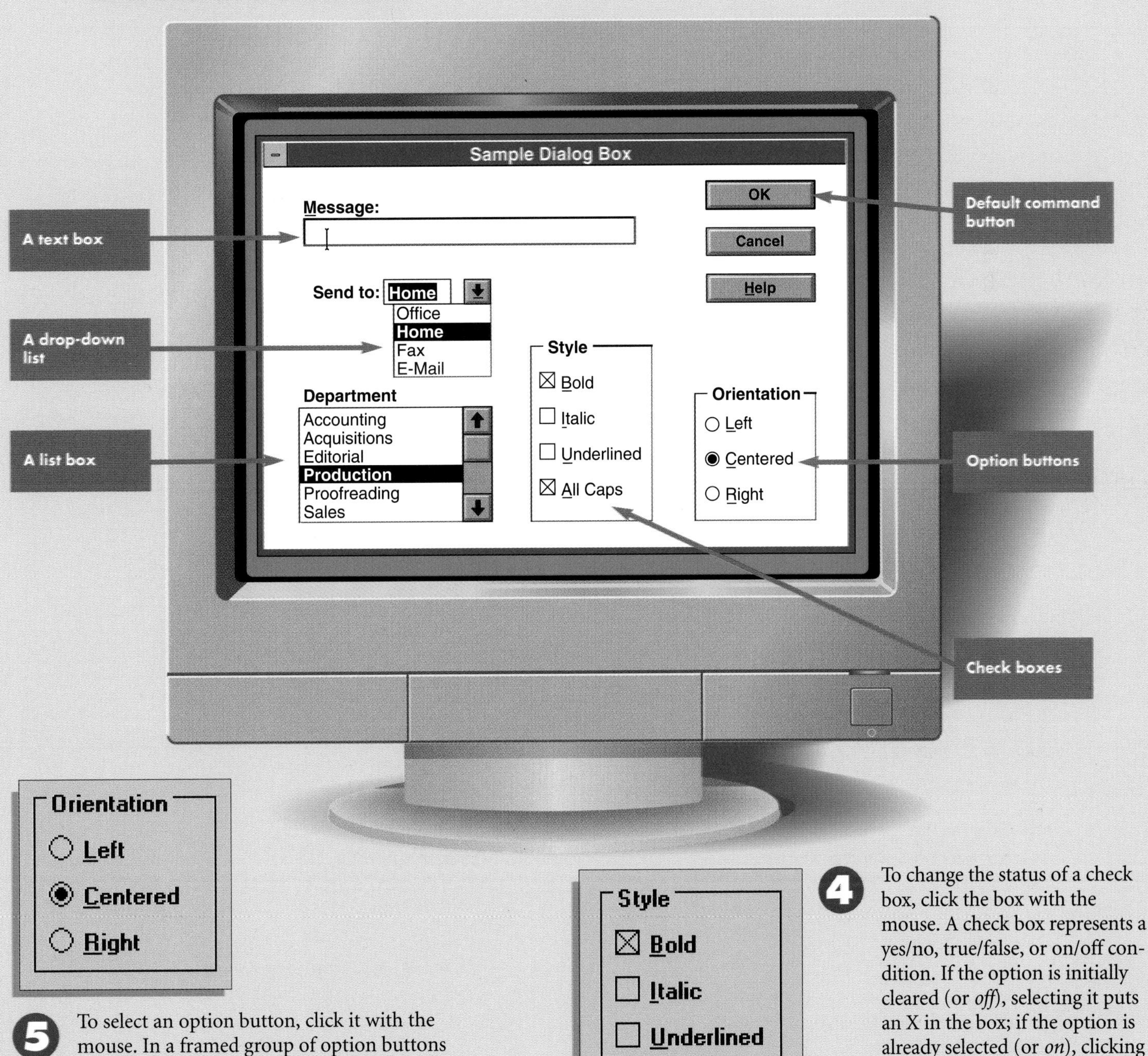


Orientation
Left
Centered
Right

**5** To select an option button, click it with the mouse. In a framed group of option buttons (also known as *radio buttons*), only one can be selected at a time; in other words, these options are mutually exclusive. Windows displays a bold black dot in the selected option button.

Style
Bold
Italic
Underlined
All Caps

**4** To change the status of a check box, click the box with the mouse. A check box represents a yes/no, true/false, or on/off condition. If the option is initially cleared (or *off*), selecting it puts an X in the box; if the option is already selected (or *on*), clicking it clears the X. Each check box is independent; you are free to select or clear any combination of these options.

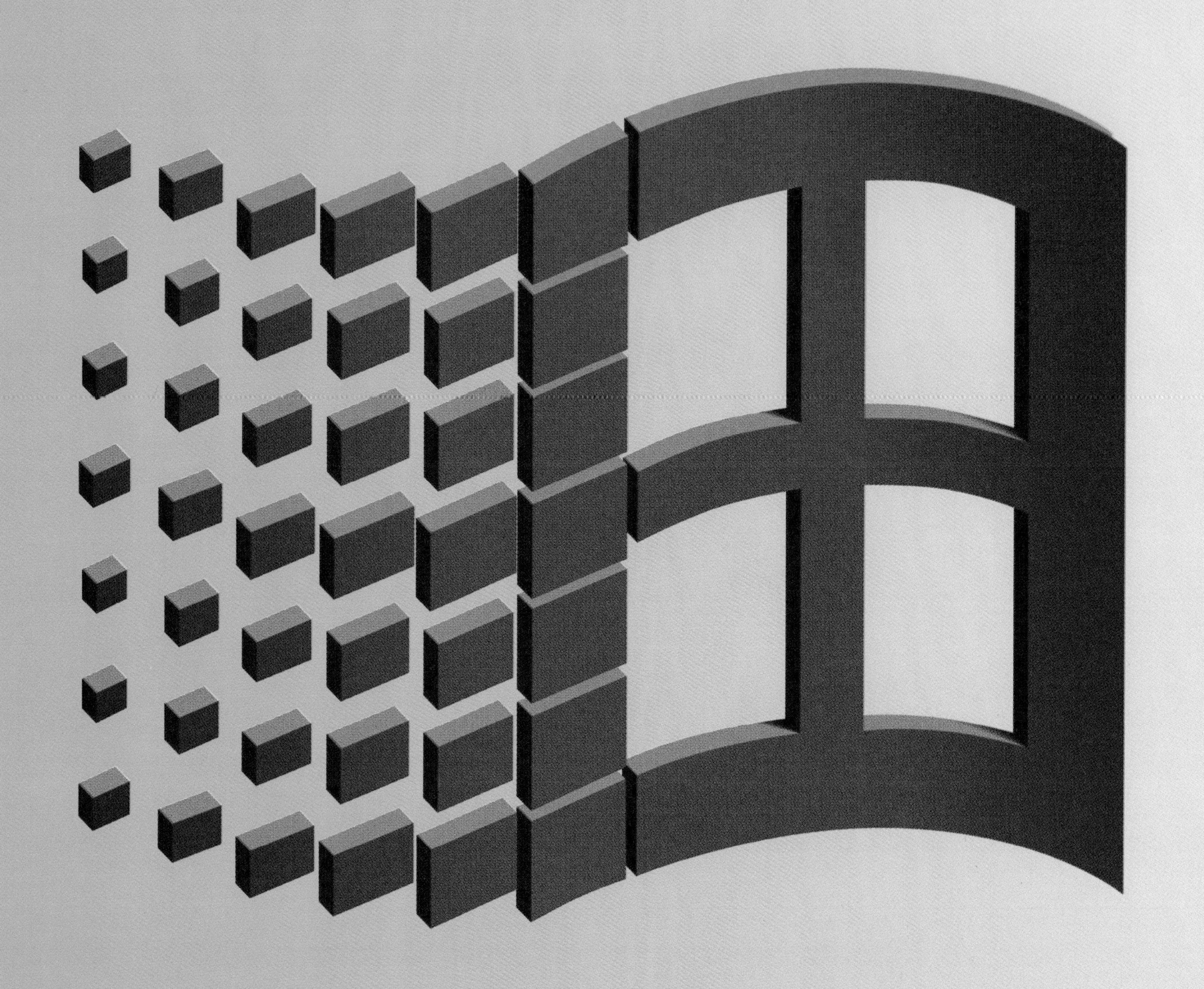

# CHAPTER 4

# Reorganizing Groups in the Program Manager

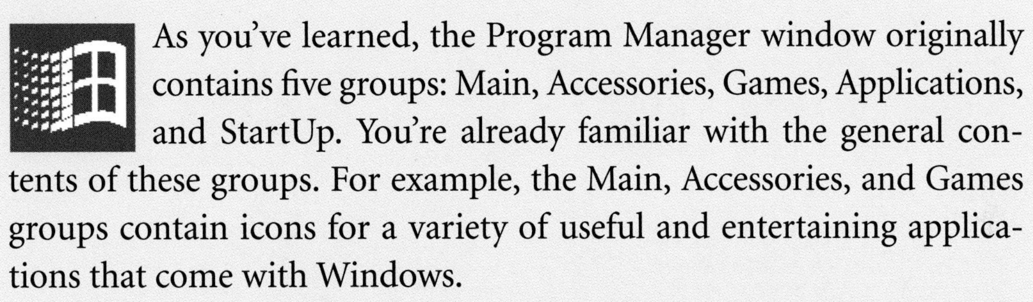

As you've learned, the Program Manager window originally contains five groups: Main, Accessories, Games, Applications, and StartUp. You're already familiar with the general contents of these groups. For example, the Main, Accessories, and Games groups contain icons for a variety of useful and entertaining applications that come with Windows.

But Windows allows you to reorganize your program icons to suit your own daily work routine. In this chapter you'll explore several methods for changing the groups in the Program Manager window. You'll learn to create new groups for organizing icons, copy or move icons from one group to another, and add new icons to a group for applications that are not already represented by icons in the Program Manager. In addition, you'll learn how to create *automatic applications*—programs that start automatically at the beginning of each Windows session—by adding icons to the StartUp group. As you'll see, the Program Manager is a very flexible control center for your operations in Windows.

# How to Create a New Group

The original groups in the Program Manager window are organized in broad categories that may or may not be convenient for you. At the beginning of a Windows session, you might have to open two or more group windows and search for the icons you need. To solve this problem, you can create your own custom group windows within the Program Manager. Then you can copy selected program icons from groups that already exist to bring together a convenient group. By creating one or more new groups, you can reorganize the program icons in a way that makes sense for your own day-to-day activities.

## TIP SHEET

- **If you prefer, you can use the Copy command on the Program Manager's File menu to copy a program icon from one group to another. Select the icon you want to copy; then pull down the File menu and choose Copy. The Copy Program Item dialog box identifies the icon you have selected. Pull down the To Group list and select the group to which you want the icon copied. Then click OK.**
- **Alternatively, you can move an icon from one group to another. To do so, drag the icon from its original group to the new group *without* holding down the Ctrl key.**
- **Copying a program icon is not the same as copying the program file itself. In fact, the process of copying a program icon does not affect the application at all. Copies of icons take up little space on your hard disk.**

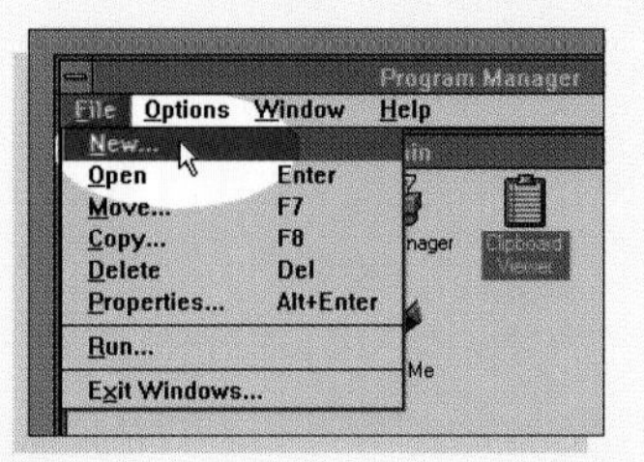


1. If the Program Manager window is not already open, double-click its icon with the mouse. Then pull down the File menu and click the New command.

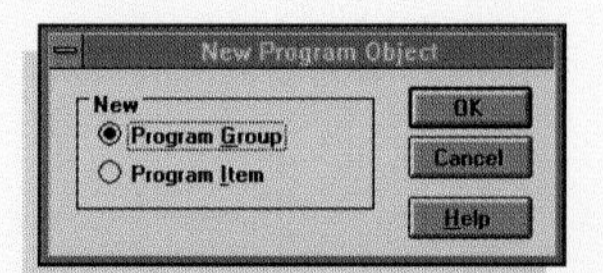


2. The New Program Object dialog box appears on the desktop. The options in this dialog box allow you to create a new group or add a new program icon to an existing group. Click the Program Group option button if this option is not already selected. Then click the OK button.

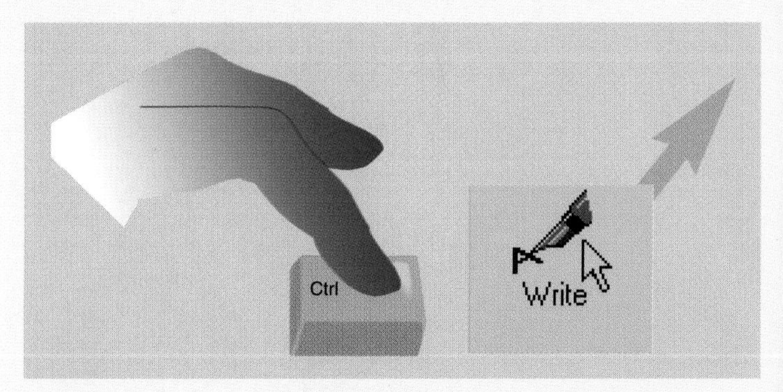


6. To copy a program icon, hold down the Ctrl key and drag the icon from its original group to your new group. When the icon arrives in the new group, release the mouse button and then the Ctrl key. The icon remains in the original group and a copy appears in the new group. Repeat this step for each icon you want to include in your new group.

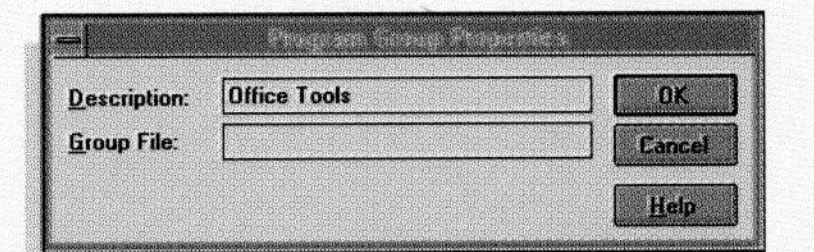


3 The Program Group Properties dialog box appears next on the desktop. In the Description text box, enter a name for your new group. This name will appear in the group window's title bar. You can leave the Group File box blank.

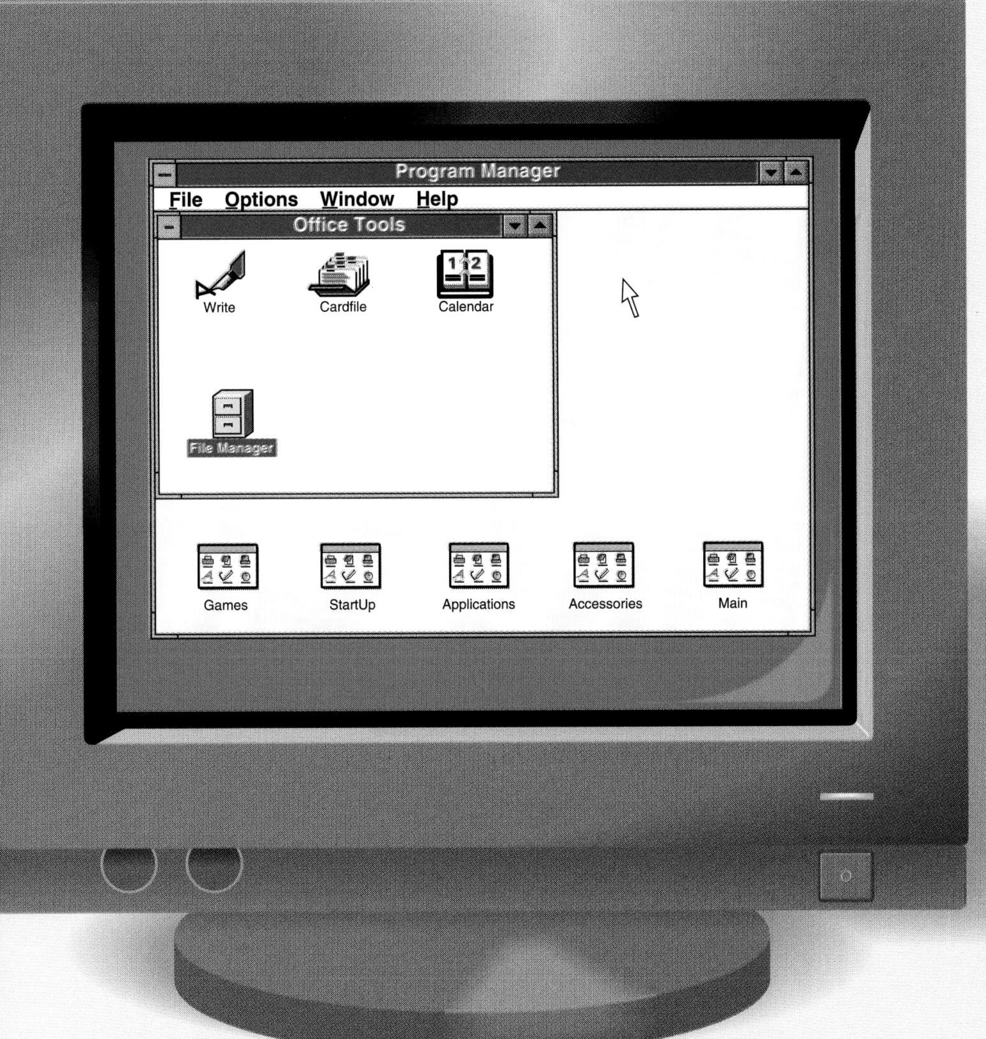


4 Click the OK button. In response, Windows creates the new group and opens it in the Program Manager window.

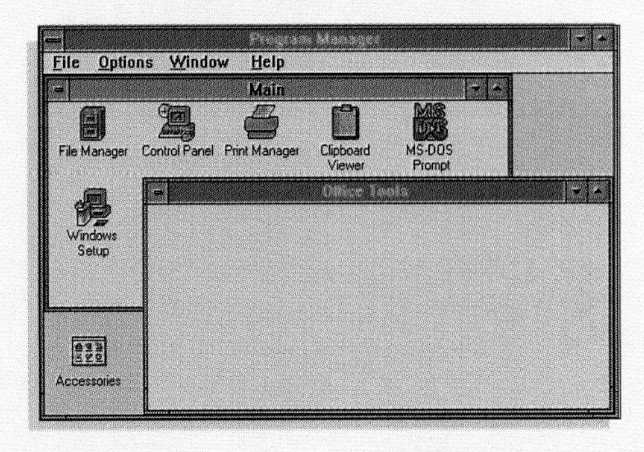


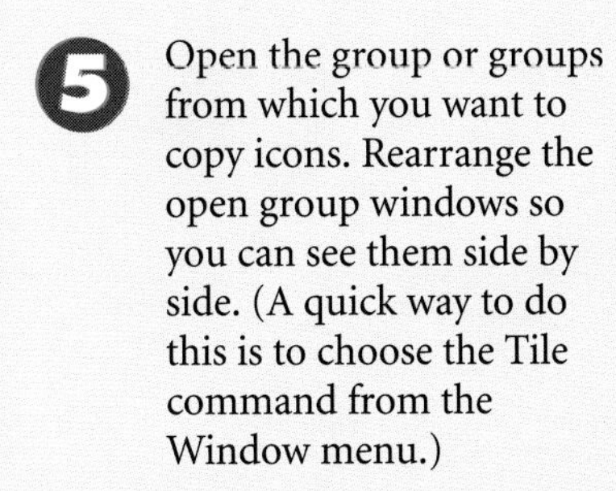

5 Open the group or groups from which you want to copy icons. Rearrange the open group windows so you can see them side by side. (A quick way to do this is to choose the Tile command from the Window menu.)

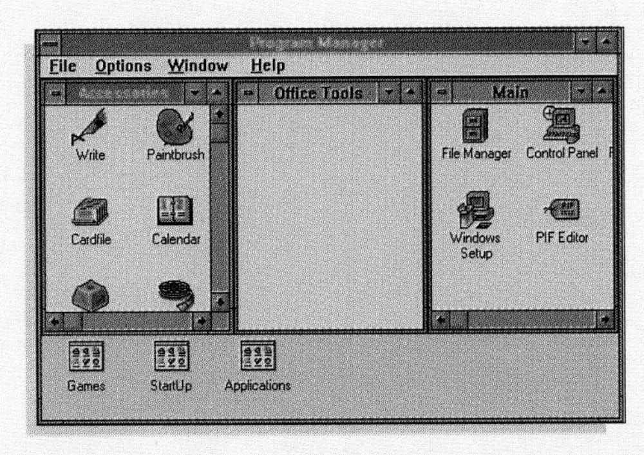

# How to Add a New Program Icon to a Group

Sometimes your computer's hard disk may contain a Windows program that is not yet represented by an icon in the Program Manager. In this case, you can use the New command on the Program Manager's File menu to add the program's icon to a group. Before you begin, you need two pieces of information: the name of the program file on disk and the directory location, or *path*, of the file. Once you know a program's name and location, you can easily install an icon for it in any group you choose.

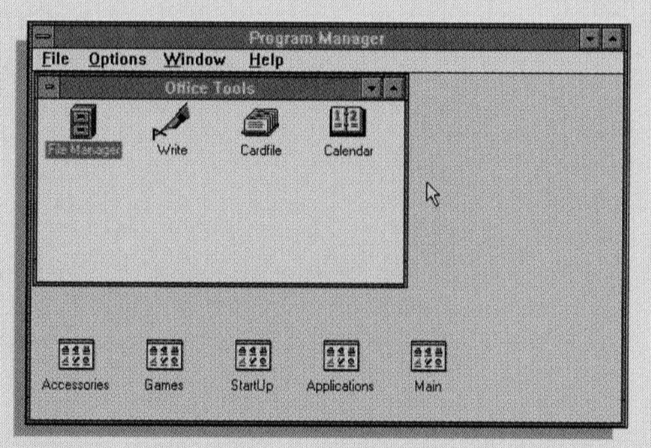


**1** Select the group in which you want the new program icon to appear. If the group window is closed, double click its icon to open it.

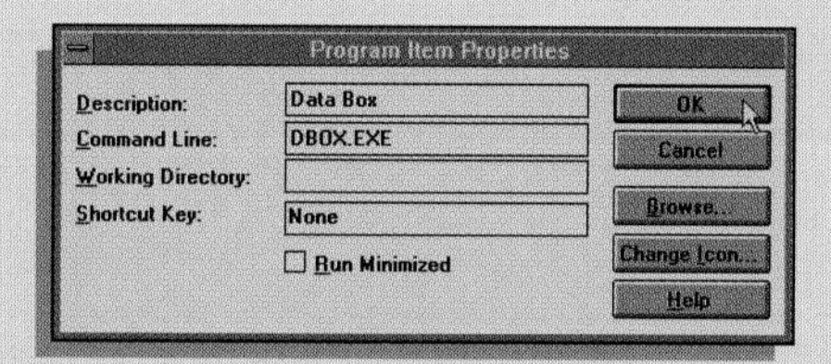


**4** The Program Item Properties dialog box appears next on the desktop. In the Description text box, enter a caption for the icon you are adding to the group. Then press Tab to select the Command Line text box and enter the path and file name of the program this new icon will represent. (If the program file is located in the Windows directory, you can omit the path name, as shown here.) Click the OK button to confirm these entries. As shown in the central graphic on these pages, the new program icon appears in the current group. You can now double-click this icon to start the application.

## TIP SHEET

- **If you're not sure where the program file you want is located on your hard disk, click the Browse button in the Program Item Properties dialog box. You can use the resulting Browse dialog box to locate the application you want to add to the current group. To find out what program files a particular directory contains, double-click the directory's name in the Directories box. The file list then shows the names of all the program files in the selected directory. When you find the program you want to add, select its name on the file list and then click OK in the Browse dialog box. To confirm your selection, click OK in the Program Item dialog box.**

**2** In the Program Manager's menu bar, pull down the File menu and click the New command.

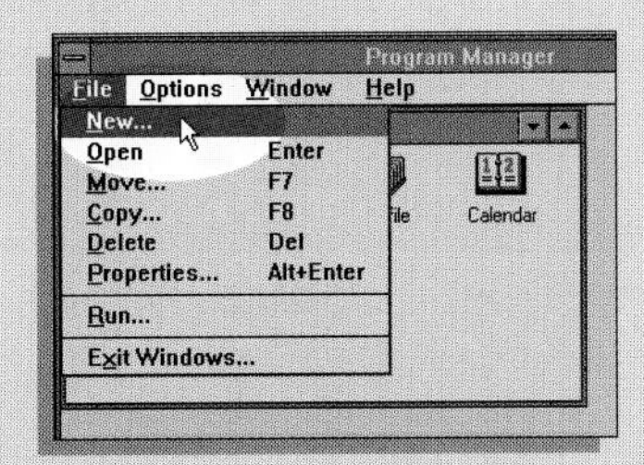

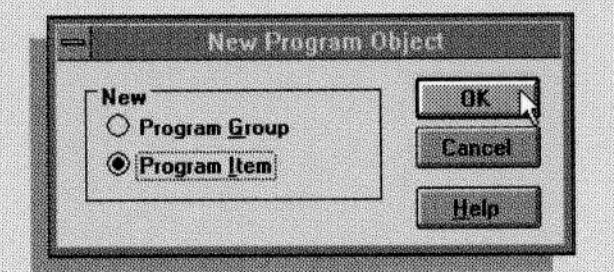


**3** The New Program Object dialog box appears on the desktop. Because you opened a group before choosing the New command, the Program Item option is already selected. This is the correct option for adding a new icon to the current group, so click the OK button to confirm the selection.

# How to Set Up Automatic Applications

StartUp is a special group window that allows you to define automatic applications. Each application you add to the group will start automatically at the beginning of every Windows session. Using techniques you have learned in this chapter, you can place one or more icons in the group. It's a good idea to place icons for applications that you use every day in the StartUp group. By doing so, you save yourself the trouble of starting these applications yourself at the beginning of each session.

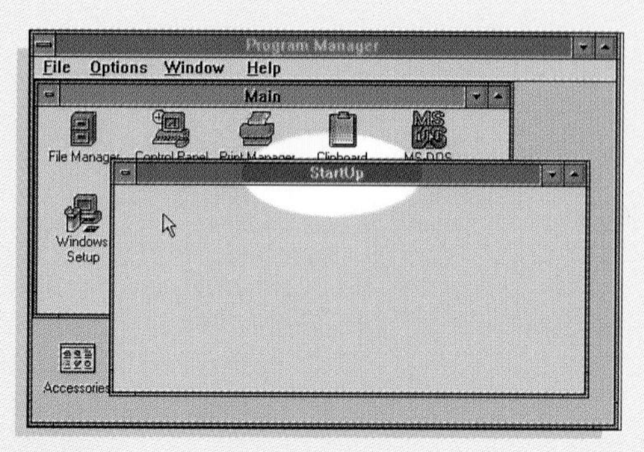


**1** Select the StartUp group. If the group is closed, double-click its icon to open it. The StartUp group remains empty until you add one or more icons to it.

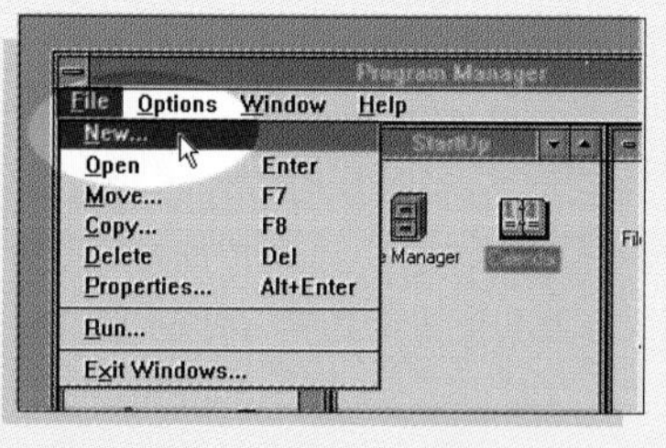


**5** To add an icon to the StartUp group for a program that is not yet represented as an icon in any other group, pull down the File menu and choose the New command. Then follow steps 3 and 4 of the previous section ("How to Add a New Program Icon to a Group").

## TIP SHEET

- **When you are finished adding icons to the StartUp group, you can minimize the group window if you wish. The next time you start Windows, all the applications in this special group will start automatically at the beginning of the session.**
- **If you copy two or more icons to the StartUp group, the applications start in the order in which they are arranged—that is, from left to right, starting with the first row of icons in the group.**
- **If you no longer want an application to start automatically, you can delete the program's icon from the StartUp group. Open the group, select the icon you want to delete, and press Del on the keyboard. Windows asks you to confirm the deletion; click the Yes button in the Delete box if you are sure you want to delete the icon.**

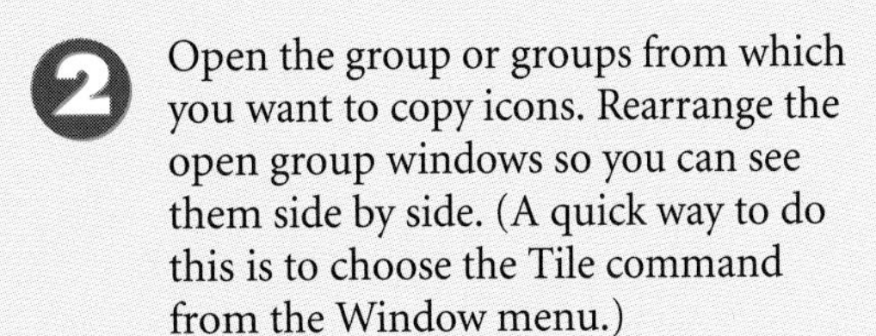


**2** Open the group or groups from which you want to copy icons. Rearrange the open group windows so you can see them side by side. (A quick way to do this is to choose the Tile command from the Window menu.)

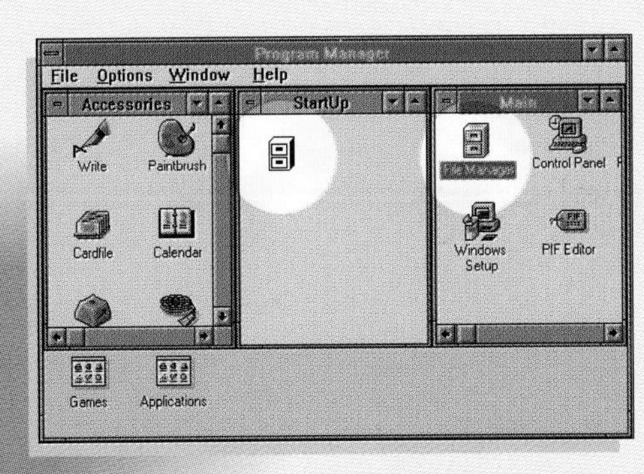


**3** To copy a program icon to the StartUp group, hold down the Ctrl key and drag the icon from its original group to the StartUp group. When the icon arrives in the StartUp group, release the mouse button and then the Ctrl key. The icon remains in the original group and a copy appears in the StartUp group.

**4** To move a program icon to the StartUp group, drag the icon from its original group to the StartUp group. When the icon arrives in the StartUp group, release the mouse button. The icon disappears from its original group and appears in the StartUp group.

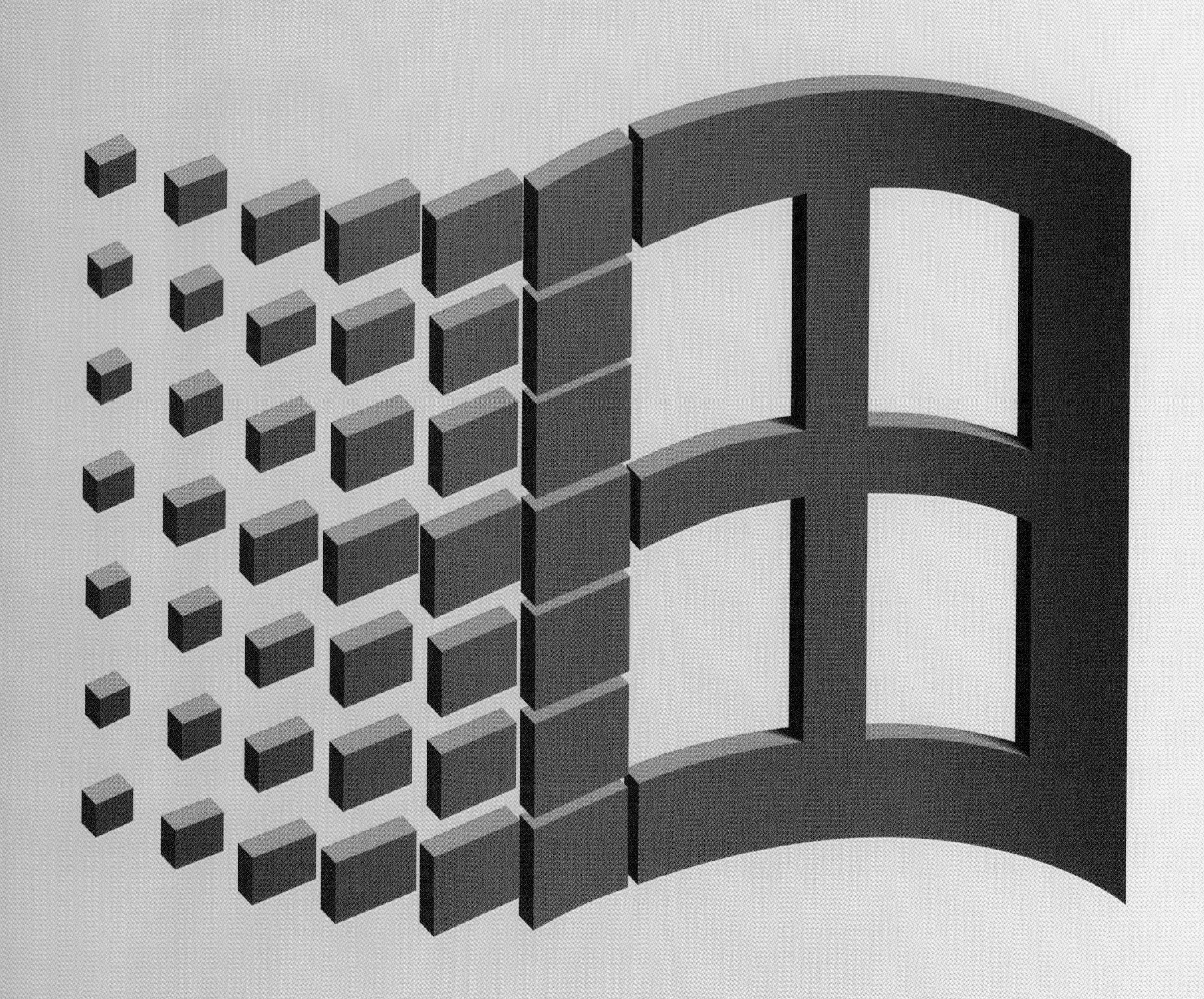

## CHAPTER 5

# Changing the Windows Settings

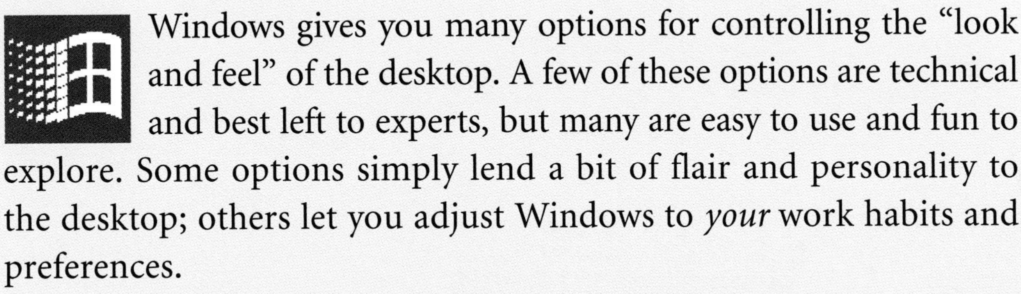

Windows gives you many options for controlling the "look and feel" of the desktop. A few of these options are technical and best left to experts, but many are easy to use and fun to explore. Some options simply lend a bit of flair and personality to the desktop; others let you adjust Windows to *your* work habits and preferences.

You gain access to these options by double-clicking the Control Panel icon in the Main group. The Control Panel window displays icons representing the various changes you can make to the Windows environment. In this chapter you'll learn to change the colors of the desktop, fine-tune the behavior of the mouse, and change the system time and date settings. Along the way, you'll also gain a better appreciation of how flexible the Windows environment is.

# How to Change the Colors of Windows

Windows allows you to change the colors that appear on the desktop. There are several reasons you might want to select new colors: Different colors may be more soothing, or at least relieve the monotony of staring at your computer screen for hours on end. Also, your screen may produce better images with particular colors. Whatever your reason, you can choose from a list of predefined color schemes that Windows supplies. You can view the list of color schemes and see screen samples of any scheme by double clicking the Color icon in the control panel window.

**TIP SHEET**

- **Once you've selected a color scheme, you can revise it by choosing your own colors for specific elements of the desktop. To do so, click the Color Palette button, near the bottom of the Color dialog box. The dialog box doubles in width, and a Basic Colors palette appears to the right of the sample screen. To make a change in the selected color scheme, click any element on the sample screen and then click a new color on the palette.**
- **Another way to change the colors and appearance of the screen is to choose one of the patterns or "wallpaper" designs that Windows supplies for the desktop background. To find these options, double-click the Desktop icon in the Control Panel.**

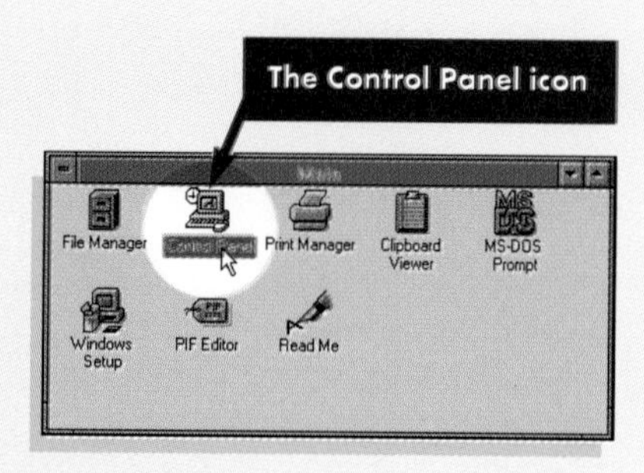


**1** In the Program Manager's Main group, double-click the Control Panel icon.

**6** When you find a scheme you like, click the OK button at the lower-left corner of the Color dialog box. Then close the Control Panel by choosing the Exit command from its Settings menu. Your desktop now displays the colors of the new scheme you have selected.

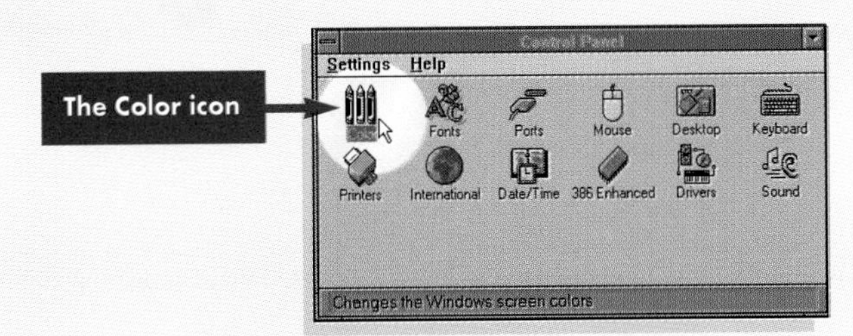


**2** The Control Panel window appears on the desktop. Double-click the Color icon, the first entry in the panel.

**3** The Color dialog box appears next on the desktop. Notice the name of the current color selection, displayed in the Color Schemes box. If this is the first time the colors have been changed in your installation of Windows, the name Windows Default is displayed. Click the down-arrow button at the right side of the box to see the drop-down list of other color schemes.

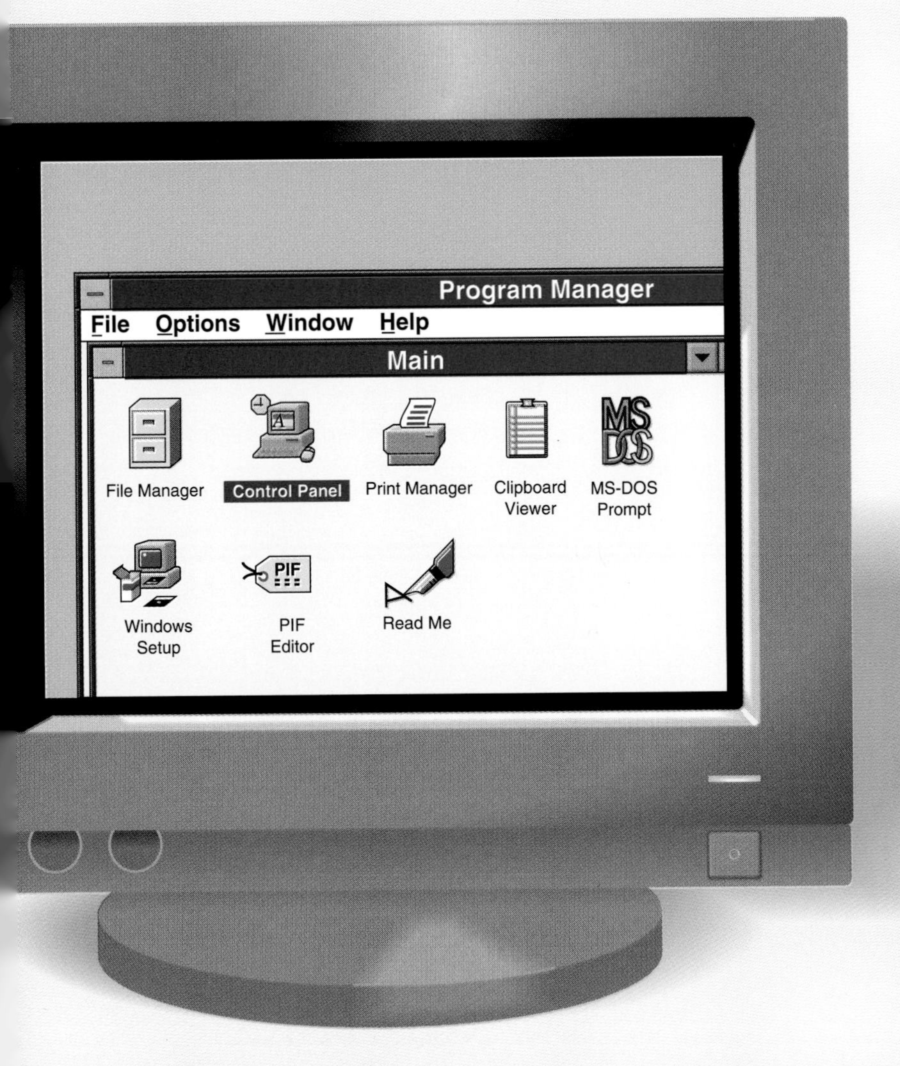


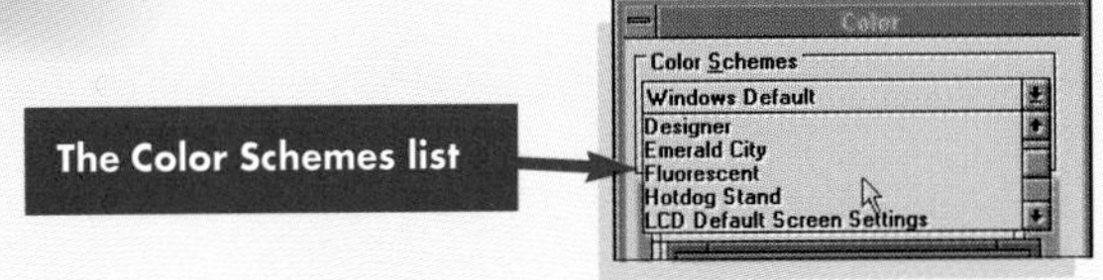


**4** Scroll through the Color Schemes list. It contains about two dozen color schemes.

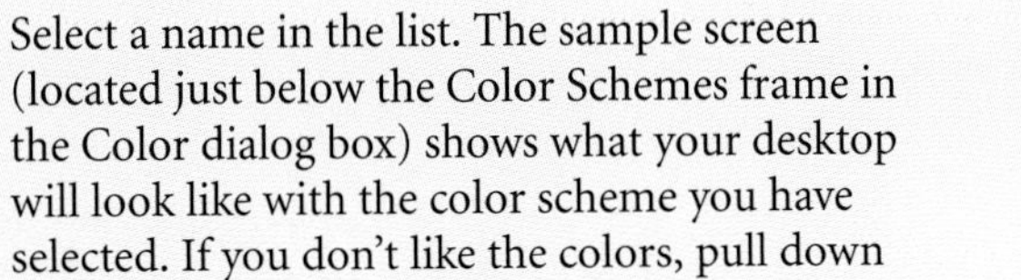

**5** Select a name in the list. The sample screen (located just below the Color Schemes frame in the Color dialog box) shows what your desktop will look like with the color scheme you have selected. If you don't like the colors, pull down the list again and try another scheme.

# How to Change the Mouse Settings

Windows allows you to change several mouse characteristics, including the clicking rate required for a successful double-click; the *tracking speed*, or speed at which the mouse pointer moves across the screen in relation to the movement of the mouse itself; and the primary button for most Windows operations. By default, the left button is the primary mouse button and the right button is reserved for application-specific uses, but Windows allows you to reverse these roles. If you are left-handed, this may be one of the most important options available through the Control Panel.

**1** Double-click the Control Panel icon in the Main group.

**6** When you have selected all the mouse options you want to change, click the OK button on the Mouse dialog box. Then choose the Exit command from the Settings menu in the Control Panel window.

**TIP SHEET**

- **If you choose the Swap Left/Right Buttons option, be aware that the change in the roles of the two buttons takes place immediately. Any subsequent Windows operations—even within the Mouse dialog box itself—must be performed with the right mouse button.**
- **The Mouse dialog box offers one additional option, known as *mouse trails.* When you activate the Mouse Trails option, any movement of the mouse produces a trail of pointer icons on the desktop. On some monitors this effect may help you follow the pointer's movement across the desktop. To display mouse trails, click the Mouse Trails option. An X appears in the check box. To test the effect, move the mouse pointer around the desktop and notice the trail of pointers it leaves behind.**

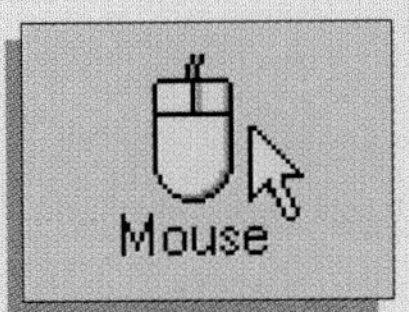


**2** Double-click the Mouse icon in the Control Panel window.

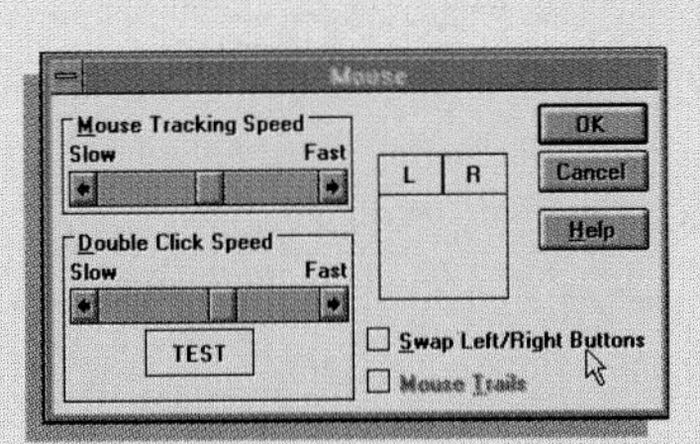


**3** The Mouse dialog box appears on the screen. If you are left-handed, begin by clicking the Swap Left/Right Buttons option. An X appears in the check box.

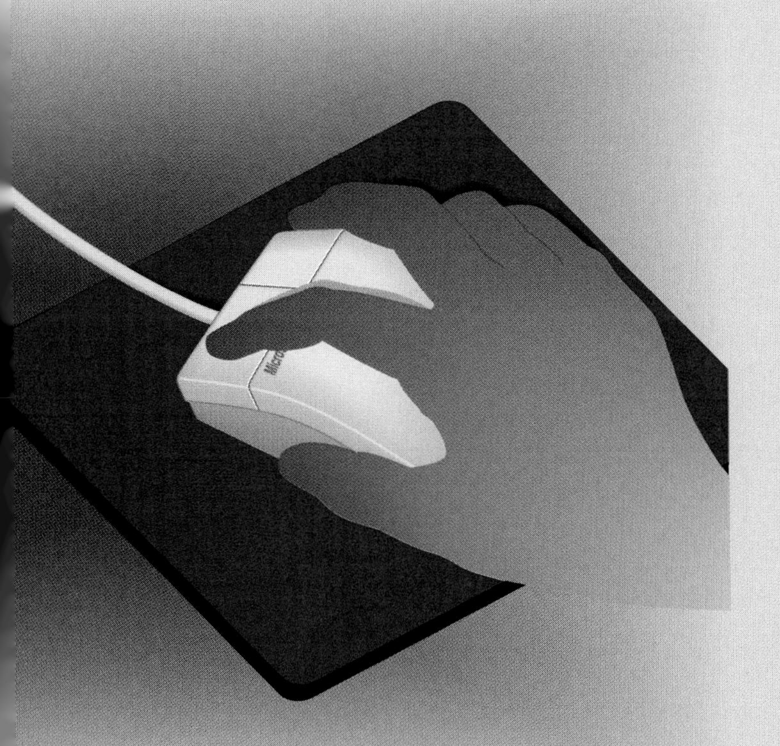

**4** To increase or decrease the tracking speed, click the left- or right-arrow button at either end of the Mouse Tracking Speed scroll bar. (Alternatively, drag the scroll box toward the left or right side of the bar.) To test the effect of this change, move the mouse and notice the corresponding movement of the mouse pointer on the desktop.

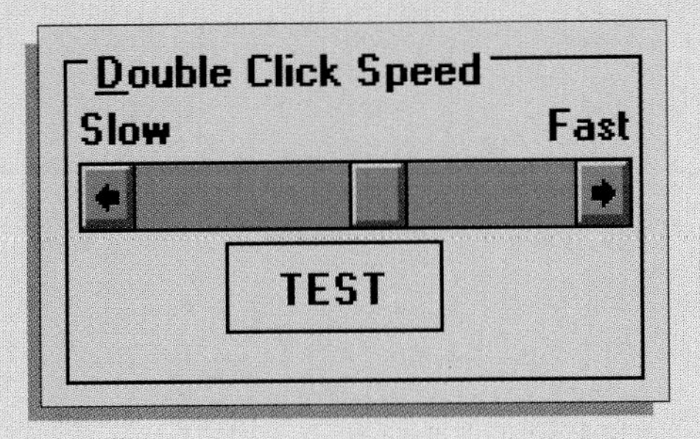


**5** To increase or decrease the double-click speed, click the arrow button at either end of the Double Click Speed scroll bar or drag the scroll box toward the left or right side of the bar. To test the effect, double-click the TEST button; if the double-click action is successful, the button changes from white to black or vice versa.

# How to Change the Date and Time Settings

Your computer's internal clock and calendar supply the current time and date for many important operations. Individual applications use these settings for their own purposes. In addition, every file you save to disk is automatically "stamped" with the current date and time. You may need to adjust the time and date occasionally to keep them accurate. The Control Panel's Date/Time icon supplies a dialog box in which you can change these two settings quickly and efficiently.

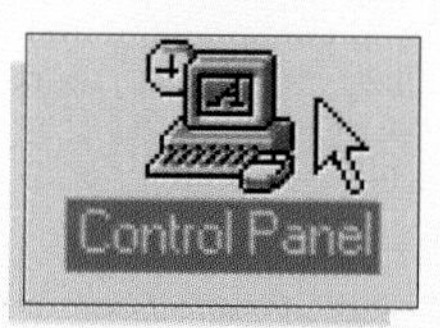


1. Double-click the Control Panel icon in the Main group.

2. The Control Panel window opens on the desktop. Double-click the Date/Time icon in the Control Panel.

6. Click the OK button to confirm any changes you make to the date or time.

- **If you inadvertently enter an invalid setting for the time or date—for example, a date entry of 2/30/94—the invalid entry automatically reverts to its previous value in the Date & Time dialog box.**
- **The date and time formats in the Date & Time dialog box are determined by options you can choose in the International dialog box. For example, you can change the separators between the elements of the date and time, or select a new month-day-year order for the elements of the date. To open the International dialog box, double-click the International icon in the Control Panel window.**

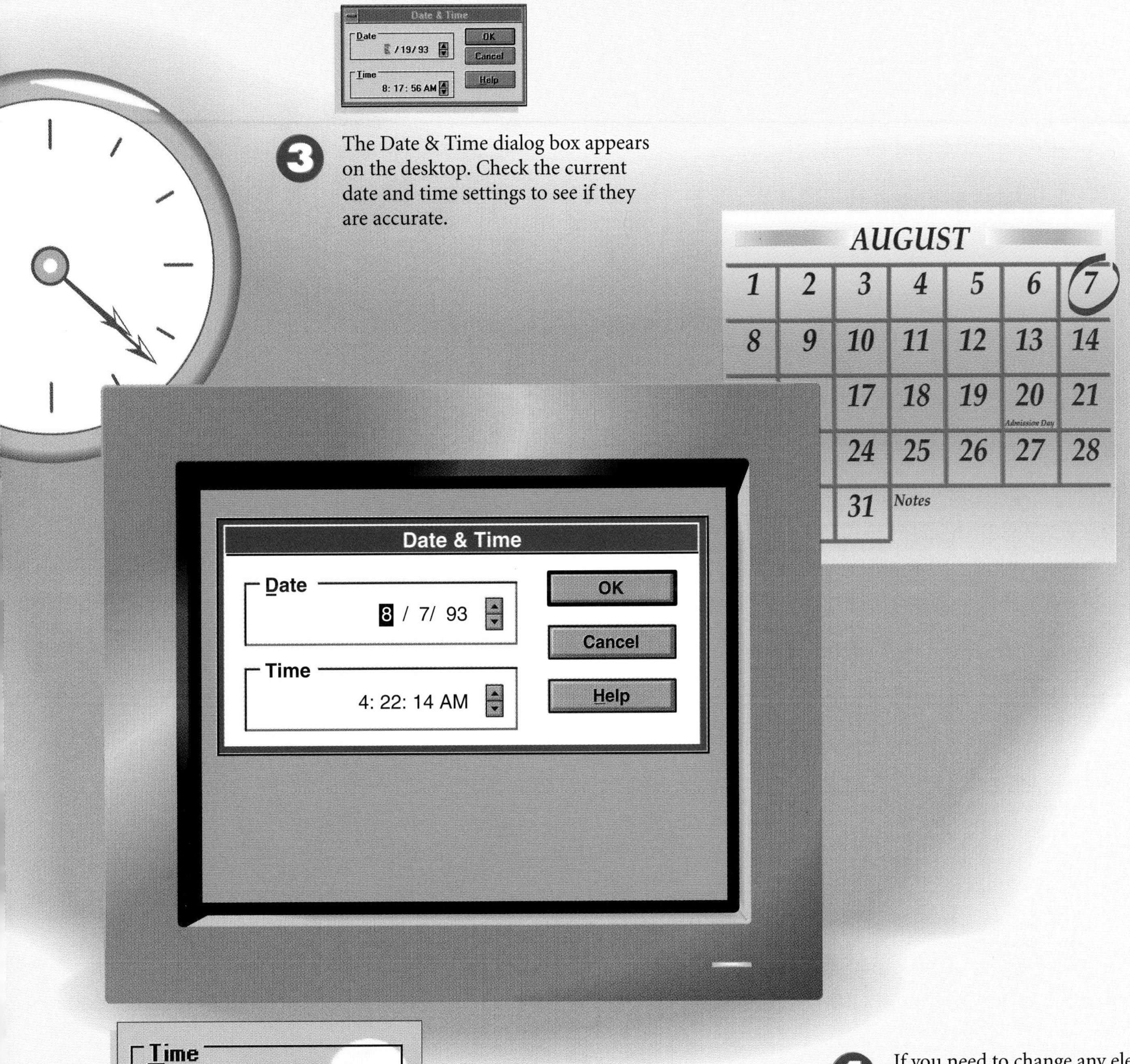


**3** The Date & Time dialog box appears on the desktop. Check the current date and time settings to see if they are accurate.

**4** If you need to change any element of the date——month, day, or year—double-click the appropriate value to select it. (The mouse pointer appears as an I-beam when positioned over an individual element of the date or time.) Then enter a new value from the keyboard, or click the up- or down-arrow button to increase or decrease the current value.

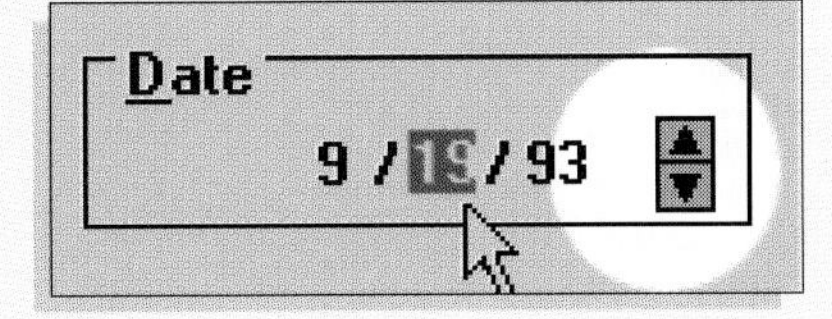


**5** If you need to change any element of the time—hour, minute, or second—double-click the appropriate value to select it. Then enter a new value from the keyboard, or click the up- or down-arrow button to increase or decrease the current value.

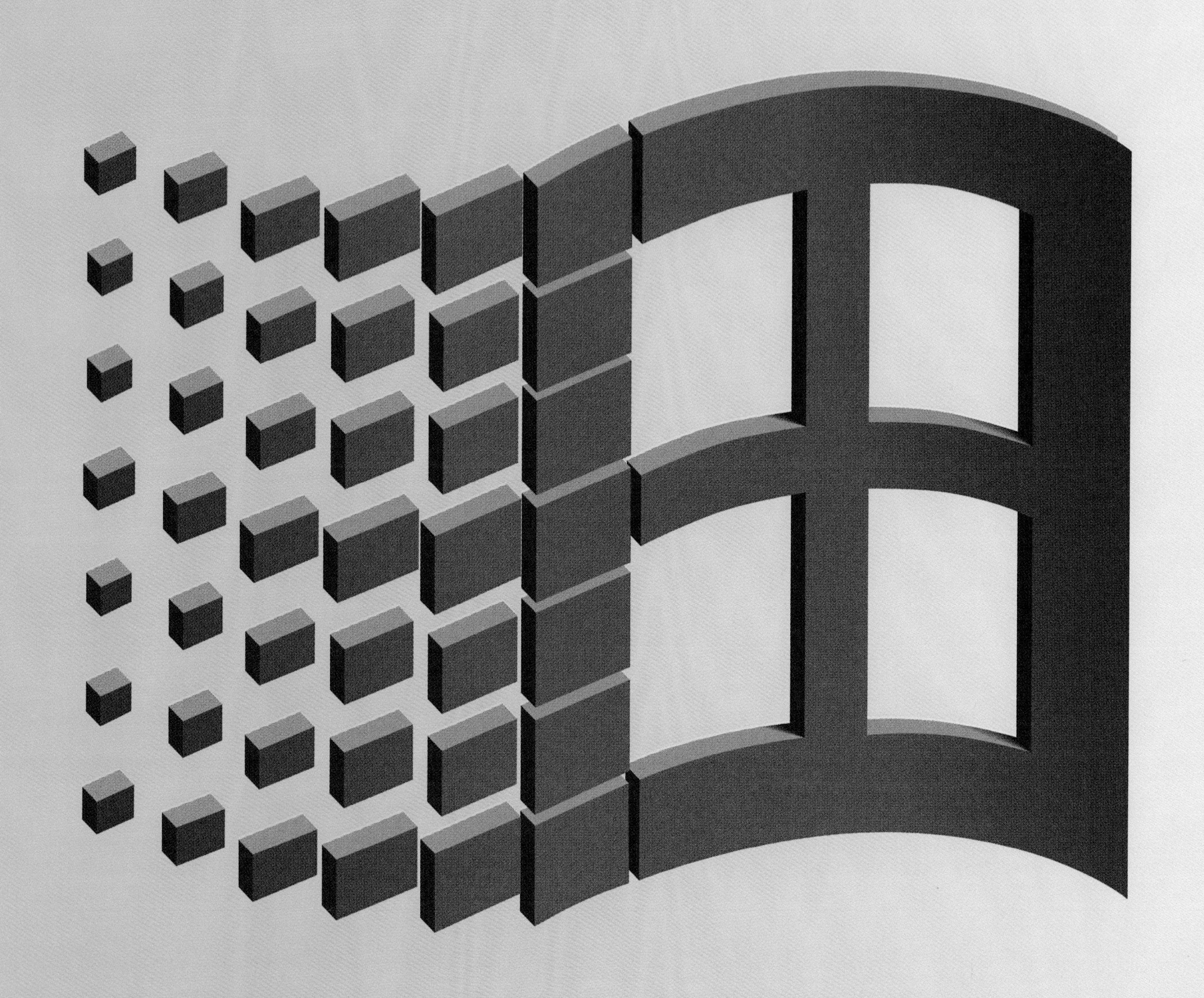

## CHAPTER 6

# Using the File Manager

Before you began using Windows on your computer, you probably learned to perform a variety of disk operations directly from the DOS prompt. For example, you can use DOS commands to list the names of files in a directory, to copy files from one place to another, to format floppy disks, to create new directories on a disk, and to change to a new directory on the current disk. You can also do all these things conveniently in Windows, using the File Manager application. Unless you are a long-time DOS user, you're likely to find these tasks easier to perform with the File Manager than with the equivalent DOS commands.

In this chapter you'll have the opportunity to practice some of the simple techniques available in the File Manager. Before you begin, you need to be familiar with a few terms you'll encounter along the way. A *file* is the basic unit for storing information on disk. A *file name* may contain two parts—a base name with up to eight characters, and an optional *extension* with up to three characters. A period separates the two parts of the name. A *document* is a file that you create with a particular application—for example, a word processed report, a spreadsheet, a database, or a drawing. A *directory* is a way of organizing the space on a disk into practical divisions. A directory can be further divided into *subdirectories.* Both directories and subdirectories can contain files. The structure of directories on a disk is sometimes represented as a *directory tree.* The top directory in the structure is known as the *root directory.* A *path* is a way of representing a file's location in the directory tree of a disk.

# How to Work with Directories and Files

When you first start the File Manager application, it displays a two-part *directory window*. On the left side of the window is a directory tree, showing the organization of directories on your hard disk. You can quickly open any directory simply by clicking its name in the tree structure. On the right side of the directory window is the *contents list* for the current directory. The list initially contains the name and icon for each item in the directory. (The generic icons represent subdirectories, program files, document files, and other files.)

- You can change the relative sizes of the two sections in the directory window—the directory tree and the contents list. To do so, choose the Split command from the View menu. Then move the mouse pointer (or press the Left or Right Arrow key on the keyboard) to position the split wherever you want it. Click the mouse button (or press Enter) to confirm the change.
- In the By File Type dialog box, you can enter a file name with wildcard characters (* or ?) to view files of a particular type. For example, enter *.DOC in the Name box to view all the files with .DOC extentions.
- To close the File Manager application, pull down the program's File menu and choose the Exit command.

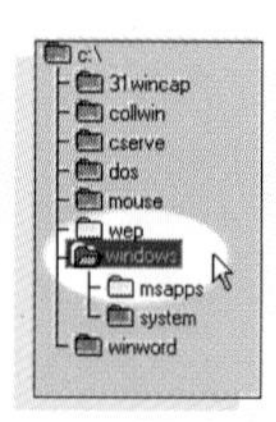


**2** To change to a different directory, position the mouse pointer over any directory icon in the directory tree and click the mouse button once. The contents list at the right side of the directory window immediately displays the files stored in the directory you selected.

**1** Double-click the File Manager icon in the Main group. The File Manager window opens onto the desktop, displaying a directory window for the current directory.

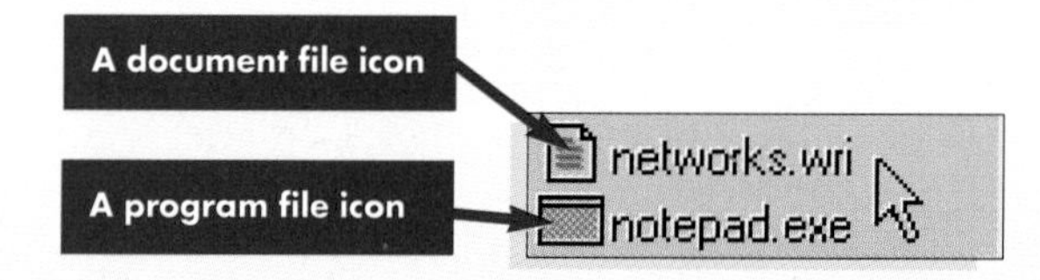


**7** To run a program, click the directory in the directory tree that contains the program; then double-click the program's icon in the directory's contents list. Alternatively, you can double-click a document icon to run the program associated with the document and then open the document itself.

Click here to see more of the contents list.

**3** To scroll through the contents of a directory, click the right- or left-arrow button at either end of the horizontal scroll bar beneath the file contents. (Alternatively, drag the scroll box right or left along the bar.)

**4** To view the names of a particular category of files in the current directory, pull down the View menu in the File Manager menu bar and choose the By File Type command. The By File Type dialog box contains several check boxes that you can select or deselect to indicate which files you want to see in the contents list. Select the categories you want to include and click OK. Back in the directory window, the contents list now shows only the file types you have selected.

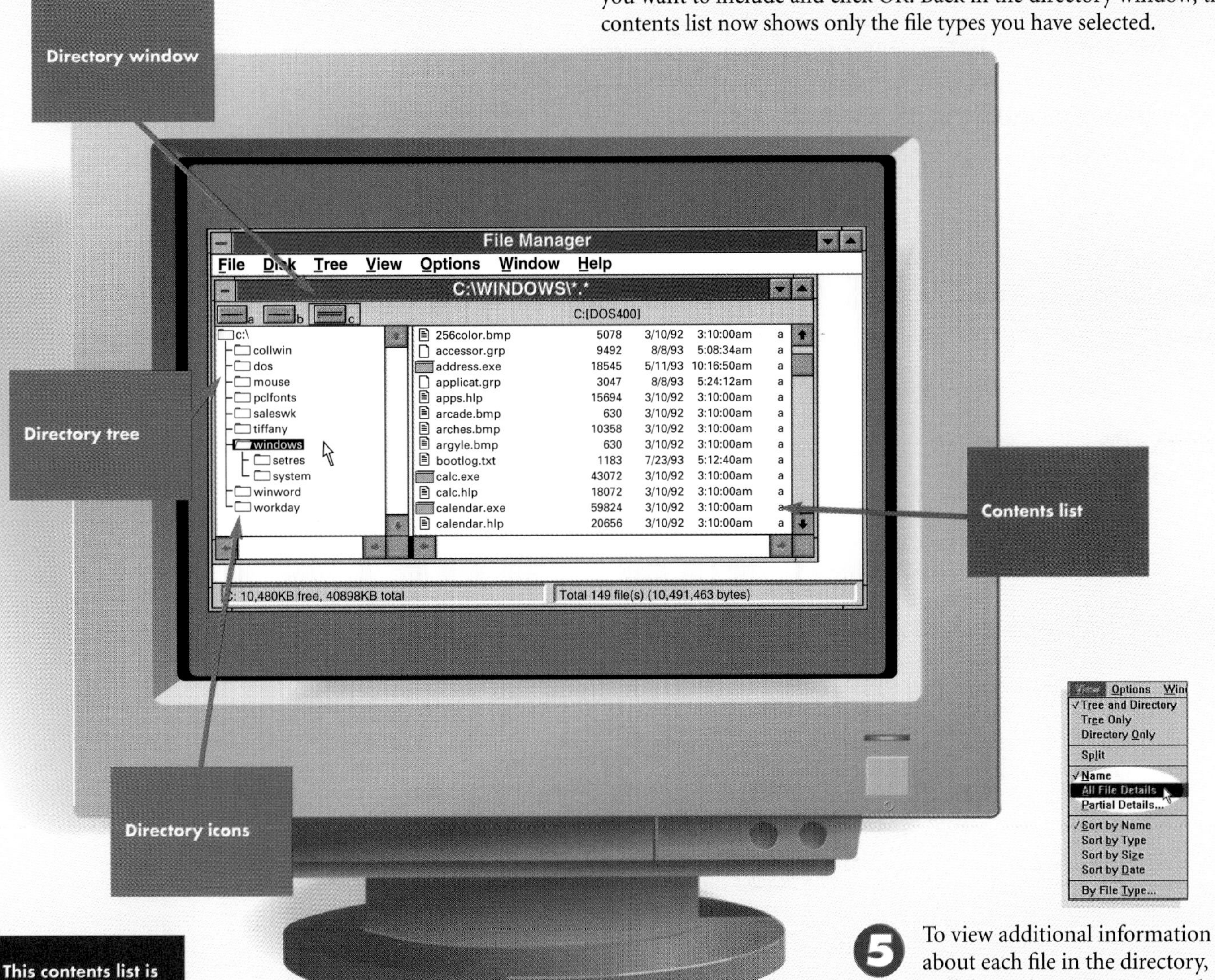


**5** To view additional information about each file in the directory, pull down the View menu in the File Manager menu bar and choose the All File Details command. The contents list now shows five columns of information, including the name, size, date, time, and attribute of each file.

**6** To display the contents list in a different order, pull down the View menu and choose one of the four Sort commands: Sort by Name, Sort by Type, Sort by Size, or Sort by Date.

This contents list is sorted by file size.

# How to Work with Two or More Directories

The File Manager allows you to open multiple directory windows at once. This gives you the opportunity to compare the contents of different directories. As you might expect, you can move and resize each open window independently, or choose the Tile or Cascade command to rearrange all the open windows in a single operation. When you want to copy or move a selected file from one directory to another, you use the mouse to perform a *drag-and-drop* operation from the source directory to the destination directory.

**TIP SHEET**

- **To move a file from one directory to another on the same disk, drag the file without holding down the Ctrl key. To print a document, drag the file from its directory to the Print Manager icon on the desktop. (You have to start the Print Manager application first. See Chapter 9 for more information.) To add a program or document to a group in the Program Manager, drag the file to the group from any open directory in the File Manager.**
- **You can also perform a drag-and-drop operation with several files at once. To select multiple files in the contents list of a directory window, hold down the Ctrl key and click each file you want to include. (To select several contiguous files, click the first file and then hold down the Shift key while you click the last file in the series.) You can then drag the entire selection to a new directory or disk.**

**1** Double-click the File Manager icon in the Main group. Initially, the File Manager displays a directory window for the current directory.

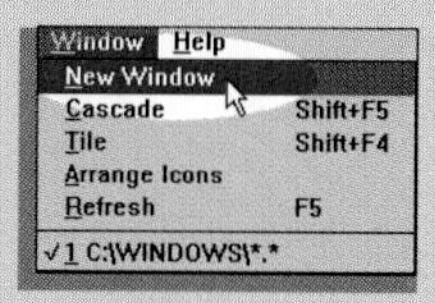


**2** To open an additional directory window, pull down the Window menu on the File Manager menu bar and click the New Window command.

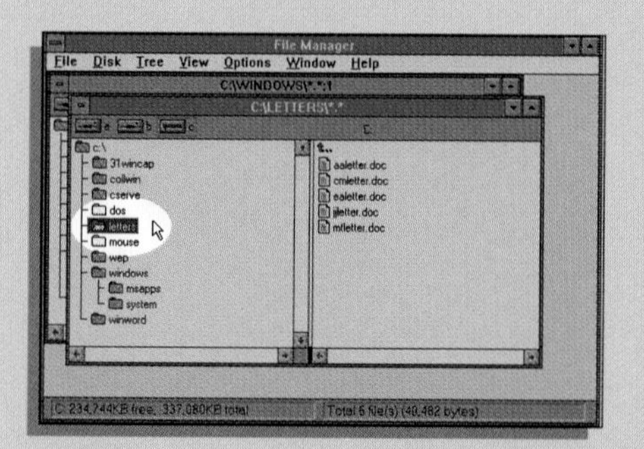


**3** In the new window's directory tree, click the directory you want to view.

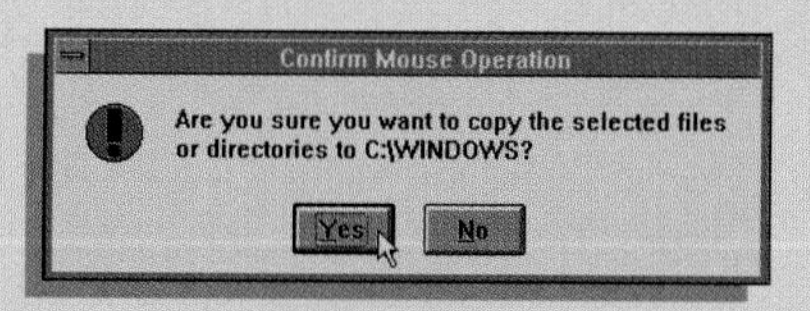


**6** A dialog box named Confirm Mouse Operation appears on the desktop. The message in the box describes the operation you are about to complete. Click the Yes button to confirm or No to cancel.

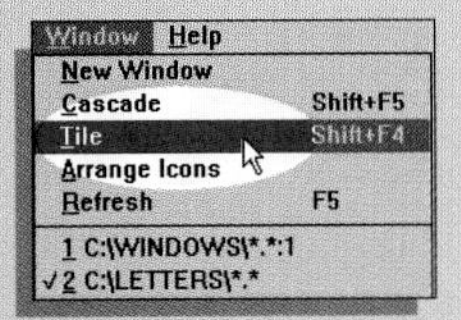

To rearrange the open directory windows within the File Manager, pull down the Window menu and choose Tile. The central graphic on these pages shows the tile arrangement. You can choose Cascade from the Window menu to return to the original "stack" arrangement.

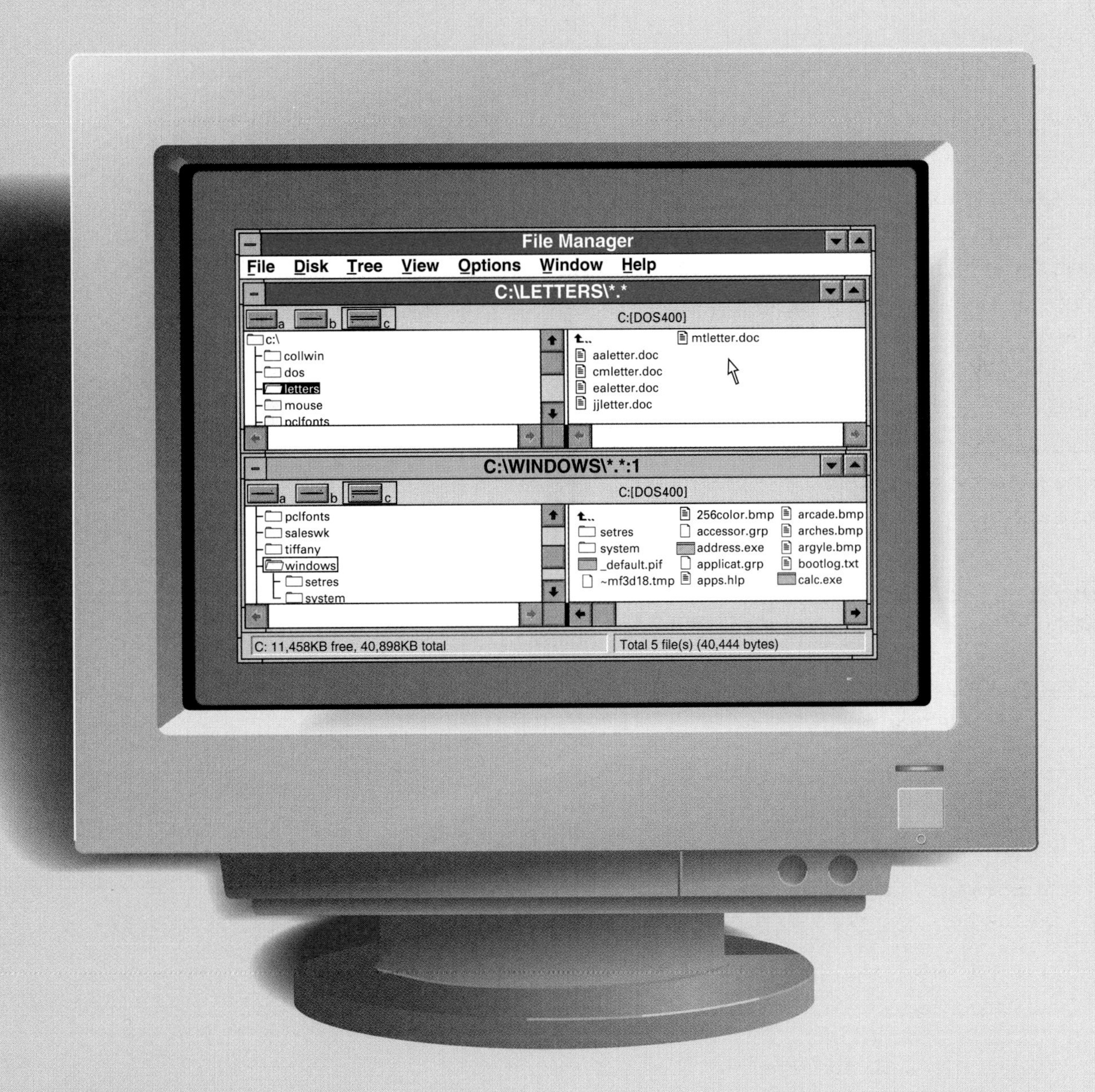

To copy a file from one directory to another in the current drive, hold down the Ctrl key and drag the file's icon from its original directory window to the destination you want—either to a directory icon or to another directory window. As you drag, the mouse pointer appears as an arrow with a document icon. The document icon contains a plus sign, indicating that you are copying, not moving, the document. When you reach the destination directory, release the mouse button first and then the Ctrl key.

# How to Format a Disk

In Windows you format a disk by choosing the Format Disk command from the File Manager's Disk menu. You can then use the File Manager to create new directories and copy files to the disk. You can open directory windows for any disk in your system. At the upper-left corner of each directory window you'll see a row of drive icons representing the available disk drives. To view the directory tree and contents list for a particular drive, you simply click the appropriate icon.

**1** Select a floppy disk that you want to format and insert it into the appropriate drive. If File Manager is not yet running, double-click the File Manager icon in the Main group window.

**2** Pull down the Disk menu on the File Manager menu bar and choose the Format Disk command.

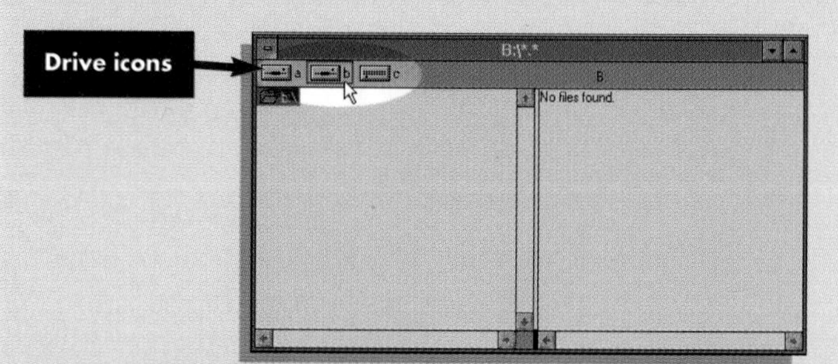


**6** To open a directory window for the newly formatted disk, pull down the Window menu and choose the New Window command. Then click the appropriate drive icon at the upper-left corner of the window. You can now use drag-and-drop operations to copy or move files from your hard disk to the floppy.

- **The Format Disk dialog box contains a Label text box in which you can enter a name for the disk you are about to format. In addition, you can click the Make System Disk check box if you want the disk to contain the basic DOS files necessary for starting your computer system.**
- **To copy a file from one disk to another, drag the file from the source directory window to the destination. The destination disk can be represented either by an open directory window or by a drive icon.**
- **To move a file to another disk, hold down the Shift key while you drag the file.**
- **To create a new directory on any disk pull down the File menu in the File Manager menu bar and choose the Create Directory command.**

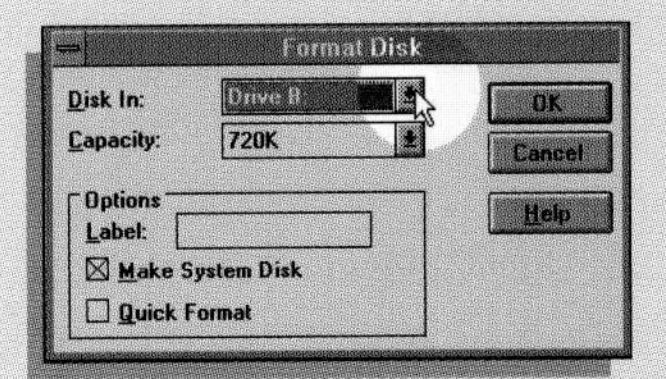


**3** The Format Disk dialog box appears on the desktop. Look at the drive name displayed in the Disk In box. If this is not the drive in which you have inserted the new disk, pull down the Disk In list and choose the name of the correct drive.

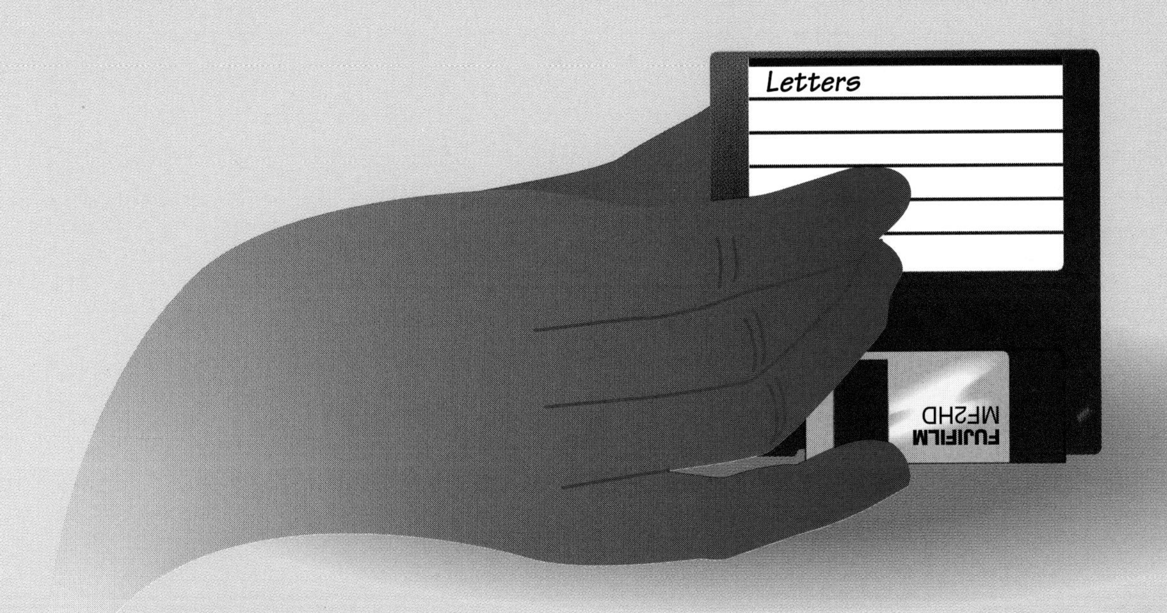


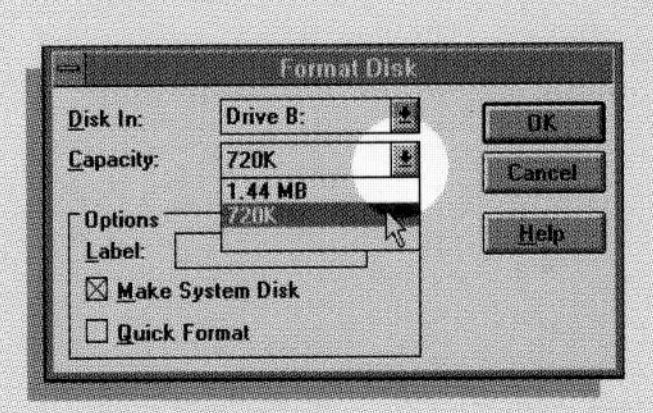


**4** Pull down the Capacity list and choose the correct memory setting for the disks you have purchased. (The settings are 1.2MB or 360K for 5¼-inch disks and 1.44MB or 720K for 3½-inch disks. In general, *high-density* disks can be formatted at the higher memory setting, but *double-density* disks should be formatted at the lower setting.)

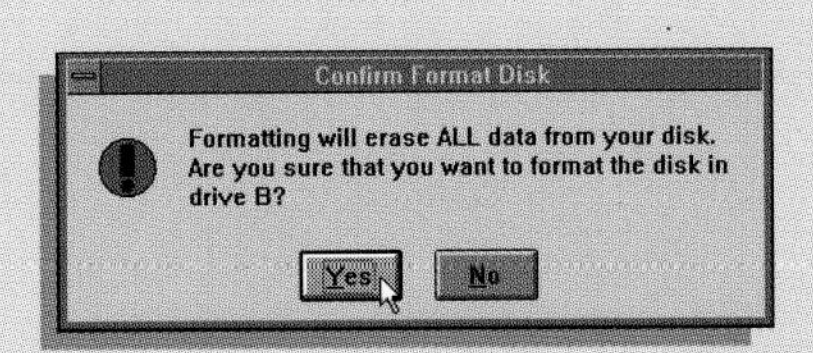


**5** Click OK to begin formatting the disk. A Confirm Format Disk warning message appears on the desktop. Click the Yes button if you're sure you want to format the disk. As the process proceeds, a Formatting Disk message box shows how much of the disk has been formatted. Finally, the Format Complete box shows the formatted capacity of the disk and gives you an opportunity to format another one. Click No unless you have additional disks to format.

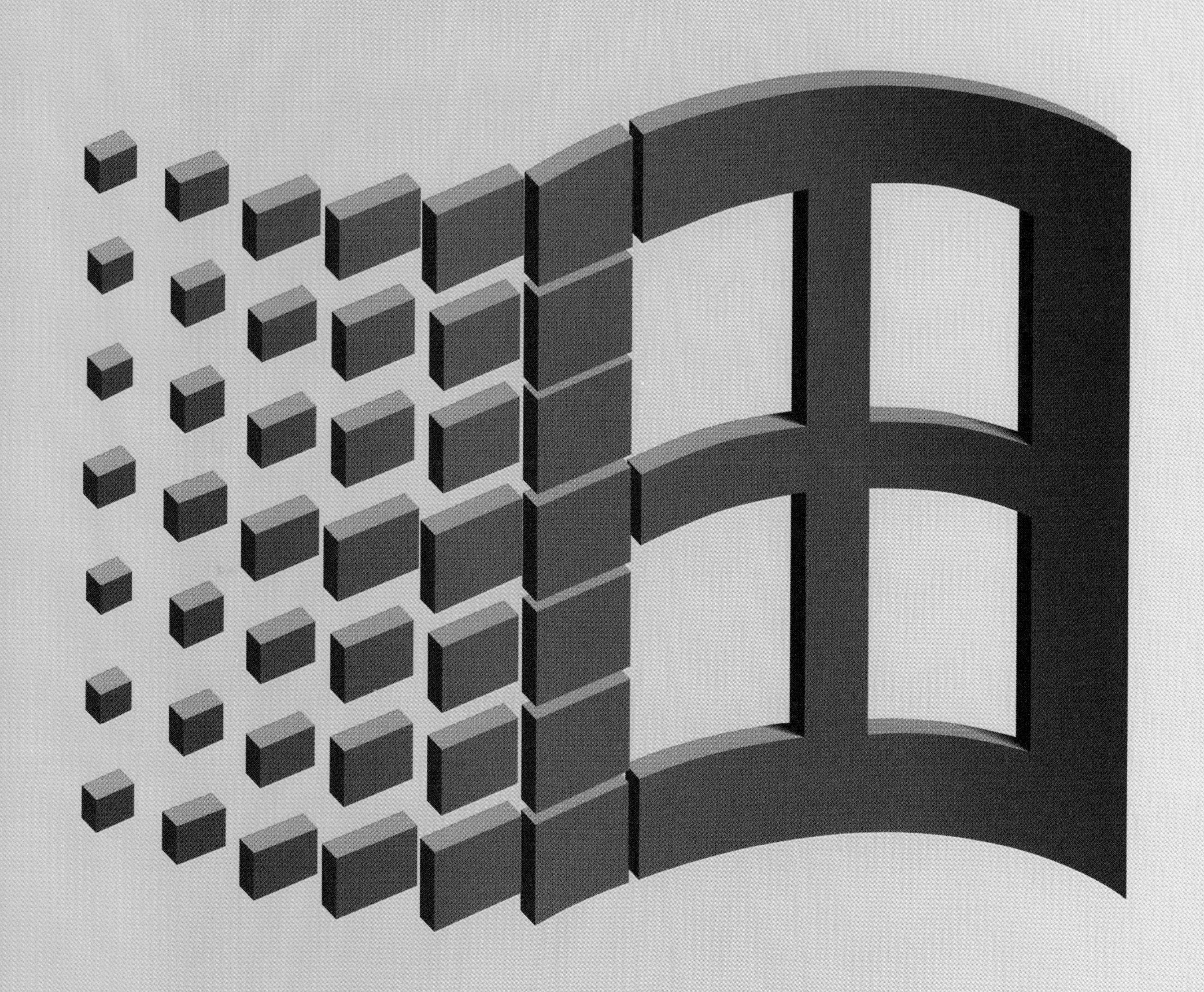

## CHAPTER 7

# Word Processing

Word processing has forever changed the lives of people who write. Whatever you put down on paper—letters, memos, reports, speeches, essays, stories, poems, plays, novels, recipes, grocery lists, homework assignments, term papers, dissertations, or your personal journal—word processing simplifies the process and inevitably improves the result. A good word processing program gives you tools to streamline every step along the way—from composing the initial draft, to revising and correcting the text, to producing attractive and readable copy on paper.

*Write* is name of the word processing program that comes with Windows. It's simple enough to master in a short time, yet has the features you need for most day-to-day word processing tasks. This chapter introduces you to some of the most important Write procedures. You will learn how to type and correct the text of a document, select typographical effects to make your text easier to read, and format paragraphs in your document. You will also see how to save your work as a file on disk or print it on paper.

In the Windows environment, word processing is enhanced by a feature called the *Clipboard*, which allows you to copy or move information from one place to another within a document, or from one document to another. Although you open only one document at a time in Write, you can use two simple procedures, *copy-and-paste* and *cut-and-paste*, to transfer text between documents. You'll learn about these procedures in Chapter 8.

# How to Get Started in Write

If you've never used a word processing program before, you'll be pleasantly surprised at how easy it is to get started in Write. You simply open the application and start typing—almost as you would on a typewriter. But there are several big differences between a typewriter and a word processor. Most importantly, the Write application makes it very easy for you to revise your work. You use the mouse or the keyboard to move to any part of your document; then you can erase parts of the text that you've already typed, or insert new text.

**TIP SHEET**

- **To insert new text in an existing section of your document, use the mouse or keyboard to move the insertion point, and start typing. You can also insert a new paragraph: Move the insertion point to the beginning of an existing paragraph and press Enter to make room for the new one.**
- **After you've typed some practice text, you may want to abandon the current document and start a new one. To do so, pull down the File menu and choose the New command. Then click No when Write asks you if you want to save the current changes.**
- **To close the Write application, pull down the File menu and click the Exit command. Alternatively, you can minimize the Write window and switch to other work.**
- **Like all major Windows applications, Write has its own on-line help. To see the list of available topics, pull down the Help menu and click the Contents command.**

**2** Pull down the Document menu and click the Ruler On command. The Ruler appears just beneath the menu bar in the Write window; it shows the current indent settings within which you'll type your document. (In addition, the Ruler contains a collection of icons designed to streamline your work in Write. You'll learn to use these icons later in this chapter.)

**1** If the Accessories group is not open in the Program Manager window, double-click the group icon to open it. Inside the group window, double-click the Write icon. When the Write application appears on the desktop, click the window's maximize button.

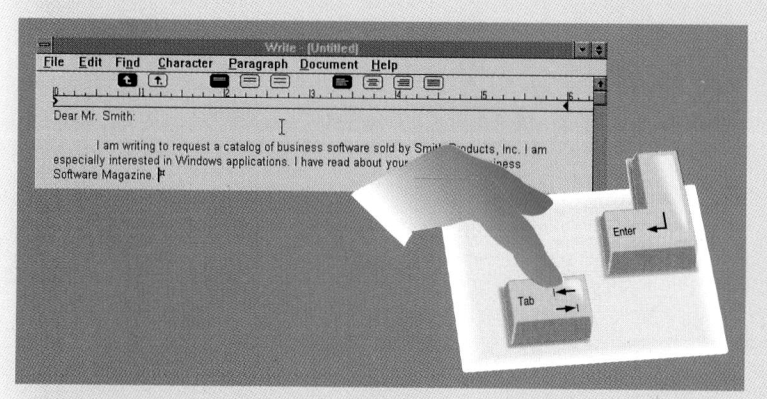


**5** Press Enter to start a new paragraph. (Optionally, press Enter again to insert a blank line in your document.) Then press Tab to indent. Try typing a paragraph containing two or three lines of text. When you reach the end of a line, notice that Write automatically moves the insertion point to the beginning of the next line. In other words, you do *not* press the Enter key to start a new line within a paragraph; the *word-wrap* feature takes you to the next line automatically.

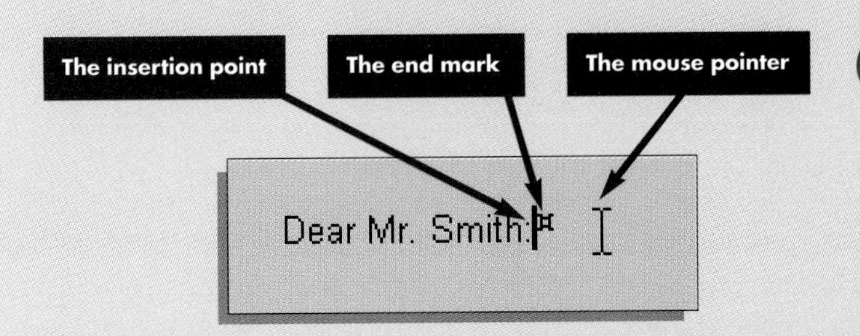


**3** From the keyboard, start typing the text of a practice document. Notice two important visual elements of the Write window: The flashing *insertion point* (|) marks the place where text will appear in your document as you type from the keyboard, and the *end mark* (¤) shows where your document ends. The mouse pointer is shaped like an I-beam when positioned within the Write work area.

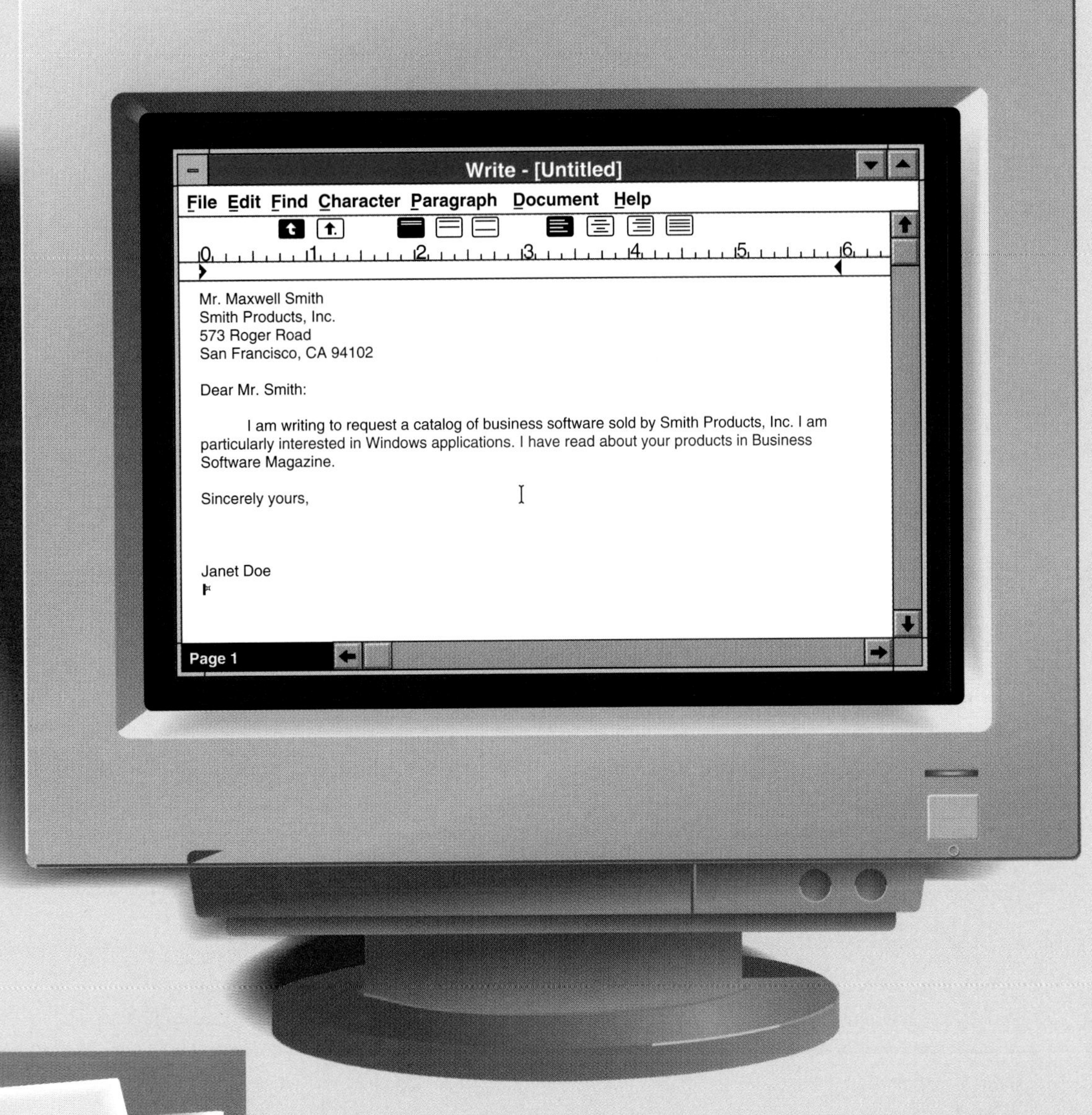


**4** If you make a mistake, press Backspace one or more times to erase the characters just to the left of the insertion point. To move the insertion point to a new place within the document, position the mouse pointer and click, or press any of the arrow keys on your keyboard. Press the Delete (or Del) key to erase a character to the right of the insertion point.

# How to Apply Styles and Fonts

Special typographical effects—including styles, sizes, and fonts—can enhance the appearance of documents you create in Write. The three main type styles you can choose in Write are boldface, italics, and underlining; these can be applied individually or in combinations. In addition, you can increase or decrease the type size in an entire document or a selected portion of it.

Selecting a new *font*, or typeface design, sometimes produces a more subtle change. The Font dialog box in Write lists all the fonts available in your installation of Windows.

**TIP SHEET**

- **The blank column at the far-left side of the Write window is called the *selection area.* In this area, the mouse pointer becomes a white arrow pointing up and to the right. To select an entire line of text, move the pointer into the selection area just to the left of the line and click the mouse button. To select two or more lines of text, drag the mouse pointer down the selection area. To select a paragraph, double-click in the selection area to the left of the paragraph. Finally, to select all the text in the document, move the mouse pointer into the selection area, hold down the Ctrl key, and click the left mouse button.**
- **You can also use the keyboard to select text. Move the insertion point to the beginning or end of the text you want to select. Then hold down the Shift key and press the Right or Left Arrow key repeatedly to select text within a line, or the Up or Down Arrow key to select entire lines.**

1. Drag the mouse over the text to which you want to apply a style, size, or font. To select a line or part of a line, drag the mouse horizontally. To select two or more lines, drag vertically. (See the Tip Sheet on this page for additional text-selection techniques.) The Write program *highlights* your selection—that is, it displays the text in white against a dark background.

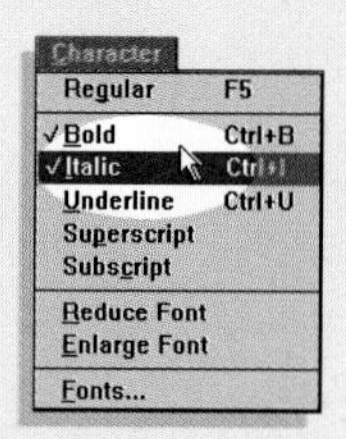


2. Pull down the Character menu and click the Bold, Italic, or Underline command. When you next look at the menu, you'll see a check mark—✓—next to the style you have chosen. Repeat this step to apply additional styles to the selected text. For example, you can produce bold italic text by choosing both the Bold and Italic commands. (Note that Ctrl+B, Ctrl+I, and Ctrl+U are the keyboard shortcuts for applying boldface, italics, and underlining to a selection of text.)

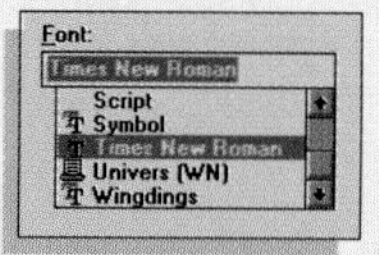


5. At the left side of the dialog box is a list of the available fonts. Use the scroll bar to move up or down the list; then click the name of the font you want to apply. (*TrueType* fonts are marked with a double-T icon. These are normally the best choice for Write documents, because you can rely on them to look the same on paper as they do on the screen.) Click OK to switch to the font you have selected.

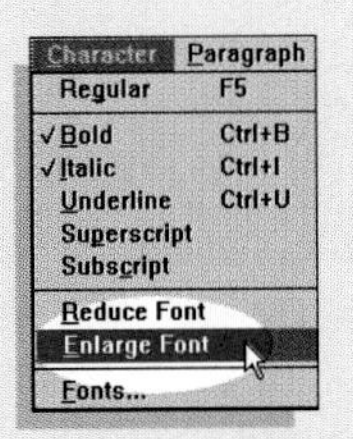


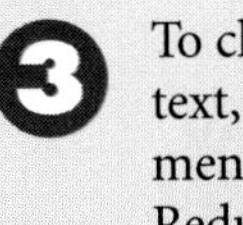

To change the size of the selected text, pull down the Character menu and choose Enlarge Font or Reduce Font. Repeat this step to make further changes in the size.

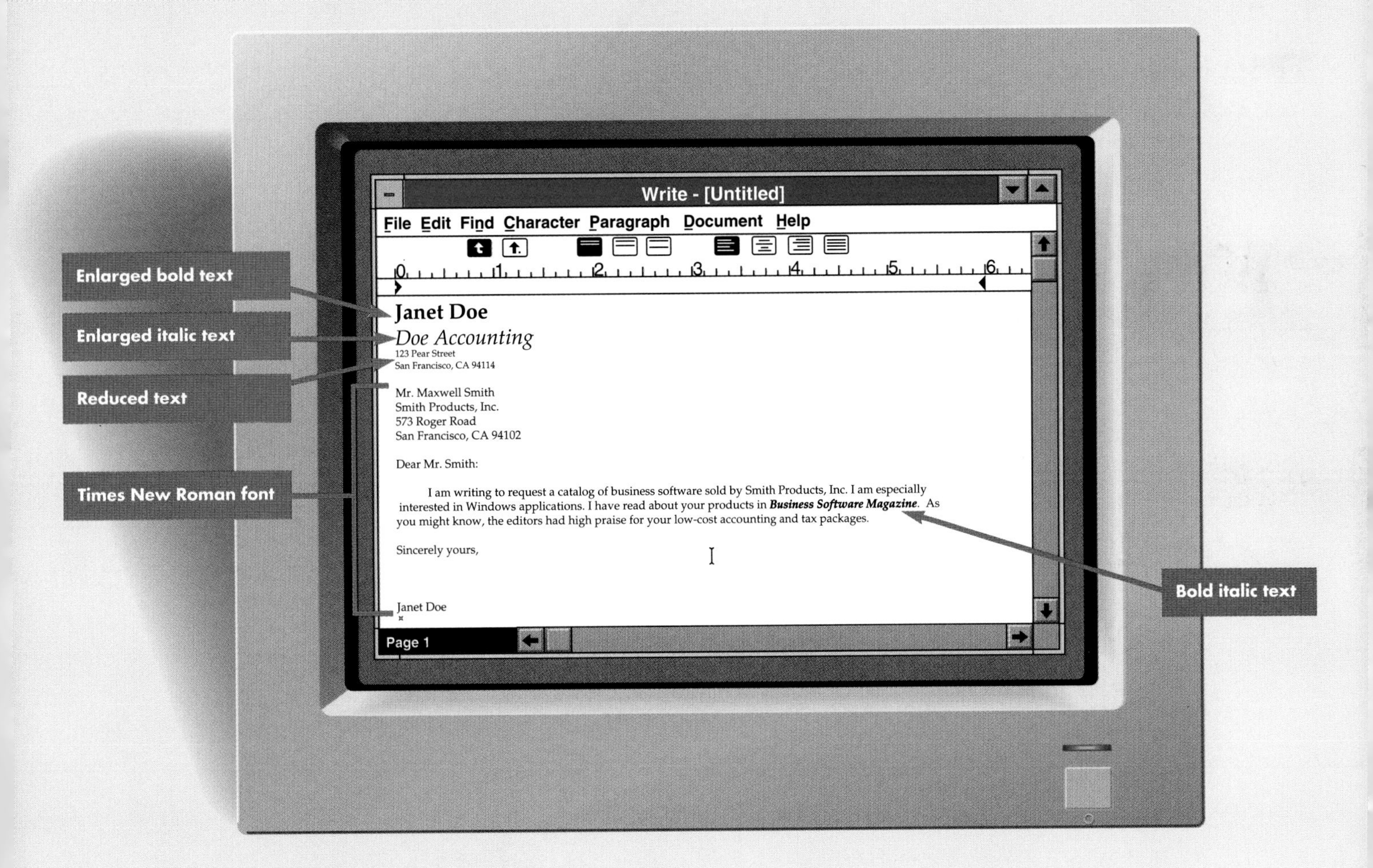


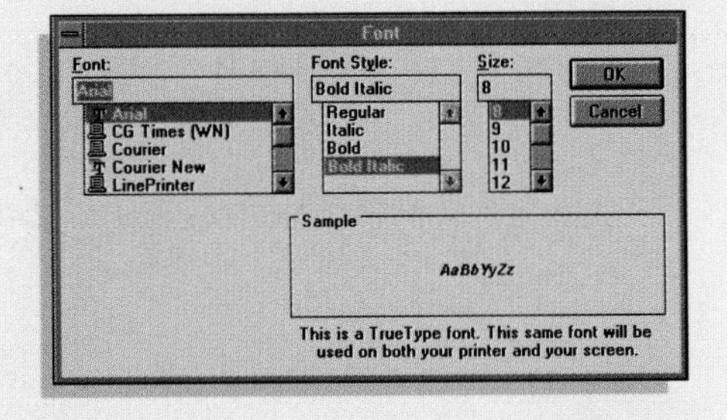

To change the font of the selected text, pull down the Character menu and choose the Fonts command. The Font dialog box appears on the desktop.

# How to Adjust Spacing and Alignment

Line spacing and alignment are two additional settings you can use to improve the appearance of a document. Write allows single spacing, 1½ spacing, and double spacing. There are four alignment options. With left alignment, the left side of a paragraph is aligned but the right is not. In a centered paragraph, each line is centered horizontally between the margins. Right alignment means that a paragraph is aligned on the right but not on the left. In justified text, both the left and right sides are aligned.

## TIP SHEET

- **The Ruler provides the easiest tools for adjusting the appearance of a paragraph. If the Ruler is not displayed at the top of the Write window, pull down the Document menu and choose Ruler On.**
- **At the left side of the Ruler, the left indent marker and the first-line indent marker move independently. Initially, they appear at the same position. To change both settings, drag first the first-line indent marker, and then the left indent marker.**
- **To change the margin settings for your document, pull down the Document menu and choose Page Layout. In the resulting dialog box, you can enter numeric settings for the left, right, top, and bottom margins. A margin is the distance between the edge of the paper and the beginning of the text. Margin settings apply to the entire document. By contrast, an indent determines the width of a given paragraph within the current margins.**

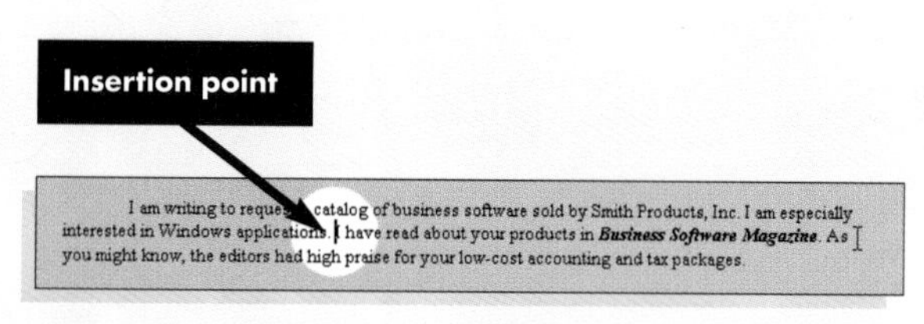


**1** Place the insertion point inside the paragraph where you want to change the spacing or alignment.

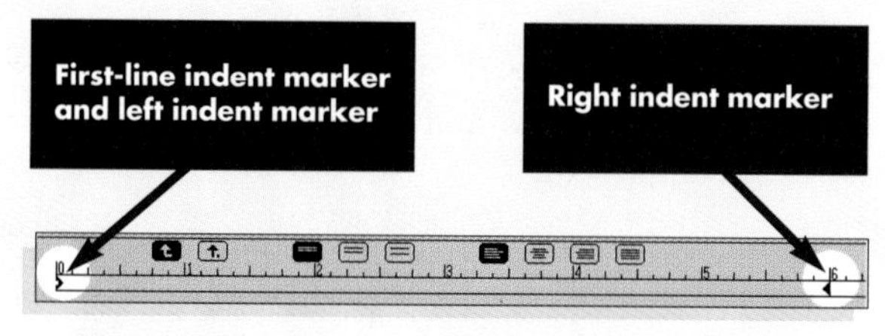


**4** To change the indent settings for the paragraph, drag any of the indent markers to new positions along the Ruler. At both sides of the Ruler, the left- and right-indent markers appear as small black triangles. In addition, the *first-line indent marker* appears as a small dot at the left side of the ruler. This marker sets the indent for the first line of a paragraph.

**2** To change the spacing within the paragraph, click one of the line-spacing icons on the ruler—for single-spaced, 1½-spaced, or double-spaced text. (Alternatively, pull down the Paragraph menu and choose the Single Space, 1 1/2 Space, or Double Space command.)

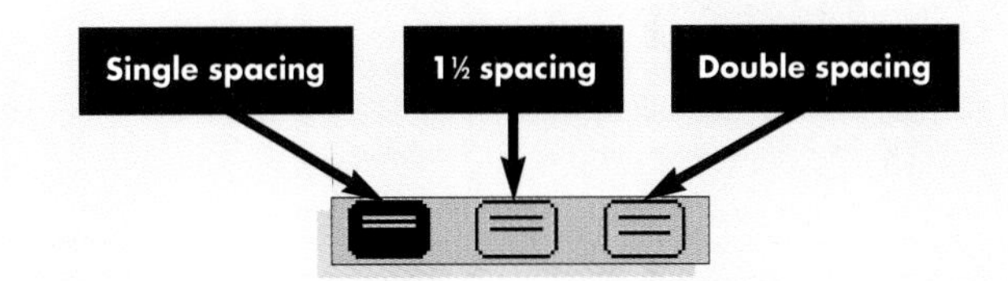


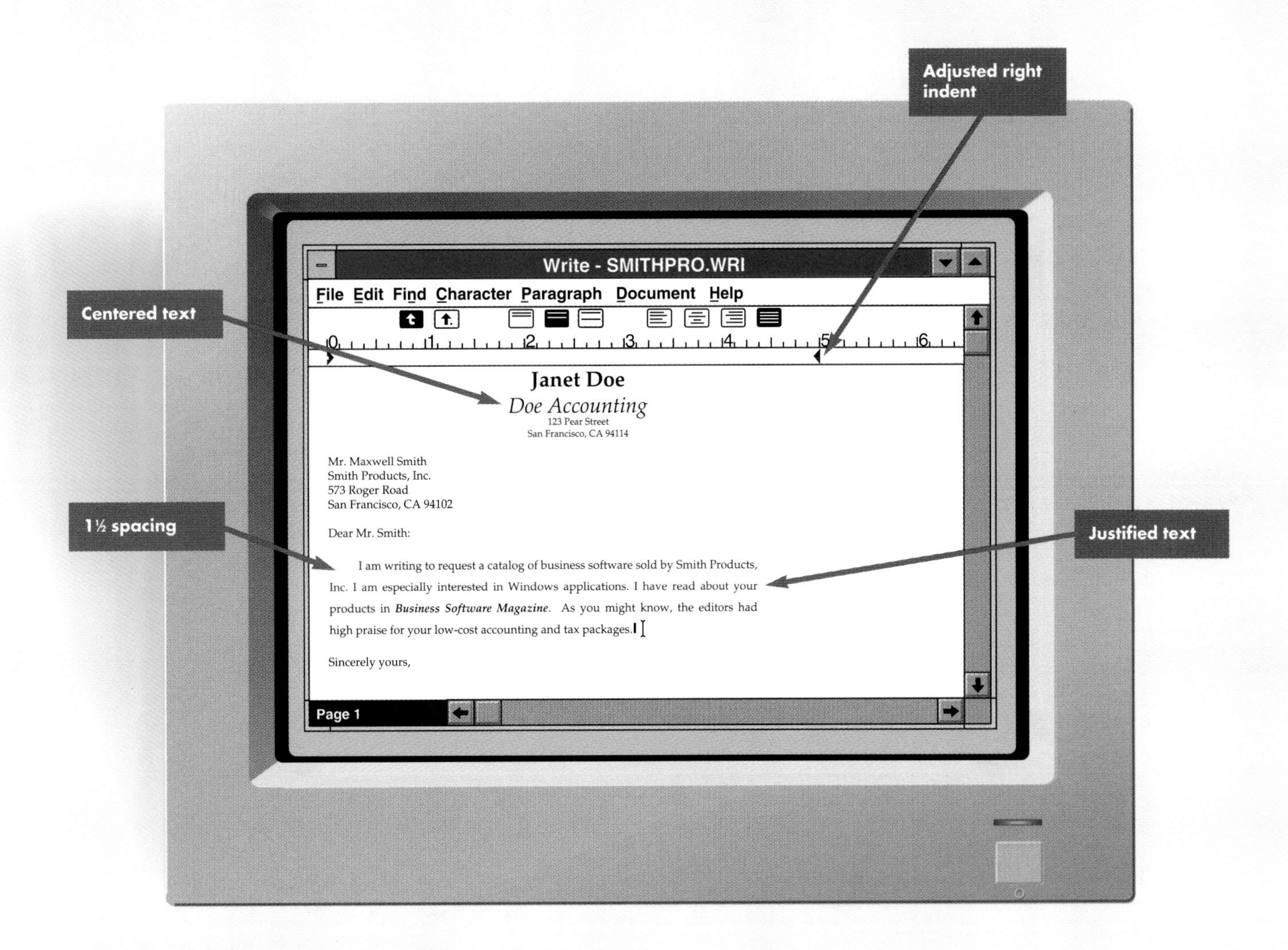


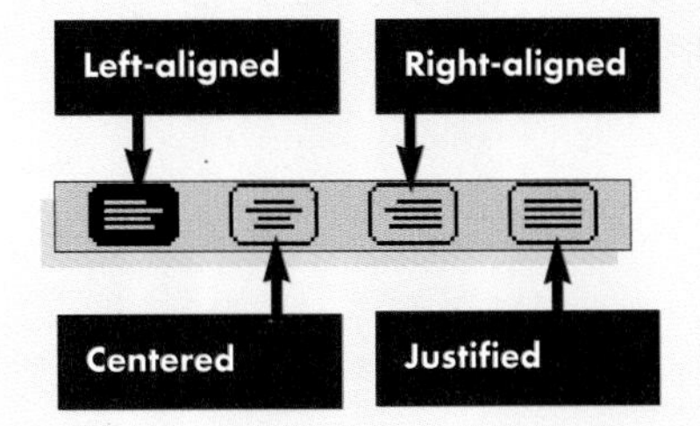


**3** To change the alignment of the paragraph, click one of the alignment icons on the ruler—for left-aligned, centered, right-aligned, or justified text. (Alternatively, pull down the Paragraph menu and choose Left, Centered, Right, or Justified.)

# How to Save a Write File

The more time you spend composing a document, the more frequently you'll want to save your work. As you type in the Write window, the text you see on the screen is initially stored in the computer's temporary memory, known as RAM. If your computer unexpectedly turns off—due to a power failure, for example—the information in RAM is lost. To protect your work from such mishaps, you simply save your document as a file on disk.

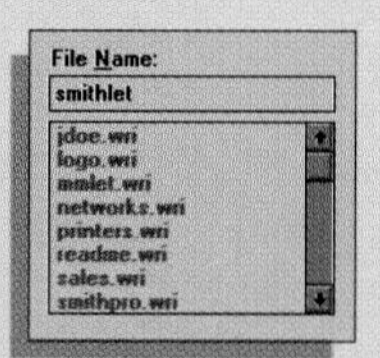


**2** In the File Name text box, type a name for your file. The name can contain up to eight characters. Write automatically supplies .WRI as the extension. For example, if you type smithlet as the name, your document will be saved as SMITHLET.WRI. Notice that the list beneath the File Name box shows the names of all existing .WRI files in the current directory.

**1** Pull down the File menu on Write's menu bar, and click the Save As command. The Save As dialog box appears on the desktop, as shown in the central graphic on these pages.

## TIP SHEET

- **For more information about files, directories, and disks, turn back to Chapter 6.**
- **Sometimes you may want to save a document in a format that can be read by an application other than Write. To do so, pull down the Save File as Type list in the Save As dialog box, and select one of the available formats. (Conversely, another Windows word processing program may be able to convert Write files into its own format. If you don't see the format you need in the Save File as Type list, try opening the .WRI file directly from the other application.)**
- **To reopen a .WRI file that you have saved in a previous Write session, pull down the File menu and choose the Open command. The Open dialog box presents a list of all the .WRI files in the current directory. Select the file you want to open and click the OK button.**

**6** As you continue to work on this document, pull down the File menu from time to time and choose the Save command. Each time you do so, the current version of your document will be saved to the disk.

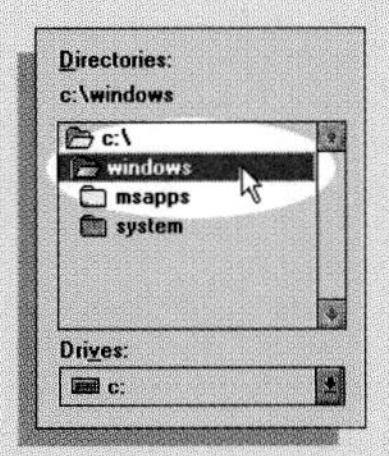


3 Take a look at the boxes labeled Directories and Drives. If you want to save your file on a disk other than the current one, pull down the Drives list by clicking the down-arrow button at the right side of the box, and make a selection. The Directories box uses an open-folder icon to indicate the directory in which your file will be saved on the current disk. To select a different directory, double-click its name with the mouse. To move up the directory tree, double-click the root directory (C:\ in this example).

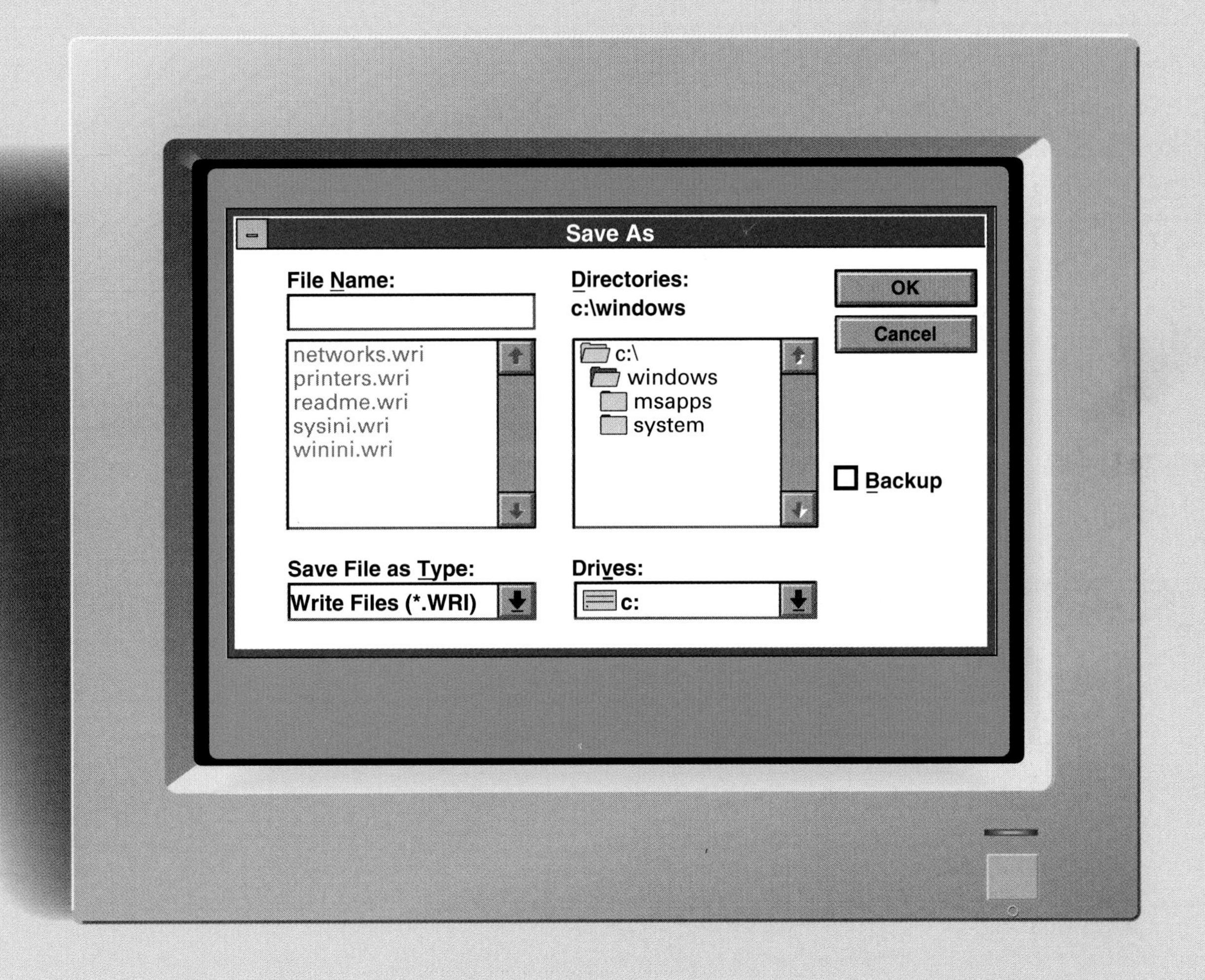

4 If you want Write to maintain a backup copy of your document, click the Backup option so that an X appears in the check box. When this option is selected, Write stores the *previous* version of your document in a backup file with the extension .BKP whenever you select Save. For example, the backup for SMITHLET.WRI would be SMITHLET.BKP.

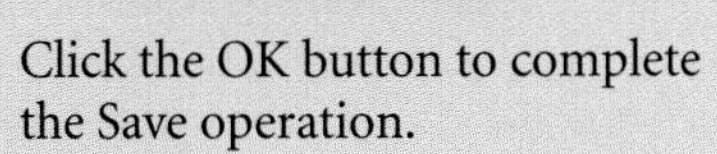

5 Click the OK button to complete the Save operation.

# How to Print a Write Document

Your final goal in Write is to produce an attractive paper document that you can mail to a friend, distribute to your colleagues, fax to a client, or maybe even submit to a publisher. When you're ready to print a document, the first and most obvious step is to make sure your printer is on and contains an adequate paper supply. After that, you're ready to open a document and choose the commands for printing.

The Print Setup command allows you to select features that are specific to your printer. The Print command gives you options for printing the current document.

## TIP SHEET

- **If you want to print only a particular passage from your document, begin by using the mouse or keyboard to select the text you want to print. Then choose the Print command from the File menu and click the Selection option button. Click OK to begin printing.**
- **The Print Manager is ultimately in charge of printing documents from Windows applications. When you choose the Print command, Windows automatically opens the Print Manager. For more information, turn to Chapter 9.**
- **A *printer driver* is a piece of software that Windows uses to communicate with a specific type of printer. When you first install Windows on your computer, the driver for your printer is copied to your hard disk. If you later attach a different printer, you'll have to install a new driver. To do so, double-click the Printers icon in the Control Panel and then click the Add button.**

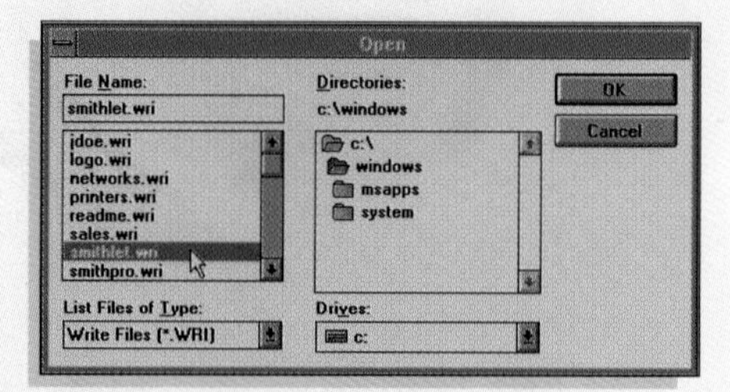


**1** If the file you want to print is not yet open, pull down the File menu and click the Open command. In the Open dialog box, select the file name of the document you want to print and click OK to open it.

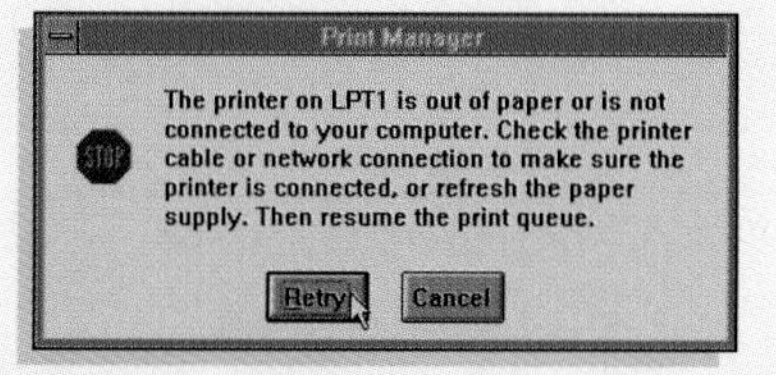


**5** If a Print Manager error message appears on the screen, Windows has not been able to connect properly with your printer. Check for all the obvious problems: Is your printer on? Is it properly connected to your computer? Is it out of paper? Once you find and correct the problem, click the Retry button to try again.

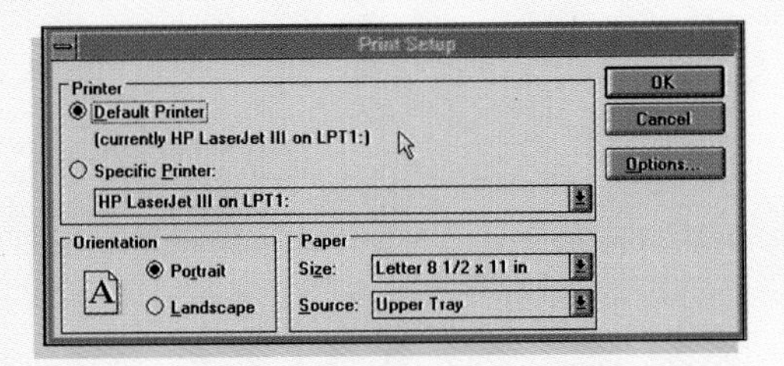


**2** Optionally, pull down the File menu and choose the Print Setup command. The resulting dialog box shows an assortment of printing options available for your printer. (It also allows you to select a different printer if more than one is available to your system.) Make your selections and click OK.

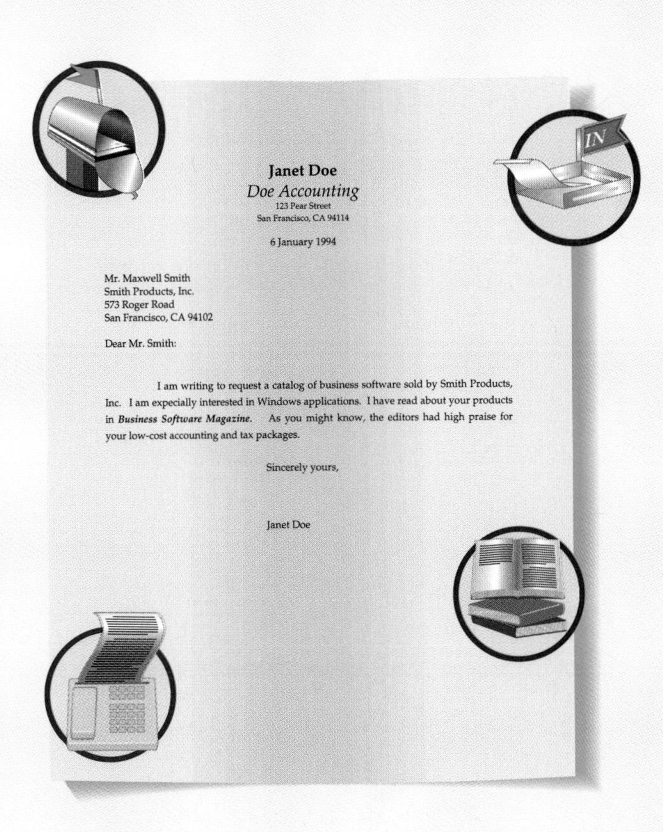
Janet Doe
*Doe Accounting*
123 Pear Street
San Francisco, CA 94114

6 January 1994

Mr. Maxwell Smith
Smith Products, Inc.
573 Roger Road
San Francisco, CA 94102

Dear Mr. Smith:

I am writing to request a catalog of business software sold by Smith Products, Inc. I am especially interested in Windows applications. I have read about your products in ***Business Software Magazine***. As you might know, the editors had high praise for your low-cost accounting and tax packages.

Sincerely yours,

Janet Doe

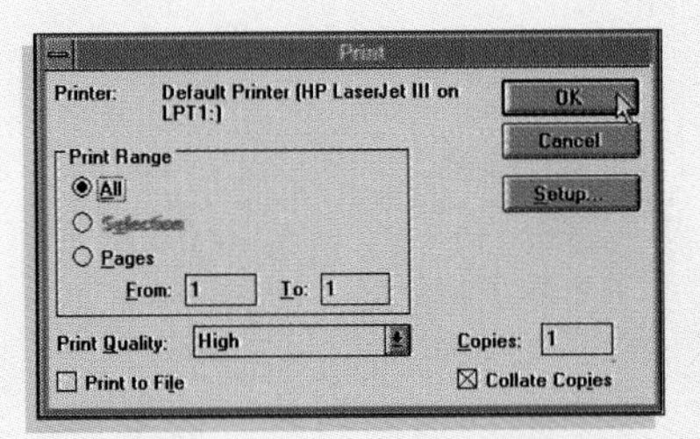


**3** Pull down the File menu a third time and choose the Print command. The Print dialog box gives you several important options. For example, you can print the entire document or a specified range of pages; you can instruct Write to print multiple copies of your document; and you can choose among several print qualities for the output. (Some options in the Print dialog box may be dimmed if they are not available for your printer.)

**4** By default, Write prints one copy of your entire document. If you want to print multiple copies or a range of pages, make the appropriate changes in the Print options. Then click the OK button, and the printing should begin.

# TRY IT!

Here's a chance to review the word processing procedures you've learned in the previous chapter. In the steps ahead you'll create the business letter shown below. You'll type the text of the document first, and then go back and reformat it. In the final steps you'll save the document to disk and print it on paper.

If Write is not yet running, open the Accessories group in the Program Manager window and double-click the Write icon. Maximize the application window. (If Write is already running, pull down the File menu and click New to start a new document.)

**Smith Products, Inc.**
573 Roger Road
San Francisco, CA 94102

15 January 1994

Ms. Janet Doe
Doe Accounting
123 Pear Street
San Francisco, CA 94114

Dear Ms. Doe:

Thank you for your interest in our business applications for Windows. Enclosed is our latest catalog. With the tax season just around the corner, you'll be glad to know that we are already shipping the firstr release of our popular DoTax program.

*Business Software Magazine* will be running another review of our products in the next issue. I hope you see it.

Sincerely yours,

Maxwell Smith

**2**

Document
Header...
Footer...
Ruler On
Tabs...
Page Layout...

Pull down the Document menu and click the Ruler On option if the Ruler isn't displayed.

**3**

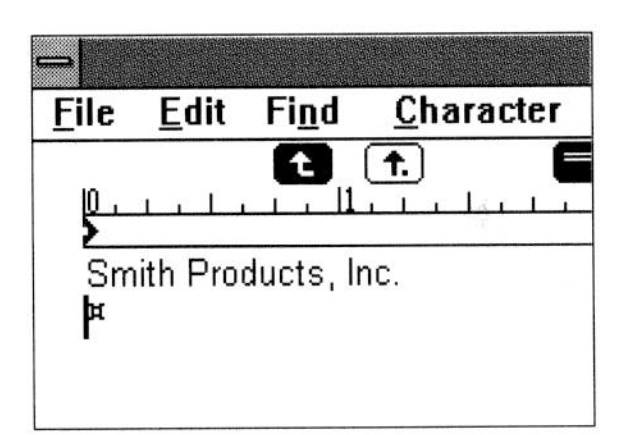


Type **Smith Products, Inc.** and then press Enter.

**4**

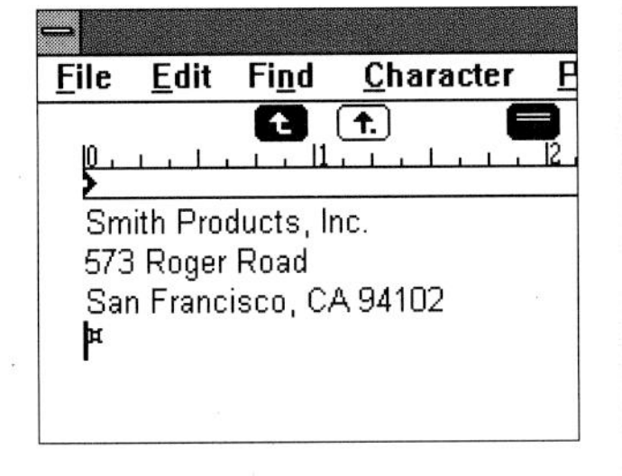


Type the remaining two lines of the return address, pressing Enter after each line.

**5**

Press Enter again to insert a blank line. Then type the date and press Enter twice.

**6**

Ms. Janet Doe
Doe Accounting
123 Pear Street
San Francisco, CA 94114

Type the four lines of the inside address, pressing Enter after each line.

**7**

Ms. Janet Doe
Doe Accounting
123 Pear Street
San Francisco, CA 94114

Dear Ms. Doe:

Press Enter, type **Dear Ms. Doe:**, and press Enter twice.

**8**

Dear Ms. Doe:

Thank you for your interest in our business applications for Windows. Enclosed is our latest catalog. With the tax season just around the corner, you'll be glad to know that we are already shipping the first release of our popular DoTax program.

Press the Tab key to indent, and then type the entire first paragraph of the letter. Remember not to press Enter to start new lines within the paragraph. Word wrap takes care of this automatically. At the end of the paragraph, press Enter twice.

**9**

already shipping the first release of our popular DoTax program.

*Business Software Magazine*

Press Tab to indent the second paragraph. Press Ctrl+I so that the next text you type will be in italics. Type ***Business Software Magazine*** and then press Ctrl+I again to turn italics off.

**Continue to next page ▸**

# TRY IT!

Continue below

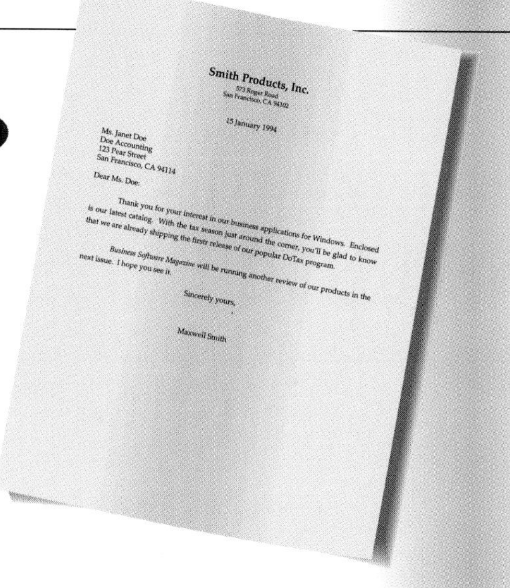

Smith Products, Inc.
573 Roger Road
San Francisco, CA 94102

15 January 1994

Ms. Janet Doe
Doe Accounting
123 Pear Street
San Francisco, CA 94114

Dear Ms. Doe:

Thank you for your interest in our business applications for Windows. Enclosed is our latest catalog. With the tax season just around the corner, you'll be glad to know that we are already shipping the firstr release of our popular DoTax program.

*Business Software Magazine* will be running another review of our products in the next issue. I hope you see it.

Sincerely yours,

Maxwell Smith

**10**

*Business Software Magazine* will be running another review of our products in the next issue. I hope you see it.

Type the remainder of the second paragraph in regular (nonitalic) text. Press Enter twice at the end of the paragraph.

**11**

Sincerely yours,

Maxwell Smith

Press Tab four times and type **Sincerely yours,**. Then press Enter four times. Press Tab four times again, and then type **Maxwell Smith**. You have now finished typing the letter.

**12**

Scroll to the top of the document and position the mouse pointer in the selection area, just to the left the first line. Click the mouse button once to highlight the line.

Press Ctrl+B to apply the boldface style to the selected text.

**14**

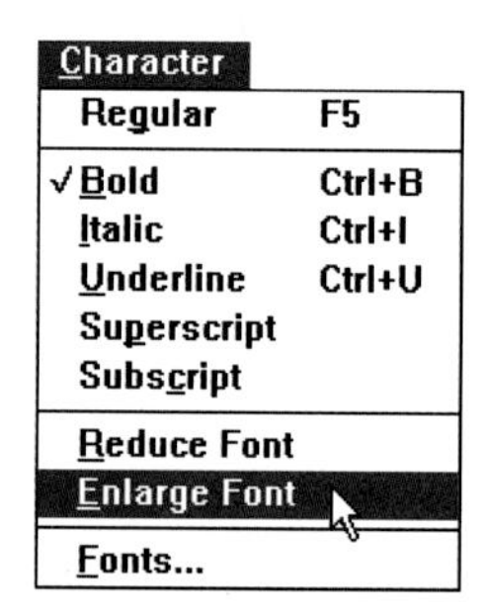


Pull down the Character menu and choose Enlarge Font. Repeat the same steps to enlarge the selected text even more.

Drag the mouse pointer down the selection area, from the second to the third line of the document. Then pull down the Character menu and choose Reduce Font to reduce the size of these two selected lines.

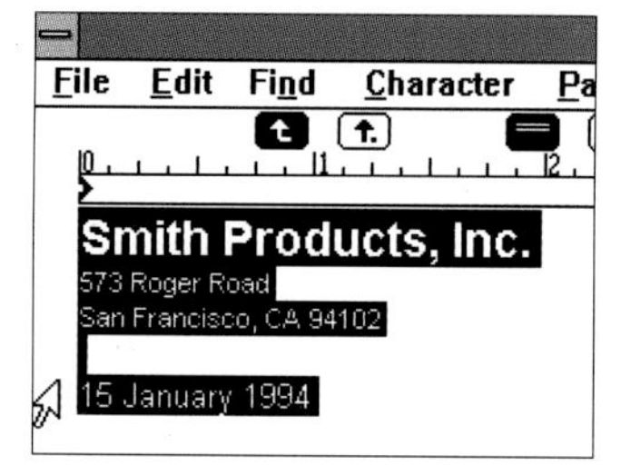


Drag the mouse pointer down the selection area from the first line down to the date. This action selects the first five lines of the document.

Click the Centered icon above the Ruler to center the lines you've selected.

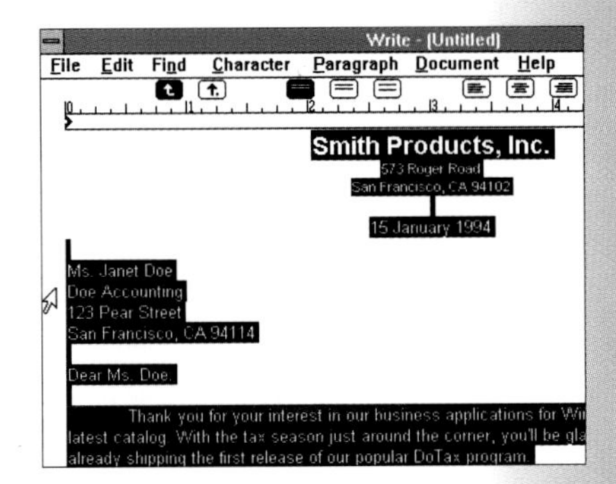


Move the mouse pointer into the selection area again. Hold down the Ctrl key and click the left mouse button to select the entire document.

Character
Regular F5
Bold Ctrl+B
Italic Ctrl+I
Underline Ctrl+U
Superscript
Subscript
Reduce Font
Enlarge Font
Fonts...

Pull down the Character menu and choose the Fonts command. The Font dialog box appears on screen.

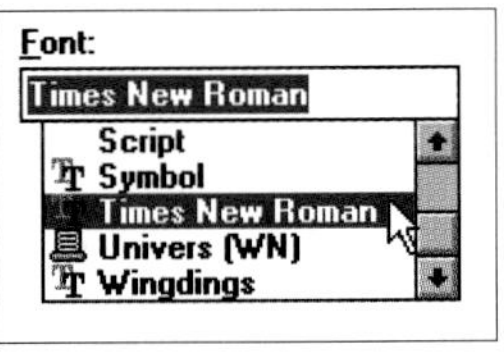


Scroll down the Font list until the TrueType font Times New Roman comes into view. Select this font, and then click OK.

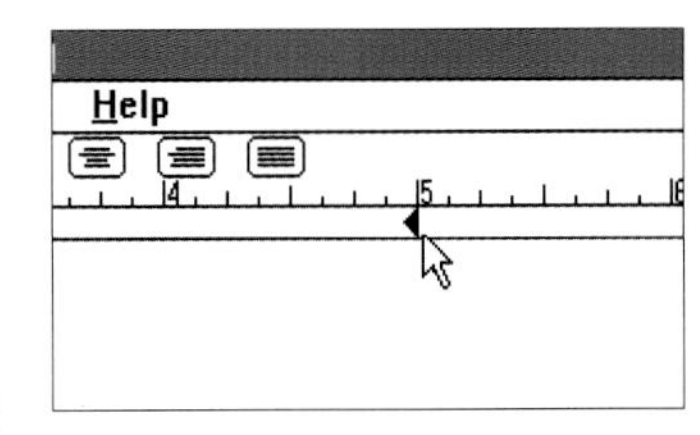


With the entire document still selected, drag the right indent marker to the 5-inch measurement along the Ruler.

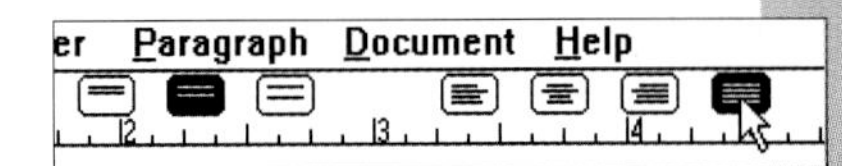


Drag the mouse down the selection area to select the two paragraphs of text in the body of the letter. In the Ruler, click the 1½-spacing icon and then the Justified icon.

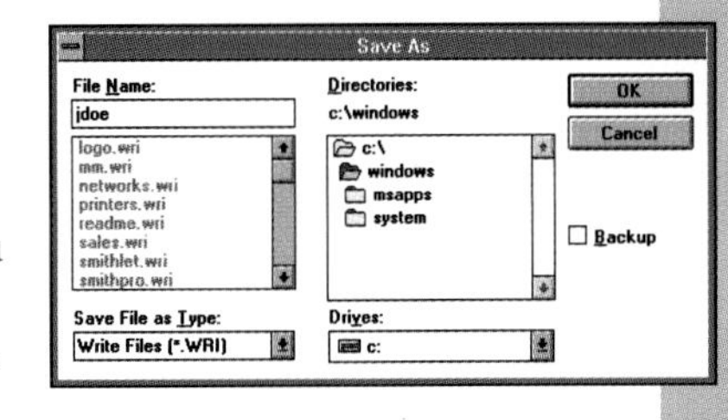


Pull down the File menu and choose Save As. Type **jdoe** as the file name and click OK.

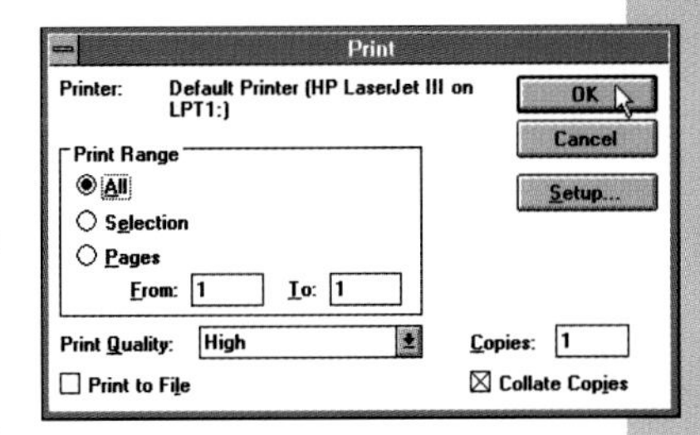


Pull down the File menu and choose Print. In the Print dialog box, click OK to print the letter.

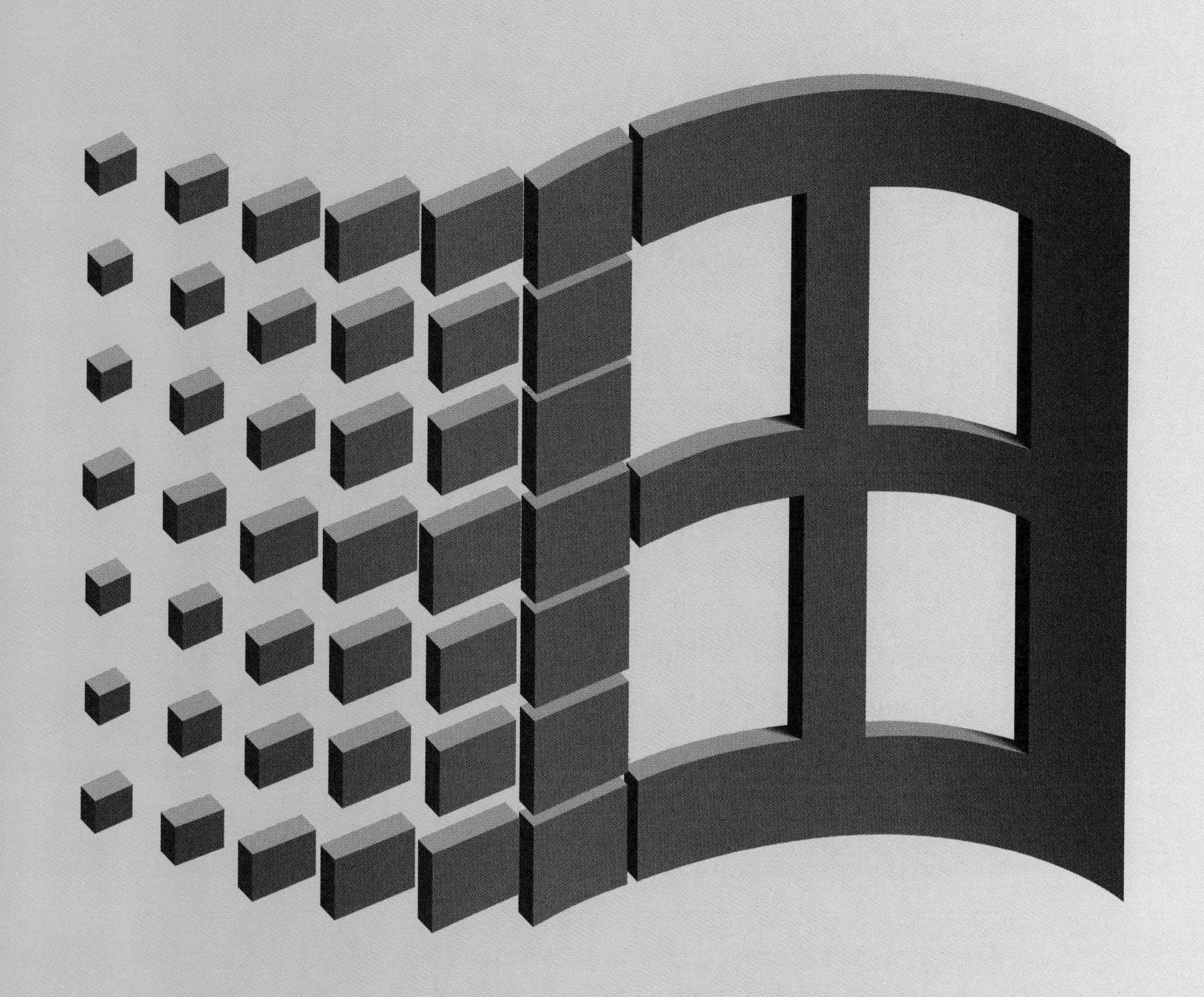

## CHAPTER 8

# Using the Clipboard

Windows gives you the power to transfer information freely from one place to another on the desktop. For example, during a typical Windows session you might move a paragraph from the middle to the beginning of a Write document or copy a block of data from one word processed document to another. Later in the Windows session, you might decide to copy an address from the Cardfile application to a letter you're composing in Write and move another drawing from the Paintbrush program to a Write document.

All these procedures make use of the Clipboard, an intermediate storage facility for information you are moving or copying from one place to another in Windows. Any time you transfer information—whether the operation involves a single document, two documents, or two applications—Windows automatically places the information in the Clipboard.

Clipboard transfers are known as cut-and-paste and copy-and-paste operations. You can perform dozens of these procedures without ever actually opening the Clipboard window. But occasionally you may want to take a look at the Clipboard's current contents. For this purpose, Windows provides a Clipboard Viewer that you can open at any time. In this chapter you'll learn how to copy and move information in Windows, and how to use the Clipboard Viewer.

# How to Copy and Paste

To copy information from one place to another in Windows you use the copy-and-paste procedure. An application that allows copy-and-paste contains Copy and Paste commands with standard keyboard shortcuts of Ctrl+C and Ctrl+V. You begin by selecting a block of information at its source and copying it to the Clipboard; then you select a destination and paste the information from the Clipboard. You can copy information within a single document, or from one document to another within or between applications.

**TIP SHEET**

- **The central graphic illustrates a copy-and-paste operation from a Write document to a Cardfile document. See Chapter 10 for an introduction to Cardfile.**
- **When you are copying from one application to another, you may want to view both the source and destination applications on the desktop at once, as shown in the central graphic. To review the techniques for arranging application windows, see "How to Display Windows in Cascade or Tile Arrangements" in Chapter 3.**
- **You can also copy drawings and graphics from one place to another in Windows. For example, you might want to copy a drawing from the Paintbrush program to a Write document. To do so, you must first mark a *cutout* in Paintbrush. Then press Ctrl+C to copy the contents of the cutout to the Clipboard. See Chapter 11 for an introduction to the Paintbrush application.**

**2** Hold down the Ctrl key and press C to copy the selection to the Clipboard.

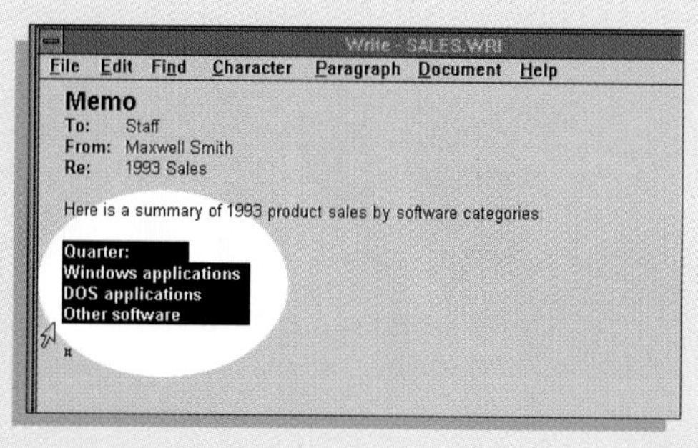


**1** To copy information from one place to another within a single document, begin by selecting the information you want to copy. Although some applications have their own special selection techniques, you can generally use either the mouse or the keyboard to select information: Drag the mouse from the beginning to the end of the selection, or hold down the Shift key and use the arrow keys to select the information. Note that the selected material is highlighted.

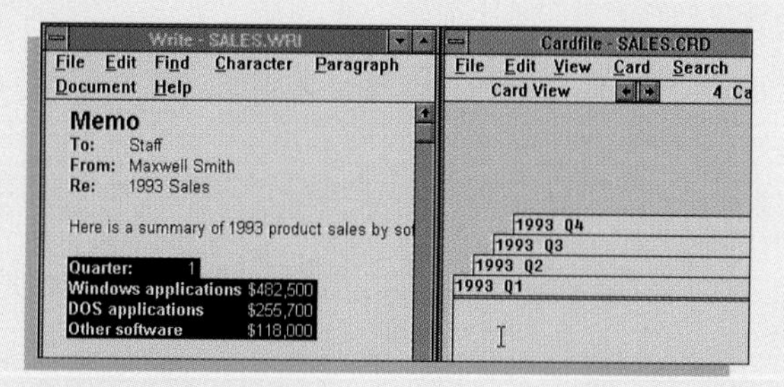


**6** To copy information from a document in one application to a document in another application, begin by selecting the information in the source document. Press Ctrl+C to copy the information to the Clipboard. Then start the second application and open the document to which you want to copy the information. Select the location where you want the copy to appear, and press Ctrl+V to paste the information from the Clipboard.

**3** Move the insertion point to the location where you want the information to appear. Then hold down the Ctrl key and press V. If you want to make additional copies, repeat this step.

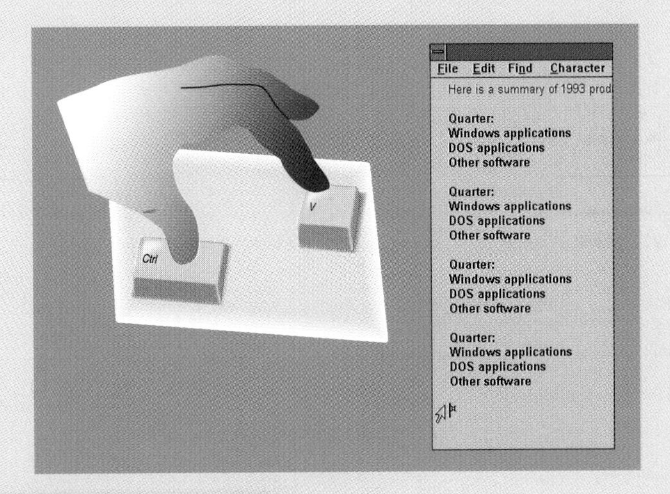


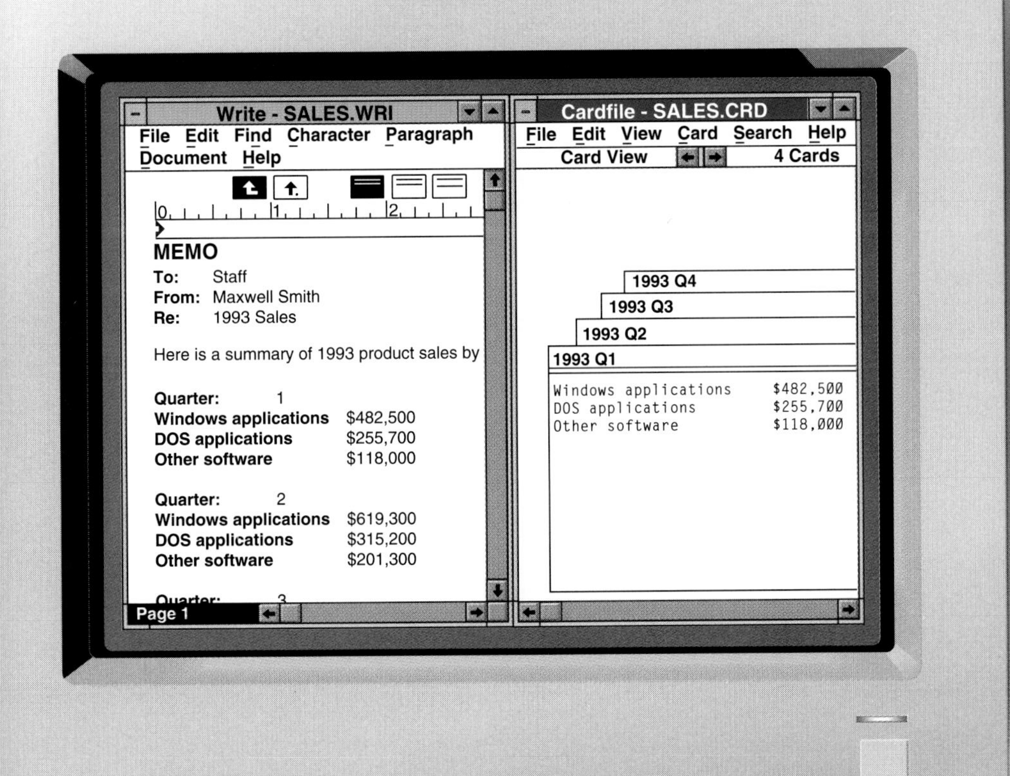


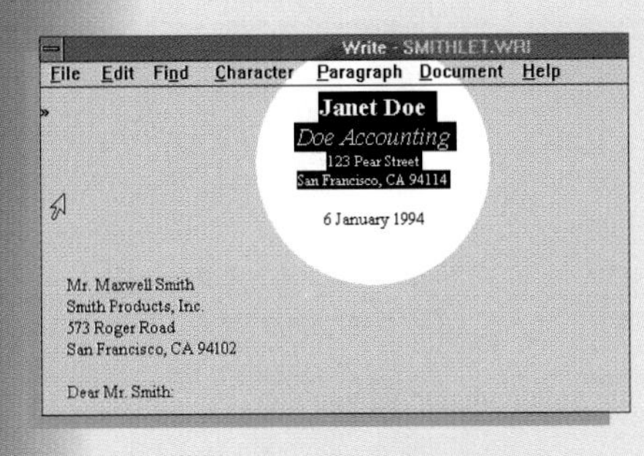


**4** To copy information from one document to another within an application, first select the information and press Ctrl+C, just as you would to copy information within a single document.

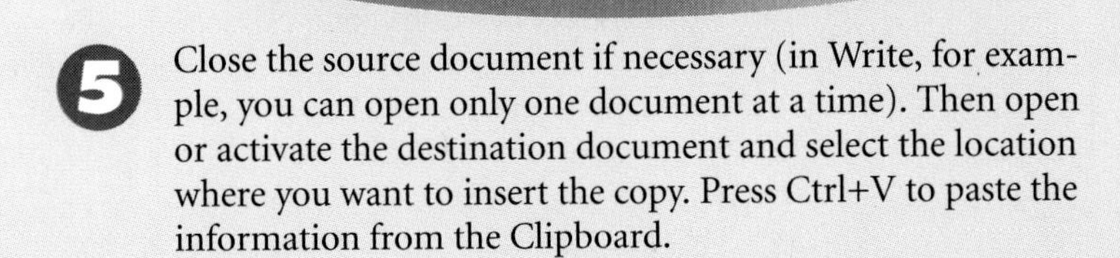

**5** Close the source document if necessary (in Write, for example, you can open only one document at a time). Then open or activate the destination document and select the location where you want to insert the copy. Press Ctrl+V to paste the information from the Clipboard.

# How to Cut and Paste

To move information in Windows you use the cut-and-paste procedure, which deletes the information from its source and places it in a new location. In any application that allows cut-and-paste, the Edit menu contains Cut and Paste commands with standard keyboard shortcuts of Ctrl+X and Ctrl+V, respectively. Like copy-and-paste, this procedure has two basic steps: You begin by selecting a block of information at its source and "cutting" it to the Clipboard; then you select a destination and paste the information from the Clipboard. Probably the most common use of the cut-and-paste operation is to move information within one document.

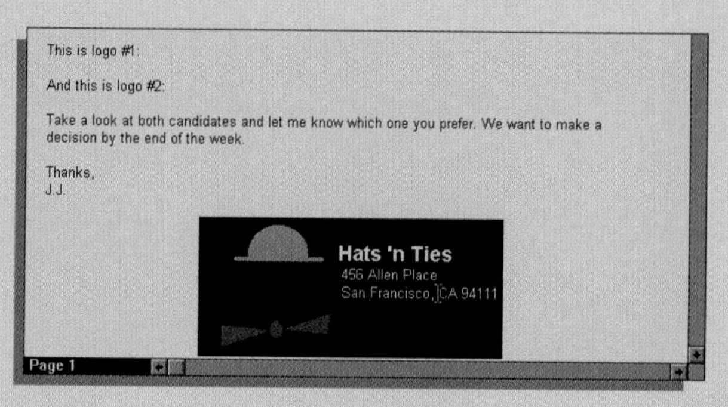


1. Select the information you want to move. You can generally use either the mouse or the keyboard to select information: Drag the mouse from the beginning to the end of the selection, or hold down the Shift key and use the arrow keys to make the selection. As with copy operations, the selection is highlighted. In this example, the selection is a graphic located near the end of a Write document. The goal is to move the graphic up into the text. To select a graphic in Write, you simply click it once with the mouse.

## TIP SHEET

- **You can use cut-and-paste to move information from one document to another or even from one application to another. But in these kinds of transfers it is usually a good idea to leave the original selection untouched at its source, so the copy-and-paste operation is often a better choice.**
- **You can paste multiple copies by pressing Ctrl+V more than once.**
- **If you cut information from a document and then change your mind about the operation, you can pull down the Edit menu and choose Undo. The Write, Cardfile, Paintbrush, and Notepad programs all have Undo commands.**
- **Chapter 11 explains how to use the Paintbrush program and how to copy a drawing from Paintbrush to Write.**

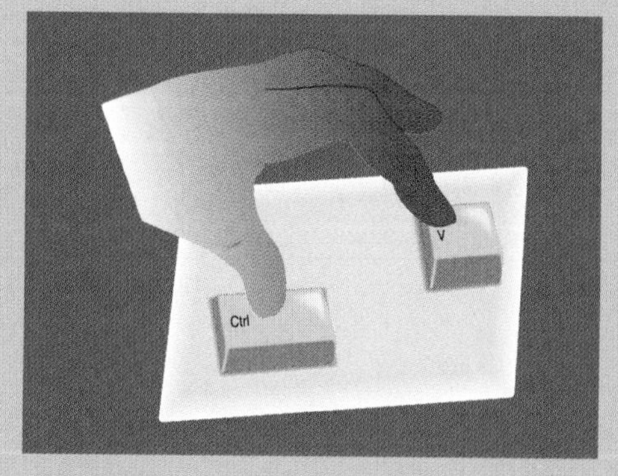


4. Hold down the Ctrl key and press V to paste the selection from the Clipboard to its new location.

**2** Hold down the Ctrl key and press X to cut the selection to the Clipboard. The selection immediately disappears from its original location.

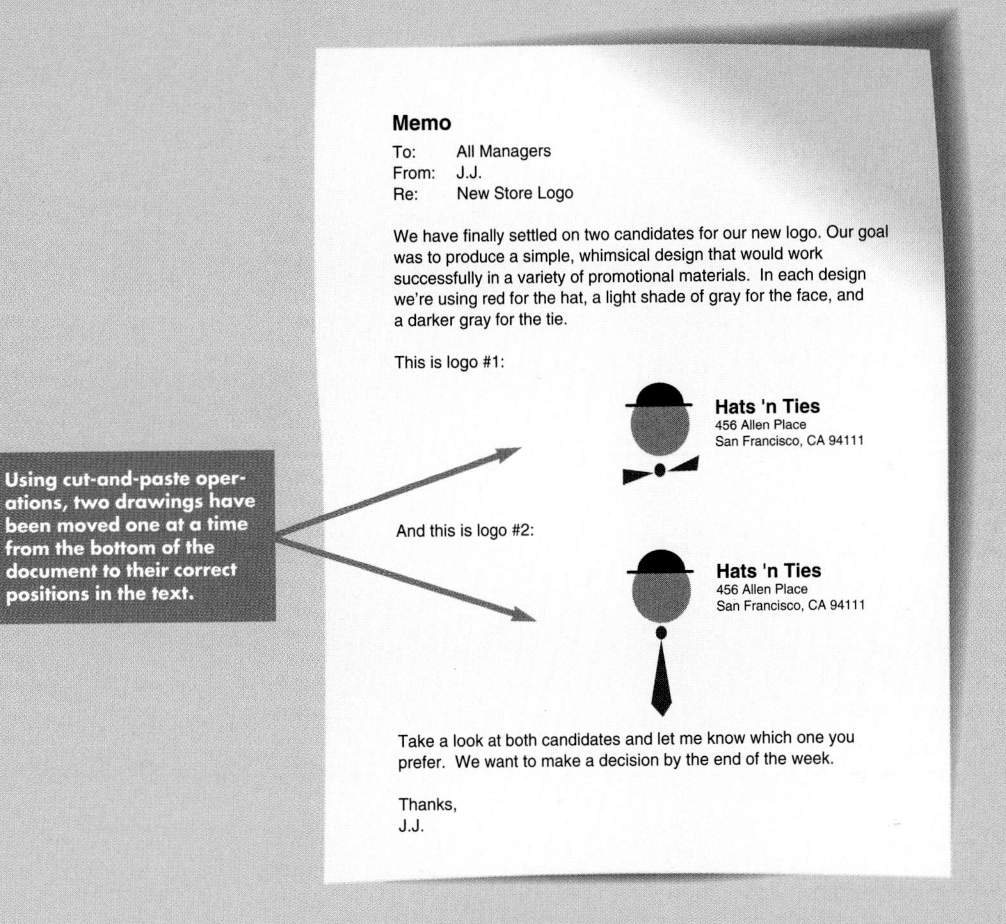

**Memo**

To: All Managers
From: J.J.
Re: New Store Logo

We have finally settled on two candidates for our new logo. Our goal was to produce a simple, whimsical design that would work successfully in a variety of promotional materials. In each design we're using red for the hat, a light shade of gray for the face, and a darker gray for the tie.

This is logo #1:

**Hats 'n Ties**
456 Allen Place
San Francisco, CA 94111

And this is logo #2:

**Hats 'n Ties**
456 Allen Place
San Francisco, CA 94111

Take a look at both candidates and let me know which one you prefer. We want to make a decision by the end of the week.

Thanks,
J.J.

**Using cut-and-paste operations, two drawings have been moved one at a time from the bottom of the document to their correct positions in the text.**

Select the location to which you want to move the information. (In Write, move the insertion point to the destination.)

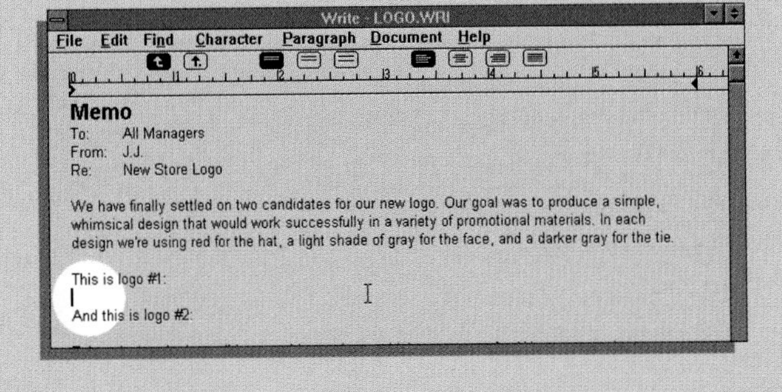

# How to Use the Clipboard Viewer

During a typical Windows session you might use the Clipboard dozens of times without ever needing to view its contents. But occasionally you may want to examine a selection that you've copied to the Clipboard. To do so, you simply open the Clipboard Viewer. Although this window has no editing capabilities, it offers some interesting features. For example, you can save the current contents of the Clipboard as a file on disk for reuse at a later time. You can also clear the contents of the Clipboard if you are finished with the selection it contains.

1. In the Main group of the Program Manager window, double-click the Clipboard Viewer icon. The Viewer window immediately appears on the desktop, displaying the last selection you copied to the Clipboard. (If you haven't copied anything to the Clipboard during the current Windows session, the window is empty.)

5. To close the Clipboard Viewer, pull down the File menu and click the Exit command. Choosing this command does *not* clear the Clipboard; the information it contains is still available for pasting.

## TIP SHEET

- **Each time you press Ctrl+C to copy a selection to the Clipboard, the previous selection is automatically deleted from the Clipboard. The Clipboard is also cleared when you exit from Windows.**
- **To open a .CLP file, pull down the File menu in the Clipboard Viewer and click the Open command.**
- **You can view the contents of the Clipboard in a variety of formats, depending on the type of information you have copied. To see a list of formats available for the current contents, pull down the Clipboard's Display menu.**
- **To capture an image of the active window to the Clipboard, hold down the Alt key and press Print Screen. To capture an image of the entire screen to the Clipboard, press Print Screen. To print a copy of a screen capture, paste the image to a Write document, and then choose the Print command from Write's File menu.**

**Here the Clipboard contains lines of text copied from a Write document.**

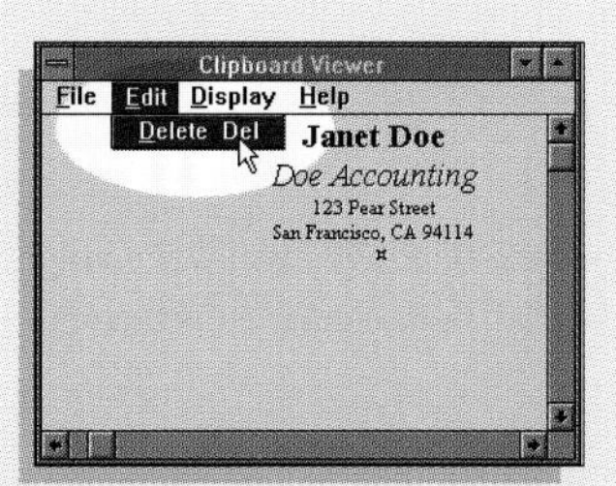


**2** To save the Clipboard's current contents to disk, pull down the File menu and click the Save As command. In the Save As dialog box, enter a name for the file; Windows automatically uses .CLP as the extension. Click the OK button to save the file.

**3** To delete the current contents of the Clipboard, pull down the Edit menu and click its only command, Delete. (Alternatively, you can press the Del key.)

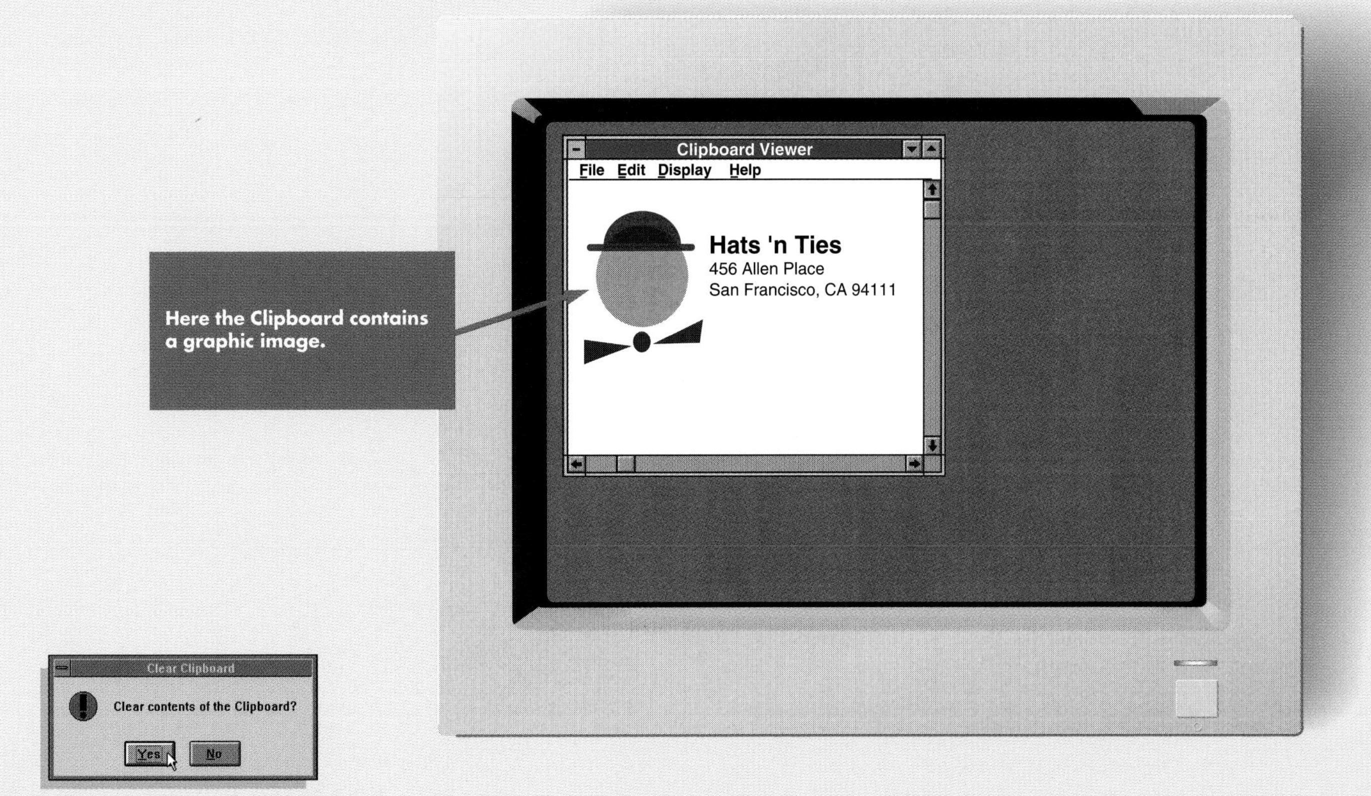


**Here the Clipboard contains a graphic image.**

**4** Before clearing the Clipboard, Windows asks you to confirm. Click the Yes button if you are sure, or click No if you change your mind.

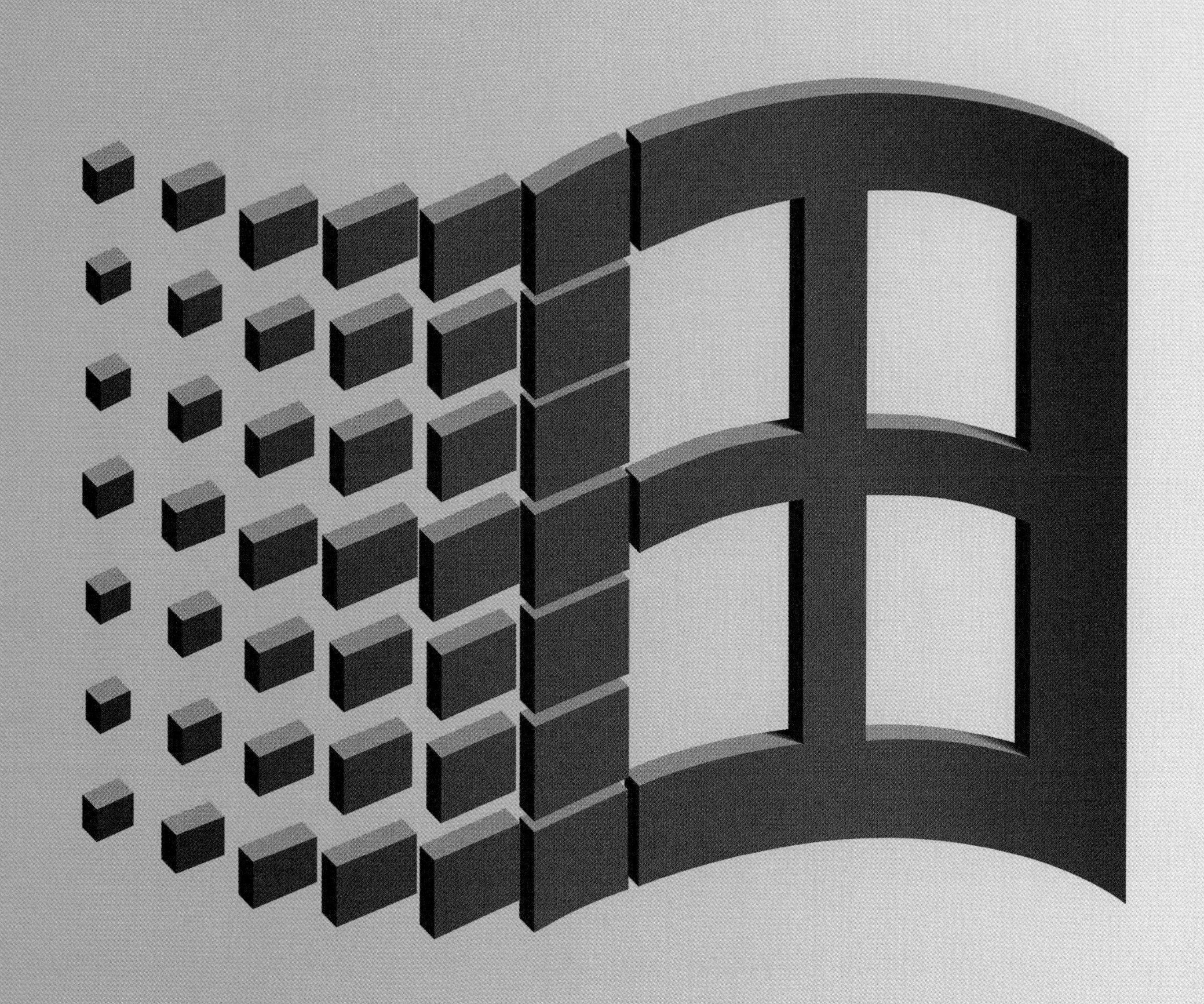

## CHAPTER 9

# Using the Print Manager

The Print Manager is in charge of printing documents from Windows applications. It coordinates the software resources needed for a successful print job—including the printer driver, the font selections, and the contents of the document itself. In general, the Print Manager is designed to do its work automatically, without distracting you from your other activities in Windows. Its icon shows up on the desktop whenever you choose an application's Print command. It allows you to place multiple documents in line for printing, creating a *print queue*, and to continue your work while the printing takes place in the background.

You may sometimes want to take direct control of printing operations. The Print Manager window gives you a variety of options for doing so. You can open the window by double-clicking its icon when it appears on the desktop. The window shows the current print queue, and allows you to pause, resume, or cancel any print job. You can also change the order in which documents will be printed. You'll learn to perform all these tasks in this chapter.

# How to Print Document Files

You typically print a document directly from the application in which the file was created. Whether you're printing a letter from Write, a data record from Cardfile, or a drawing from Paintbrush, the steps are always the same: You start the application, open the file, and choose the application's Print command.

But suppose you want a quick way to print several documents that come from different applications. For this situation, Windows provides a special shortcut that uses both the Print Manager and the File Manager. With this shortcut, printing a file becomes a simple drag-and-drop operation.

**1** Double-click the Print Manager icon in the Main group.

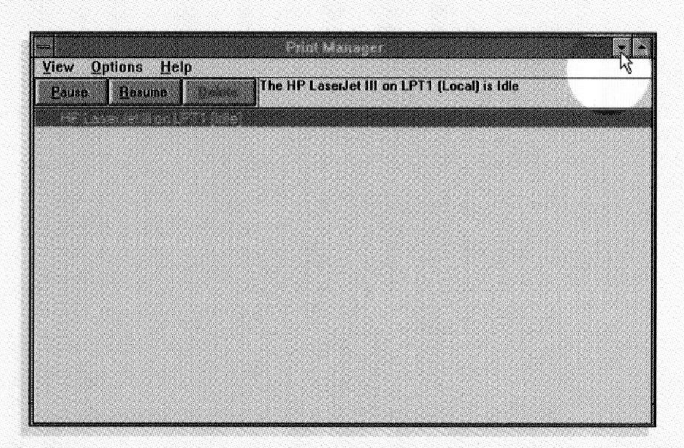


**2** The Print Manager window appears on the desktop. For convenience, click the minimize button to reduce the window to an icon.

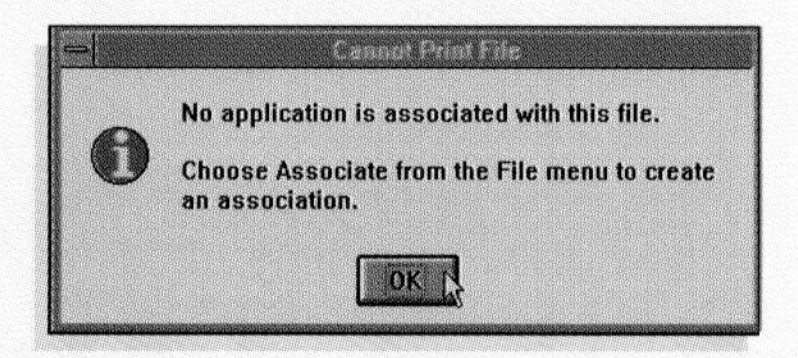


**7** If Windows displays the Cannot Print File box on the desktop instead of starting an application, the document you've selected is not associated with an application. Click OK to close the dialog box.

## TIP SHEET

- **If Windows cannot automatically determine the appropriate application from which to print a document you select, the most straightforward alternative is to start an application yourself. For example, suppose you are trying to print your AUTOEXEC.BAT file. Because this is a text file, you can print it from the Notepad application. (See Chapter 13 for information about the Notepad.)**
- **A more technical solution is to define an association between a category of documents and their appropriate application. To do this, pull down the File menu in the File Manager and click the Associate command. Enter the extension that identifies the category of files; then select an application from the Associate With list. Click OK to create the association. You can then use the drag-and-drop shortcut to print documents belonging to this category.**

**3** Double-click the File Manager icon in the Main group. When the File Manager window appears on the desktop, resize it if necessary so that you can also see the Print Manager icon.

**4** In the directory tree at the left side of the File Manager window, click the directory that contains the document file or files you'd like to print. Optionally, choose the By File Type command from the File Manager's View menu to select the file names you want to see in the directory window. (See Chapter 6 for a review of this and other File Manager operations.)

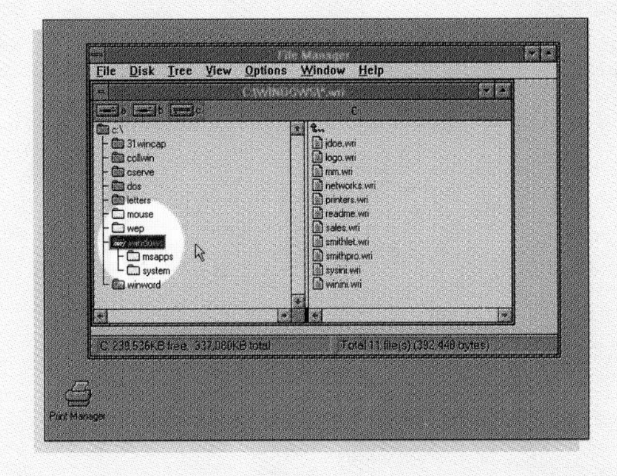


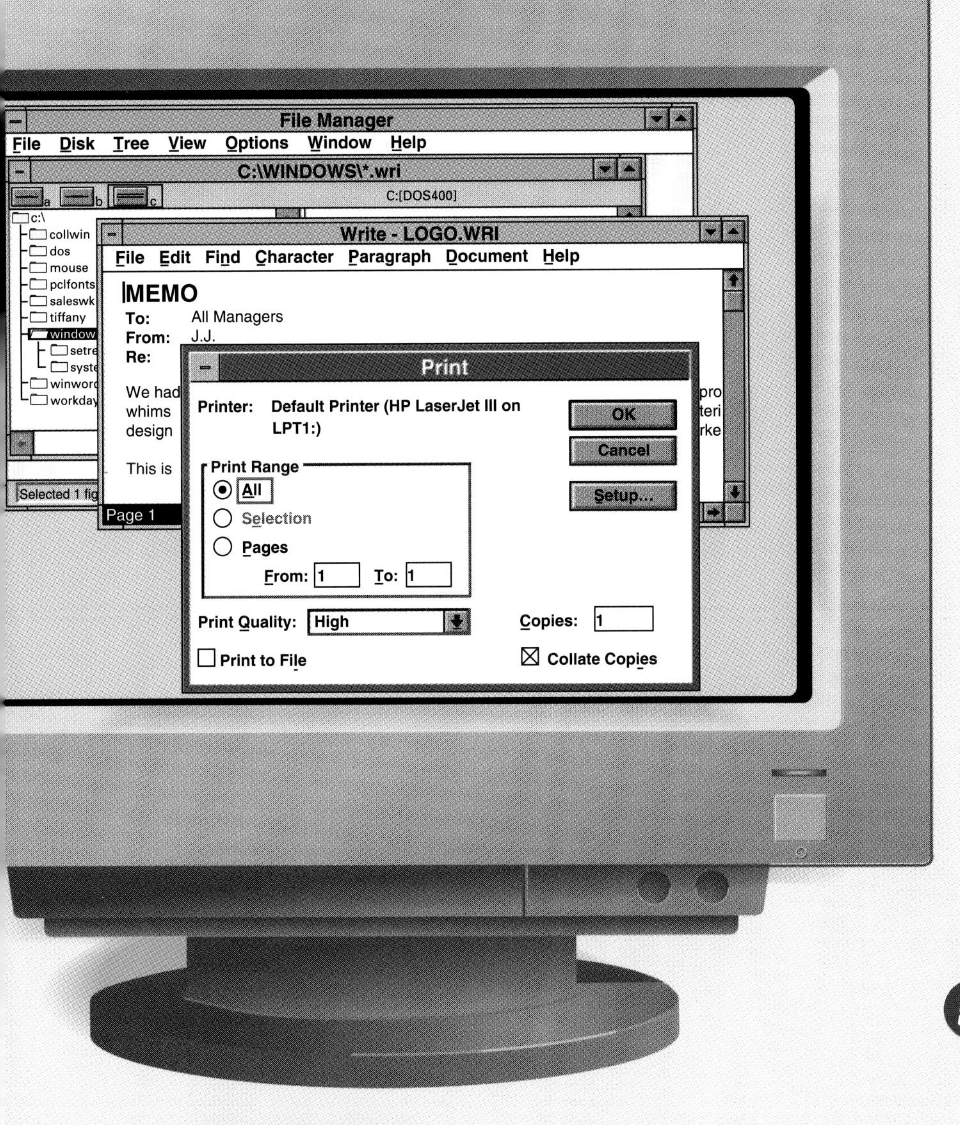

**5** In the contents list of the directory window, select the name of the file you want to print, and drag the file's icon to the Print Manager icon on the desktop. While you drag, the icon appears as a document page with a plus sign on it. Release the mouse button when the document icon is positioned directly over the Print Manager icon.

**6** Windows starts the appropriate application and opens the document you have selected. For example, if you've selected a .WRI file, Windows starts Write and opens the file, as shown in the central graphic on these pages. If a Print dialog box appears on the desktop, click OK to begin printing. When the document is ready to be printed, Windows automatically closes the application. To print additional documents, start again at step 4.

# How to Manage the Print Queue

The Print Manager window displays the current print queue—the list of documents that are waiting in line to be printed. By opening the window, you can examine the queue and, optionally, change its contents. The Print Manager allows you to pause and resume printing, change the order in which documents will be printed, and cancel one or more jobs in the queue.

**1** Send any number of documents to the Print Manager—either by choosing the Print commands in specific applications, or by using the drag-and-drop shortcut described on the previous two pages.

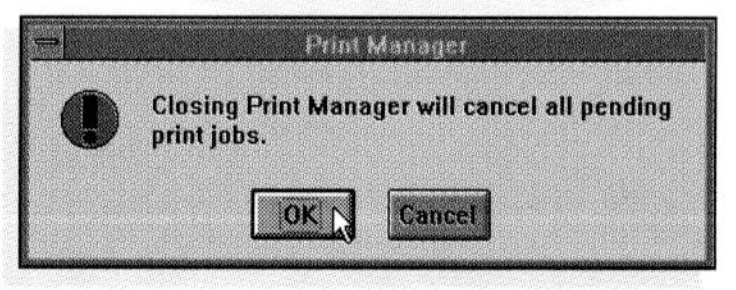


**6** To cancel all the print jobs in the queue, pull down the View menu and click the Exit command. A dialog box asks you to confirm. If you click OK, the Print Manager will be closed and the entire print queue will be canceled.

## TIP SHEET

- **When you choose an application's Print command, the Print Manager icon should automatically appear on the desktop. If the icon doesn't show up, you need to activate the Print Manager. Double-click the Control Panel icon in the Main group, and then double-click the Printers icon in the Control Panel. In the Printers dialog box, click the Use Print Manager check box. (An X appears in the box.) Then click the Close button. Close the Control Panel window by double-clicking its control-menu box.**
- **If you have several documents to send to the print queue, you might want to put your printer on pause while you are in the process of forming the queue. Double-click the Print Manager icon in the Main window and click the Pause button in the Print Manager window. Then minimize the window and begin sending documents to the queue. When you are ready to begin printing, reopen the window and click Resume. Once printing begins, you can minimize the Print Manager window and go on to other activities on the desktop.**

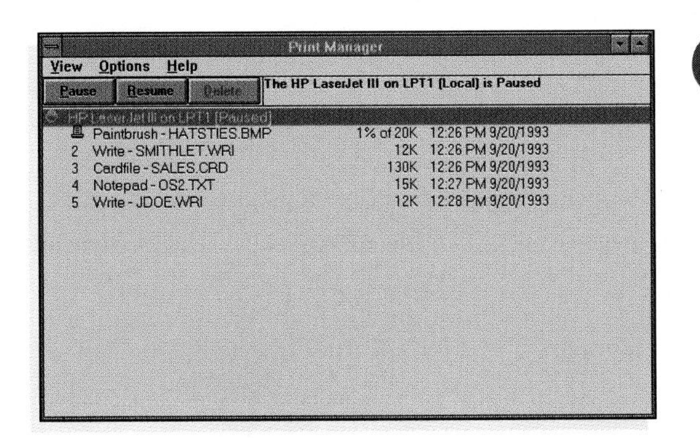


**2** To view the print queue, double-click the Print Manager icon on the desktop. The queue provides several pieces of information about each document: the file name, the application with which it is associated, its size in kilobytes, and the time and date when the file was sent to the queue. For the current file—that is, the first file in the list—the Print Manager tells you what percentage of the file has already been sent to the printer.

**3** To stop printing temporarily, click the Pause button at the upper-left corner of the Print Manager window. An open-hand icon appears next to the printer name in the queue, along with the notation *[Paused]*. To continue printing, click the Resume button.

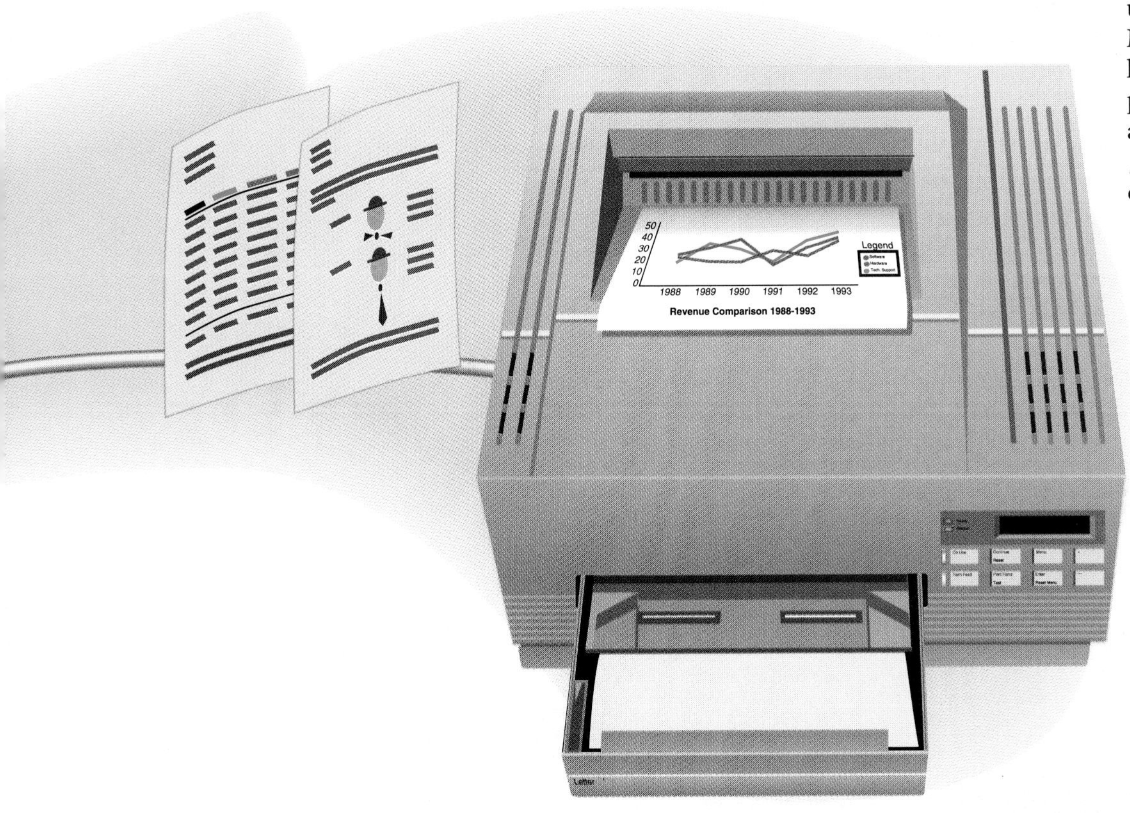


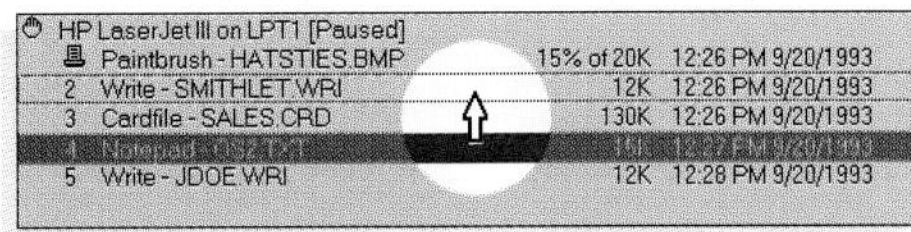


**4** To change the order in which files will be printed, select a file in the print queue and use the mouse to drag the name up or down the list. As you drag, the mouse pointer becomes an upward-pointing arrow.

**5** To remove a document from the print queue, select a file name by clicking it with the mouse, and then click the Delete button. A dialog box asks you to confirm the deletion; if you click OK, the document will be removed from the queue and will not be printed.

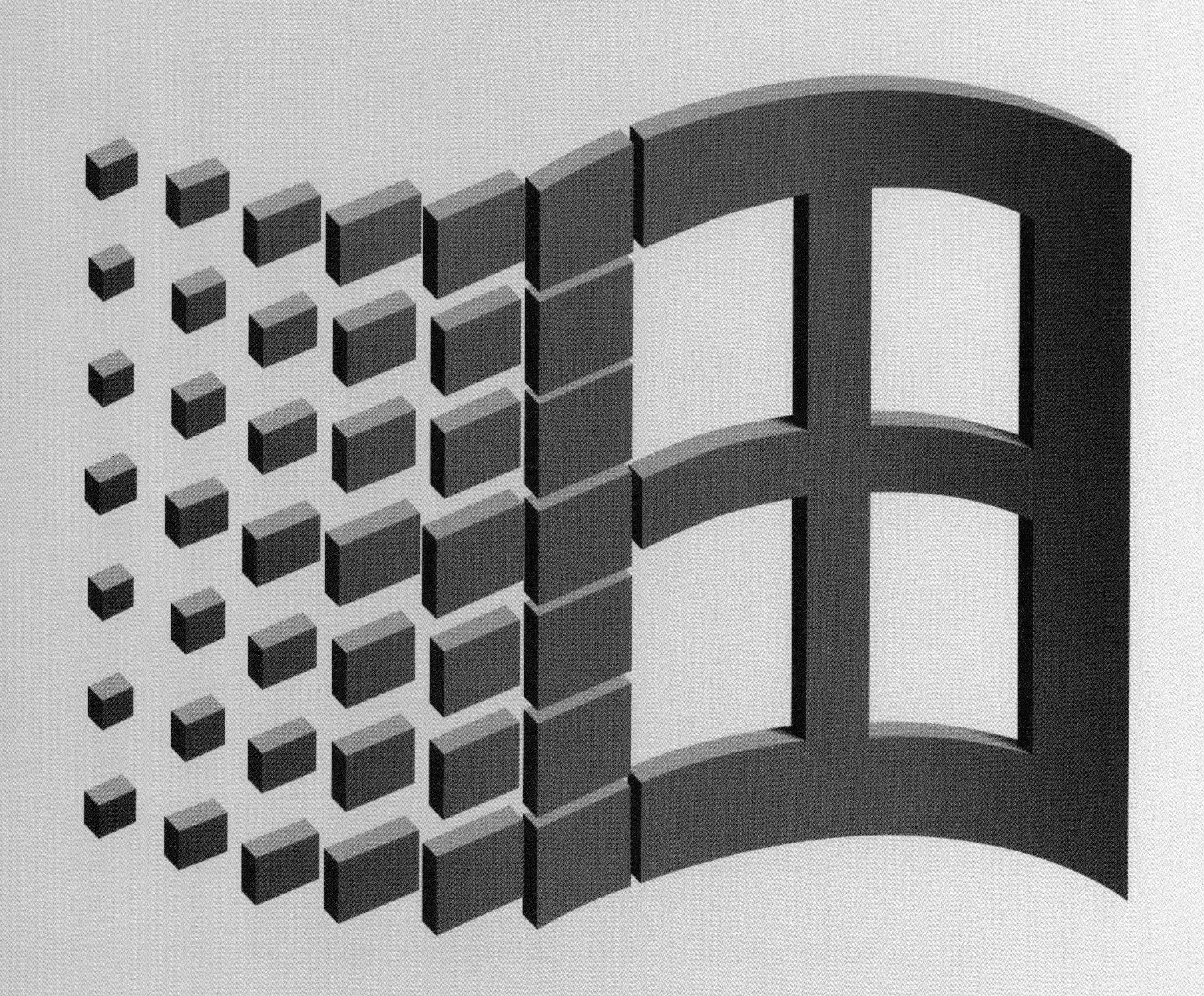

## CHAPTER 10

# Managing Information

What kinds of information do you regularly gather and use at work or at home? Addresses and phone numbers, to be sure—but probably many other kinds as well. Employee data, product descriptions, customer lists, investment ideas, loan payments and due dates, household insurance inventories, research notes, holiday lists, New Year's resolutions, birthdays and anniversaries, party invitations, cake recipes, vacation plans, letters received and owed, kids' innoculation records, garden planting schedules—the list goes on, and is as diverse as life is busy. Whether you normally keep these records stored neatly in folders or scrawled on the backs of envelopes, you can significantly improve your access to information by transferring them partially or wholly to files on the computer. In Windows, the Cardfile application is just the tool you need for this job.

Cardfile's primary charms are simplicity and visual clarity. You keep your records on individual cards, which appear as rectangular areas of information on the screen. A file may consist of dozens or even hundreds of cards, arranged in an overlapping stack. Cardfile automatically alphabetizes your cards by their index lines. The *index* is normally the first item of information you enter onto a card, and serves as a kind of topic description or title for the card.

When you want to find a particular card in a file, Cardfile gives you several quick ways of searching for information. Whether you need a friend's phone number, the name of that restaurant on Pine street, or the chocolate cake recipe with coffee in it, you can use Cardfile's Search menu to find the right card in seconds. As you'll learn in this chapter, you can also print cards, individually or in groups, whenever you need information on paper.

# How to Get Started in Cardfile

A card is the space in which you enter one record of information in the Cardfile application. Ultimately, you may add many cards to a file.

A card contains two sections: an *index line* at the top, where you enter the title, topic, or primary data item of a particular record; and the *information area*, where you type additional information. As you add new cards to a file, Cardfile automatically arranges them alphabetically by the contents of their index lines.

As you'll see, the steps for filling in the first card in a new file are a bit different from those for adding subsequent cards.

## TIP SHEET

- **You can edit the contents of a card at any time. In the information area, the mouse pointer takes the shape of an I-beam. Position the pointer at the position where you want to edit the text, and click the mouse button to move the insertion point. (Alternatively, use the arrow keys on the keyboard to move the insertion point in any direction.) Press Backspace to delete a character to the left of the insertion point, or Delete to erase a character to the right. To insert text, position the insertion point and begin typing.**
- **To select a portion of the text in the information area, drag the mouse pointer from the beginning to the end of the selection. (To select a single word, position the mouse pointer over the word and double-click the mouse button.) A highlighted selection appears as white text against a dark background. To copy or move a selection, use the standard Clipboard techniques. See Chapter 8 for details.**
- **If you want to undo the most recent change you made in the information area, pull down the Edit menu and choose the Undo command or press Ctrl+Z.**

1. Double-click the Accessories group icon if the group isn't already open. Then double-click the Cardfile icon to start the application. The application window opens onto the desktop.

5. The insertion point reappears in the card's information area. Type the information you want to store for this card. The card contains room for eleven 40-character lines of text. Within the dimensions of the card, you can organize the contents of the information area any way you wish. As with the Write application, word-wrap occurs automatically when you reach the end of a line—that is, the insertion point jumps down to the beginning of the next line, bringing the current word with it if there isn't enough space on the previous line. Alternatively, you can always press Enter if you want to start a new line.

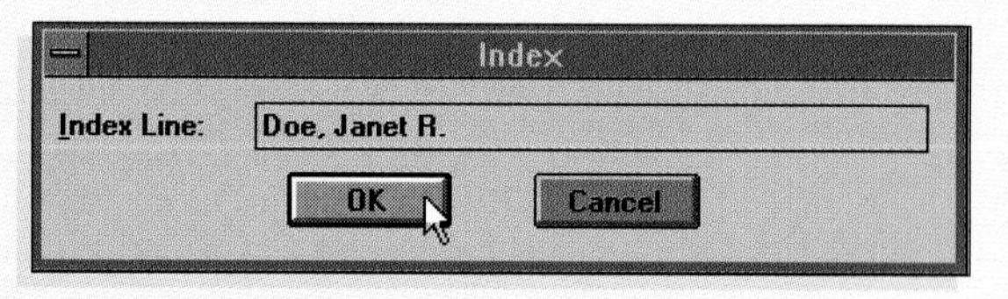


4. The Index dialog box appears on the desktop. Enter the index information for the first card into the Index Line text box, and then click the OK button. The information appears on the index line of the card itself.

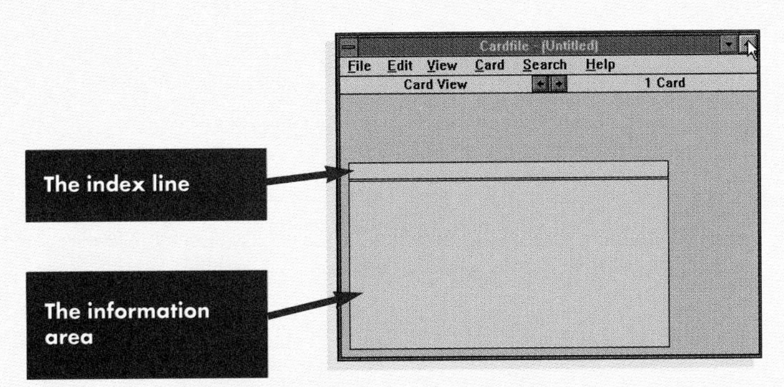


**2** In the lower-left corner of the window, you can see the first card of a new file. Within the card, the index is separated from the information area by a double line. A flashing insertion point (|) appears in the information area, indicating that Cardfile is ready for you to begin typing in this section of the card. Click the maximize button to expand the size of the application window; the card keeps its original dimensions.

**3** On the Cardfile menu bar, pull down the Edit menu and click the Index command. This is the command to choose when you want to enter or edit information on the index line of a card. Notice that the keyboard shortcut for the Index command is F6. (Another shortcut is to position the mouse pointer inside the index line area of a card and double-click the left mouse button.)

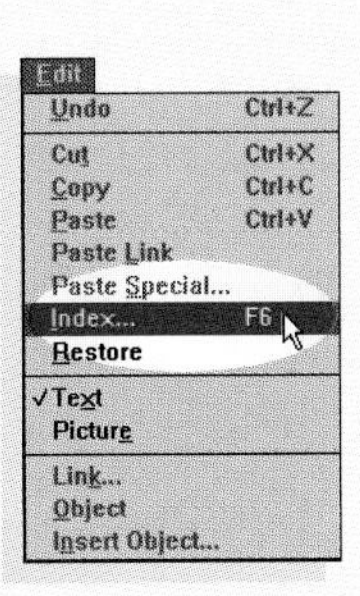


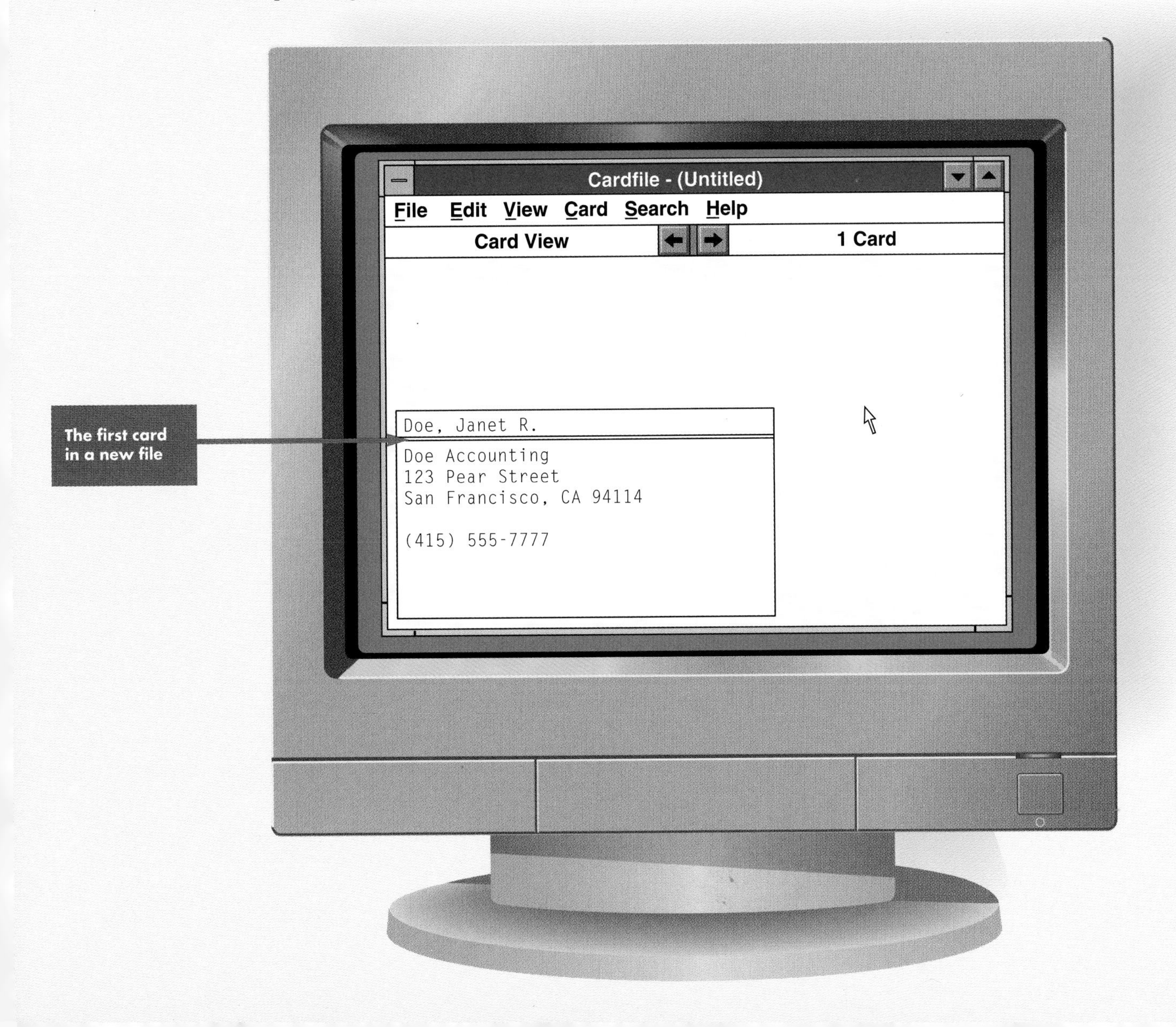

# How to Add Cards and Switch Views

On the first card of a new file you design a structure for storing your data. Most importantly, you choose a category of information to enter on the index line of each card. Then, as you add new cards to the file, you follow the pattern established on the first card.

Cardfile allows you to work with a file in either of two views. In the familiar *card view*, each record is displayed on its own rectangular card. You can see the information area on the front card, but only the index lines of the other cards. (When you add a new card, it always starts out at the front of the file.) In the *list view*, you see all the index lines in alphabetical order. Switching between views is easy, and can sometimes help you locate information in your file.

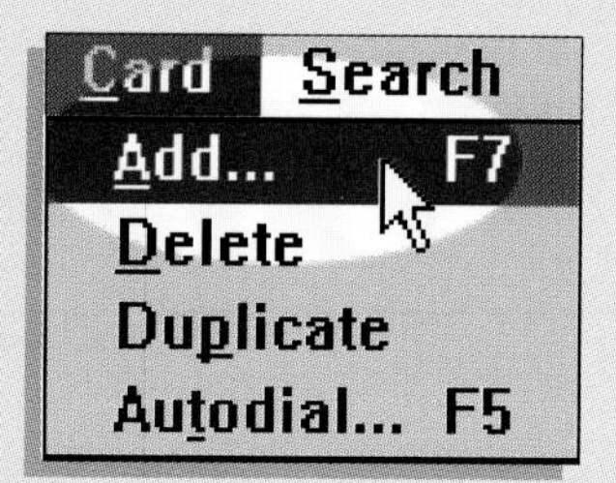


**1** To add a new card to the current file, pull down the Card menu and click the Add command, or press the F7 shortcut key.

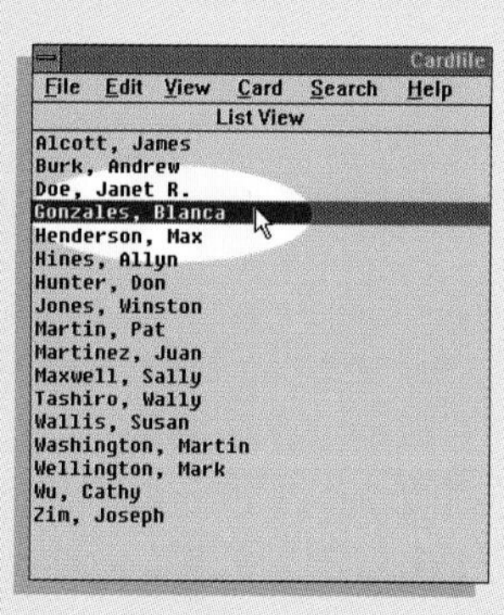


**5** The list view shows the index lines in alphabetical order. Select any card by clicking its line with the mouse. Then switch back to card view to see the card's information area by pulling down the View menu and clicking the Card command.

**TIP SHEET**

- **Before adding many new records to your file, you should save the file to disk. Turn the page to find out how to name and save a card file.**
- **Cardfile gives you several ways to bring a particular card to the front of the file; for details, see "How to Find Information in a Card File" later in this chapter.**
- **You can store a picture in the information area of a card. To do so, you begin by copying a picture to the Clipboard from an application such as Paintbrush. (See Chapter 11 for details.) Then return to the Cardfile application and select the card on which you want to paste the picture. Pull down the Edit menu and click the Picture command to designate this as a picture card. Then pull down the Edit menu again and choose Paste (or press the Ctrl+V shortcut). The picture appears in the information area of the card.**

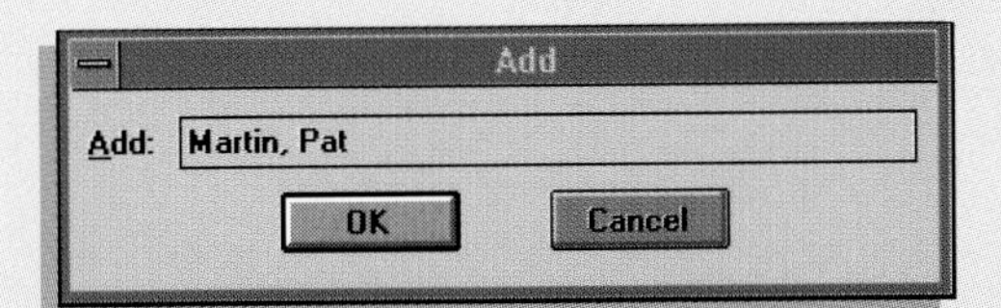


2 The Add dialog box appears on the desktop. Type the information you want to store on the index line of the new card, and then click the OK button.

3 The new card appears at the front of the file. Type the text that you want to store in the card's information area. Then start again from step 1 for each new card you want to add to the file.

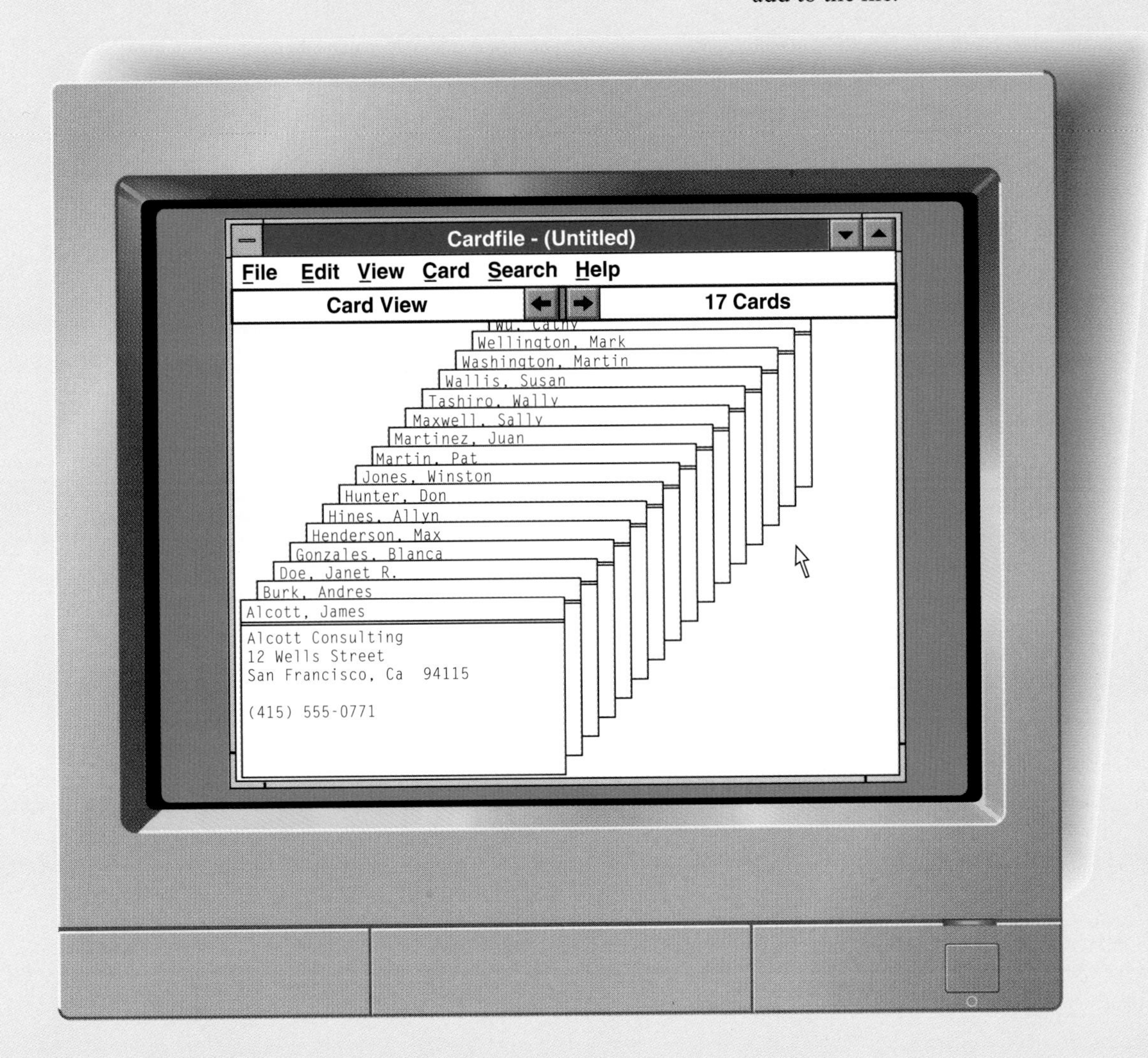


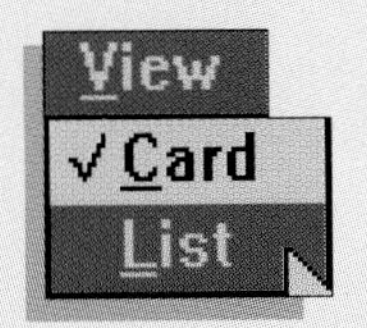

To switch to list view, pull down the View menu and click the List command.

# How to Save and Open a Card File

Like many other Windows applications, Cardfile has two Save operations. From the File menu you choose the Save As command to name a file and save it for the first time, or the Save command to update an existing file after you have made additions or changes to its cards. The File menu has other important commands for managing card files. The New command closes the current file and starts a new one, and the Open command allows you to select and open an existing card file from disk.

**1** To save a card file for the first time, pull down the File menu and click the Save As command.

**TIP SHEET**

- The Merge command on the File menu allows you to combine the cards from two or more existing files. Begin this process by opening one card file. Then pull down the File command and click Merge. In the resulting File Merge dialog box, select the name of the file whose cards you want to combine with the current file, and click the OK button. The second file's cards become part of the current file. To save the merged file under a new name, pull down the File menu and choose the Save As command; then enter a file name and click OK. This way, both of the original files are preserved on disk with their contents intact.
- The maximum practical size for a card file depends on the resources of your computer system. In general, if you anticipate creating a file that has more than about a thousand records, consider using a database management program such as Microsoft Access. This kind of program will also give you sophisticated ways to search for particular groups of records, display individual records on the screen, and print selected records in customized formats.

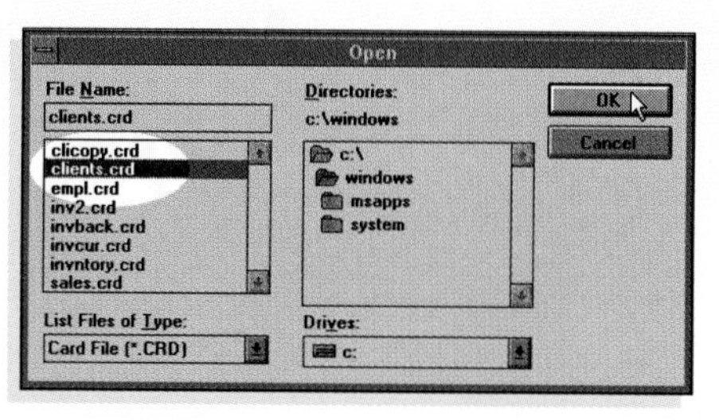


**6** In the resulting Open dialog box, select the name of the card file you want to open. (If necessary, use the Directories list to select the directory in which you have saved your card files.) Click the OK button to open the file.

**5** To open an existing card file, pull down the File menu and click the Open command.

**2** In the resulting Save As dialog box, enter the name under which you want to save the file. (Optionally, use the Directories list to select a directory for the new file. To open a directory, double-click its name in the list.) By default, Cardfile supplies a .CRD extension for the card file you are about to save. Click the OK button to complete the save operation. The new file name appears on the title bar of the Cardfile application window.

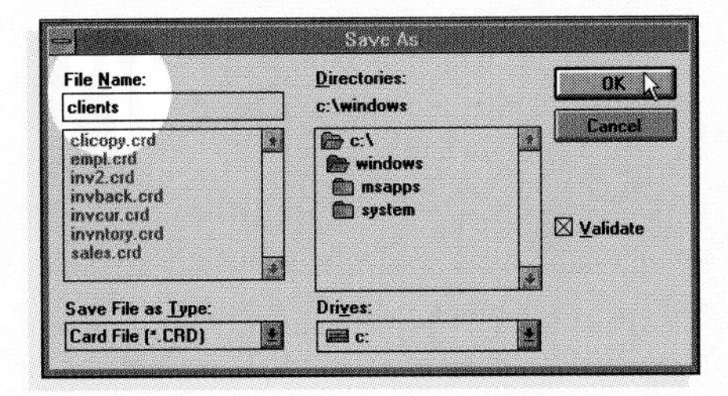


**3** To update the current card file after you have added or edited cards in the file, pull down the File menu and click the Save command.

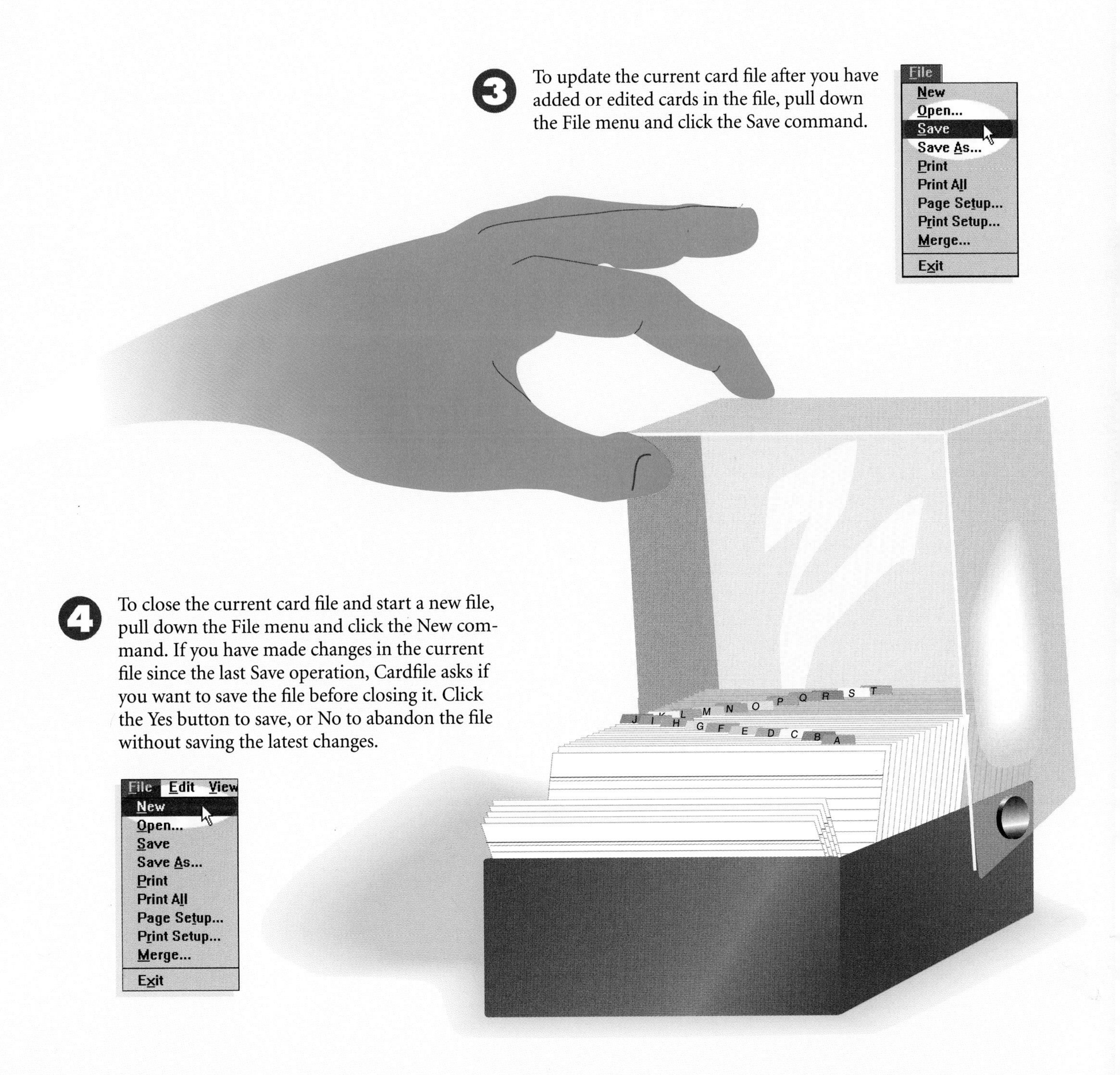


**4** To close the current card file and start a new file, pull down the File menu and click the New command. If you have made changes in the current file since the last Save operation, Cardfile asks if you want to save the file before closing it. Click the Yes button to save, or No to abandon the file without saving the latest changes.

# How to Find Information in a Card File

The front card is the current record in a file. This is the card on which you can view both the index line and the information area; in addition, the data on this card is available for editing. Cardfile gives you several convenient ways to bring a particular card to the front of a file. You can simply select a card by its index, or you can scroll through the cards one by one. But as your card file gets larger and larger, you may need more efficient ways to search for a card. The Search menu on the Cardfile menu bar provides two commands for this purpose. You can use the Go To command to search for a card containing a particular index, or the Find command to search for text in the information area of a card.

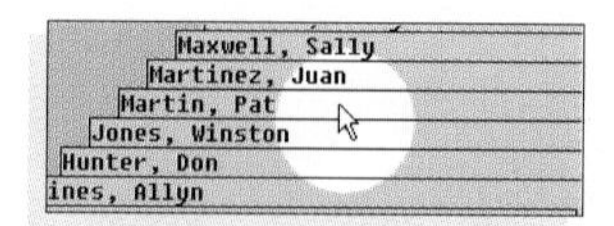


**1** To bring a card to the front of the file in card view, position the mouse pointer over the card's index line and click the left mouse button.

**7** If Cardfile cannot find the text you entered into either the Go To or Find What text box, an error message appears on the desktop. Click OK and try a different search.

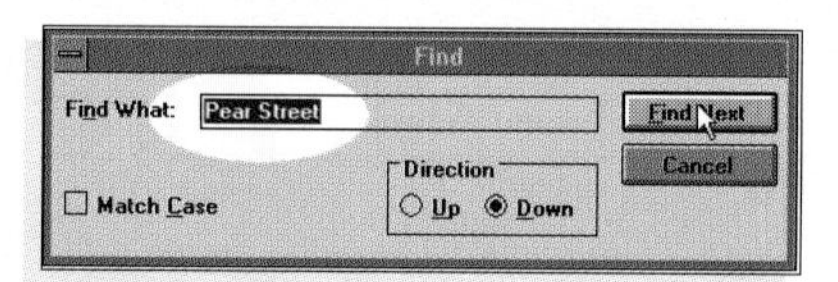


**6** In the Find What text box, enter the text you want to search for. Optionally, click Match Case if you want to search for text in the exact uppercase/lowercase pattern you have typed. Select the Up or Down option in the Direction box to indicate the direction of the search. Then click the Find Next button to begin the search. If a card with the specified text exists, it moves to the front of the file. Click Find Next again to search for another card that contains the same text, or click Cancel to close the Find dialog box.

## TIP SHEET

- **To bring the first card in a file to the front, press Ctrl+Home; to bring the last card to the front, press Ctrl+End. Here "first" and "last" refer to the beginning and end of the alphabetically arranged card file.**
- **To delete a card from a file, use any of the techniques described on these pages to bring the card to the front of the file. Then pull down the Card menu and click the Delete command. Cardfile asks you to confirm the deletion; click OK if you are sure you want to remove the card.**
- **Another command in the Card menu allows you to duplicate the current card. This is a quick way to create a new card and copy information from an existing card to it. Bring the card you want to duplicate to the front of the file. Then pull down the Card menu and click the Duplicate command.**

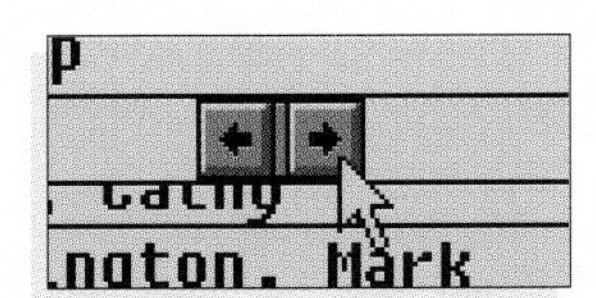


2 To scroll through the file one card at a time, click one of the two arrow buttons beneath the menu bar in the Cardfile window. Click the right-arrow button (or press the PgDn key on the keyboard) to move forward through the file. Click the left-arrow button (or press PgUp) to move backward.

3 To search for a card by its index contents, pull down the Search menu and click the Go To command. (Alternatively, you can press the F4 shortcut key.)

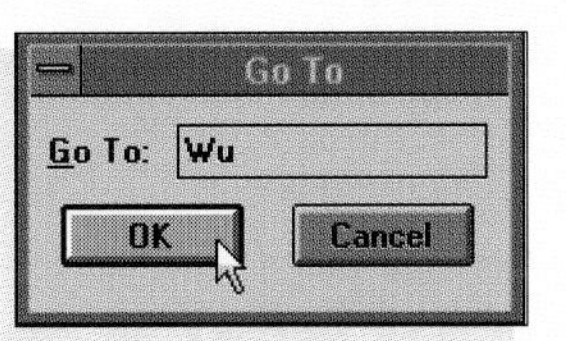


4 In the Go To text box, enter any part of the index-line text you are searching for. For example, to search for a card in an address file, you might enter a person's first name, last name, or full name. Then click the OK button. If the card exists, it instantly moves to the front of the file.

5 To search for a card by the contents of its information area, pull down the Search menu and click the Find command.

# How to Print Cards

You can print individual records from an open card file or you can print the entire file. The resulting cards look about the same on paper as they do on the screen. A box appears around each printed card, and a line separates the index from the information area. If you print the whole file, Cardfile arranges the cards in alphabetical order and prints only a few per page; a large card file can take up many printed pages.

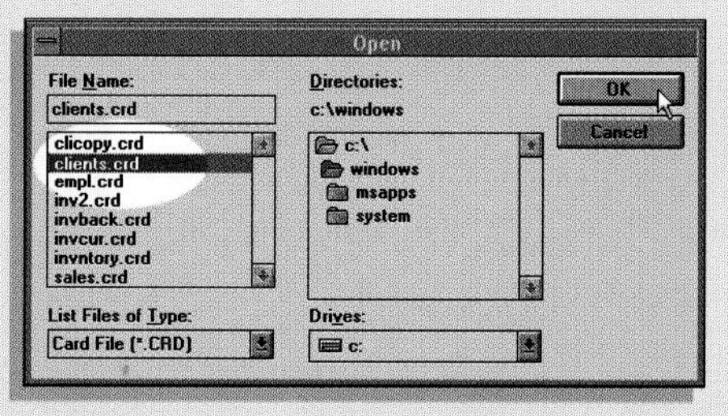


**1** To open the file you want to print, pull down the File menu and click the Open command. Select the name of the file and click OK.

**TIP SHEET**

- By default, the name of the current file appears as the *header* at the top of each page, and the page number appears as the *footer* at the bottom. You can change the header and footer (or delete them altogether) by choosing the Page Setup command from the File menu. In the resulting dialog box, change or replace the contents of the Header and Footer text boxes. Cardfile recognizes special codes for the contents of these boxes—for example, &f stands for the file name, &p for the page number, &d for the current date, and &t for the current time.
- You can also use the Page Setup command to change the top, bottom, left, and right margins of the page in the upcoming print job.
- Cardfile offers no really convenient way to print a selection of cards from a file, but here is one fairly simple approach: Open the file containing the cards you want to print. Choose the Save As command from the File menu, and make a temporary copy of the file to disk under a new name. In the copy of the file, delete all the cards you do *not* want to print. Then choose the Print All command from the File menu.

To print all the cards in the file, pull down the File menu and click the Print All command. By default, Cardfile prints a column of three cards on each 8½-by-11-inch page.

**2** To print a single card, click the card's index line to bring it to the front of the file. (Or use one of the techniques described in "How to Find Information in a Card File" to bring the card to the front.)

Alcott, James
Alcott Consulting
12 Wells Street
San Francisco, CA 94115
(415) 555-0771

Burk, Andrew
Burk Associates
9876 Missouri Drive
San Francisco, CA 91123
(415) 555-1341

Doe, Janet R.
Doe Accounting
123 Pear Street
San Francisco, CA 94114
(415) 555-7777

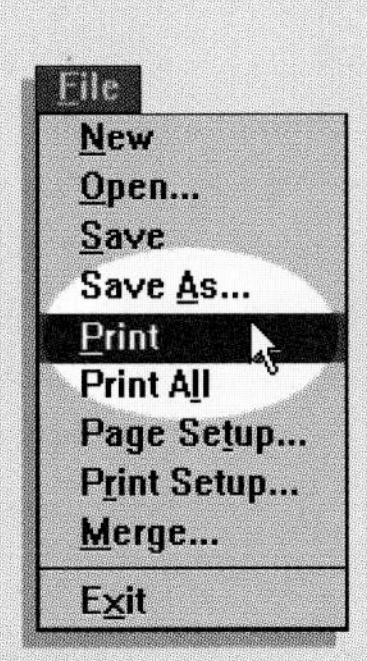


**3** Make sure your printer is ready. Then pull down the File menu and click the Print command. A copy of the front card is sent to your printer.

# TRY IT!

In this exercise, you'll try creating your own home inventory file for insurance purposes. The inventory should contain descriptions of insurable items in your home—including furniture, appliances, jewelry, and so on. In the event of an insured loss, a copy of this card file would help you describe, evaluate, and verify your claim. As you work through this exercise, you can use the imaginary inventory information suggested in individual steps, or you can actually begin building a real inventory file for the insurable items in your own home. Along the way, you'll see a practical way to organize the cards for this particular file, and you'll learn to use the Duplicate command to streamline the process.

If Cardfile isn't running yet, open the Accessories group in the Program Manager, and double-click the Cardfile icon. Maximize the application window when it appears on the desktop.

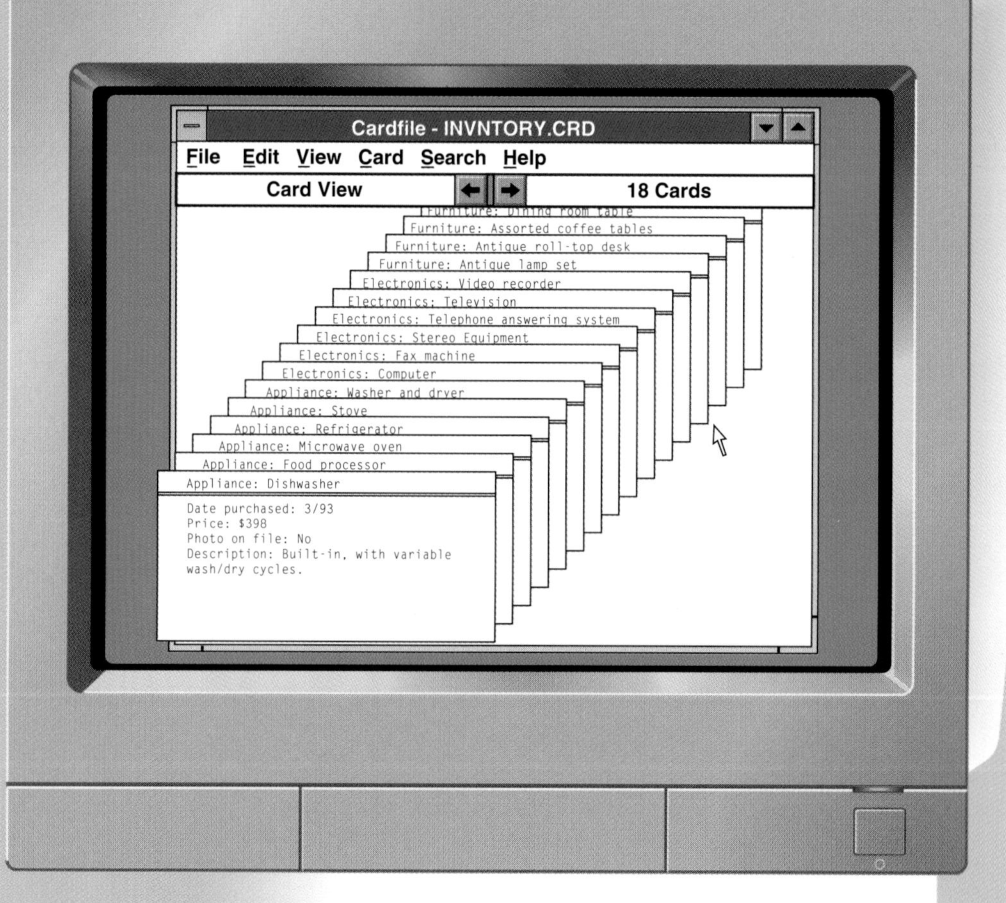

To enter an index for the first card in the file, press the F6 function key. The Index dialog box appears on the screen.

Type **Furniture:** as the index for the first card, and then click the OK button.

Furniture:
Date Purchased:
Price:
Photo on file:
Description:

On the first four lines of the card's information area, type the following four category headings: **Date Purchased:, Price:, Photo on file:, Description:**. (You'll fill in the information for these categories later.)

Pull down the File menu and click the Save As command.

Enter **invntory** in the File Name box, and click OK.

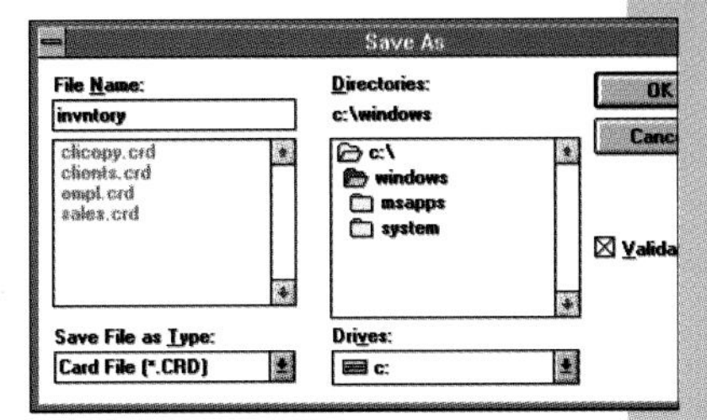

Card
Add... F7
Delete
Duplicate
Autodial... F5

Pull down the Card menu and choose the Duplicate command to make a copy of this card. Then repeat this step four more times. Your file now contains six cards.

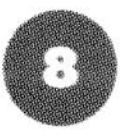

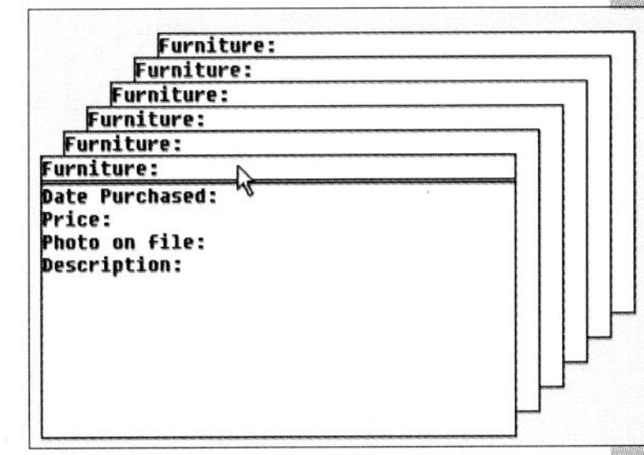


Double-click the index line on the front card to edit the index. The Index dialog box appears on the desktop.

Press the End key to deselect the text and move the insertion point to the end. Then append the words **Dining room table** to the index line, and click OK.

Continue to next page ▶

## TRY IT!

Continue below

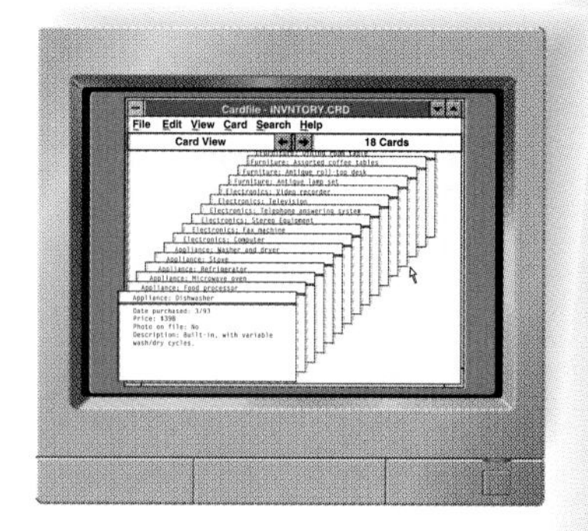

10

Furniture: Dining room table
Date Purchased: 7/92
Price: $1250
Photo on file: Yes
Description: Solid oak with si

Now fill in the description of this inventory item in the card's information area. Use your own information, or type this imaginary data—Date purchased: 7/92; Price: $1250; Photo on file: **Yes**; Description: **Solid oak with six chairs.**

11

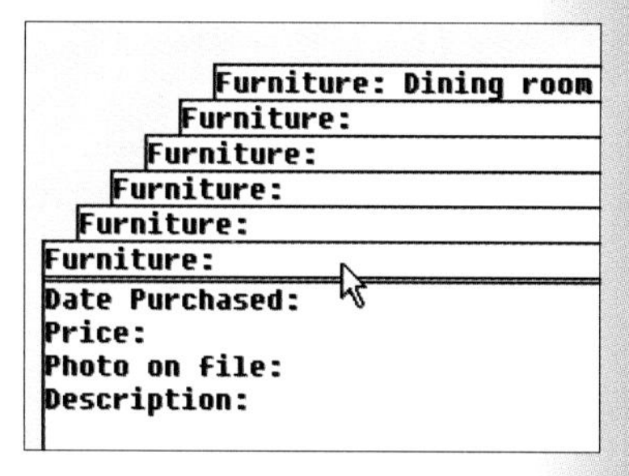


Click the index line of the next furniture card to move it to the front of the file.

Furniture: Assorted coffee tab
Furniture: Antique roll-top desk
Furniture: Antique lamp set
Furniture: Pair of antique love seat
Furniture: French-style armoire
Furniture: Dining room table
Date Purchased: 7/92
Price: $1250
Photo on file: Yes
Description: Solid oak with six chairs

Repeat steps 8 through 11 to fill in the remaining five cards currently in the file. Again, use information about the furniture in your house, or make up details.

Pull down the File menu and click Save to update the file on disk.

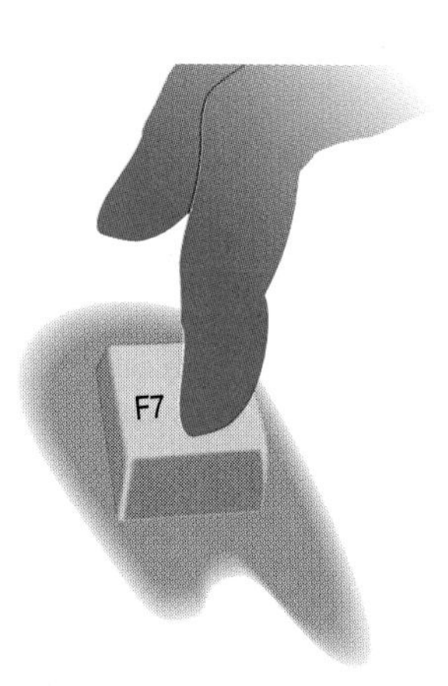


Press F7 to add a new card to the file. The Add dialog box appears on the desktop.

15

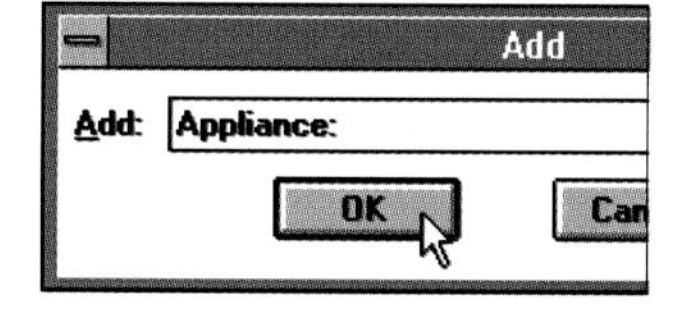


Enter **Appliance:** into the Add text box, and click OK.

16

Appliance:
Date Purchased:
Price:
Photo on file:
Description:

Type **Date Purchased:**, **Price:**, **Photo on file:**, and **Description:** on the first four lines of this new card's information area.

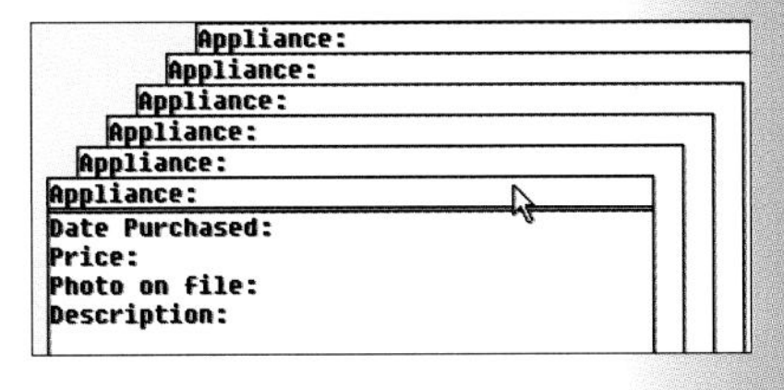


Pull down the Card menu and click the Duplicate command five times. Your file now contains twelve cards.

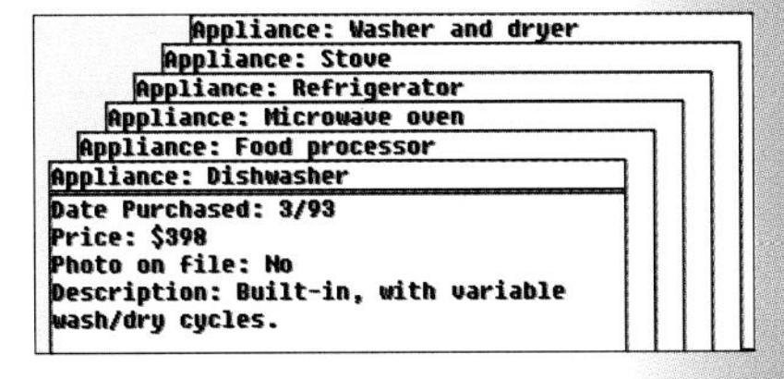


Repeat the procedure described in steps 8 through 11 to fill in the information on each of these six new cards.

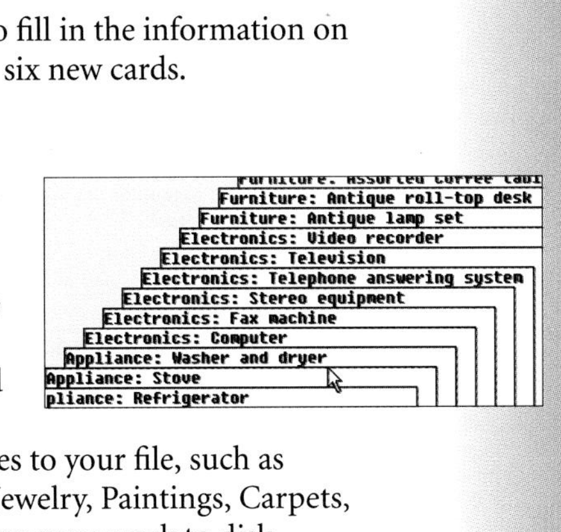


Use the same procedure as before to add more inventory categories to your file, such as Electronics, Jewelry, Paintings, Carpets, and so on. Save your work to disk periodically.

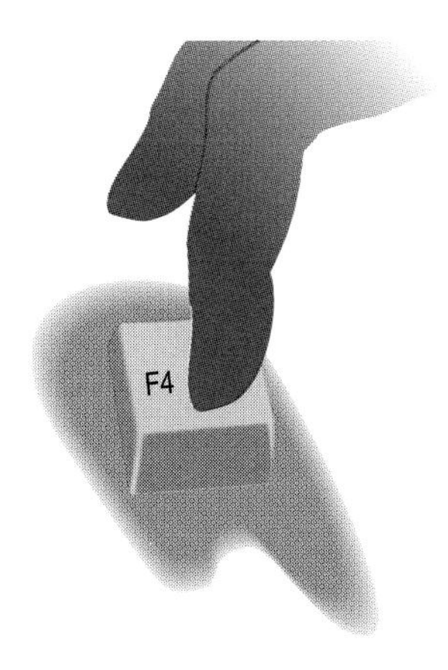


To search for a card by its index line, press F4. The Go To dialog box appears on the desktop.

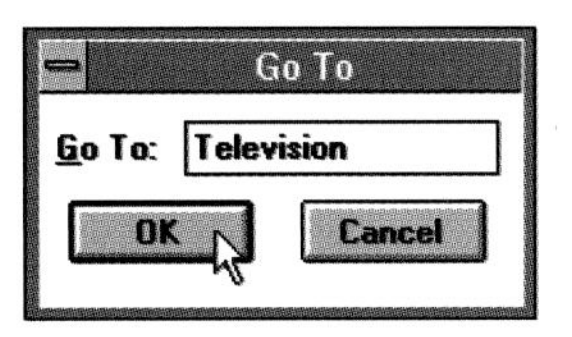


Enter the name of an inventory item in the Go To text box—**Television**, for example—and click the OK button. The matching inventory card comes to the front of the file.

Pull down the Search menu and click the Find command. The Find dialog box appears on the desktop.

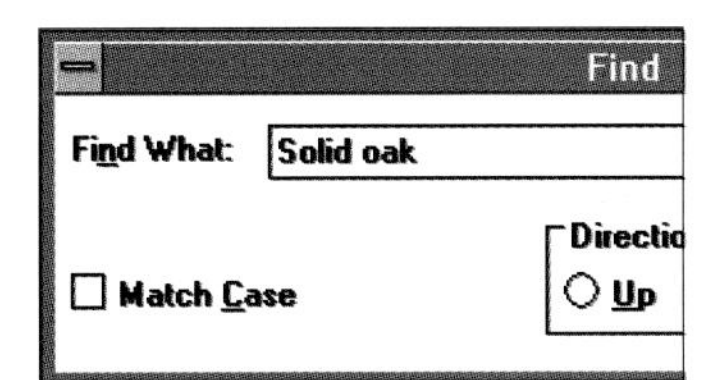


In the Find What box, enter some text you would like to find in the file—for example, a date of purchase or part of a description. Click the Find Next button to bring the matching card to the front of the file. Then click Cancel to close the dialog box.

Pull down the File menu and choose the Print All command to send the inventory file cards to your printer.

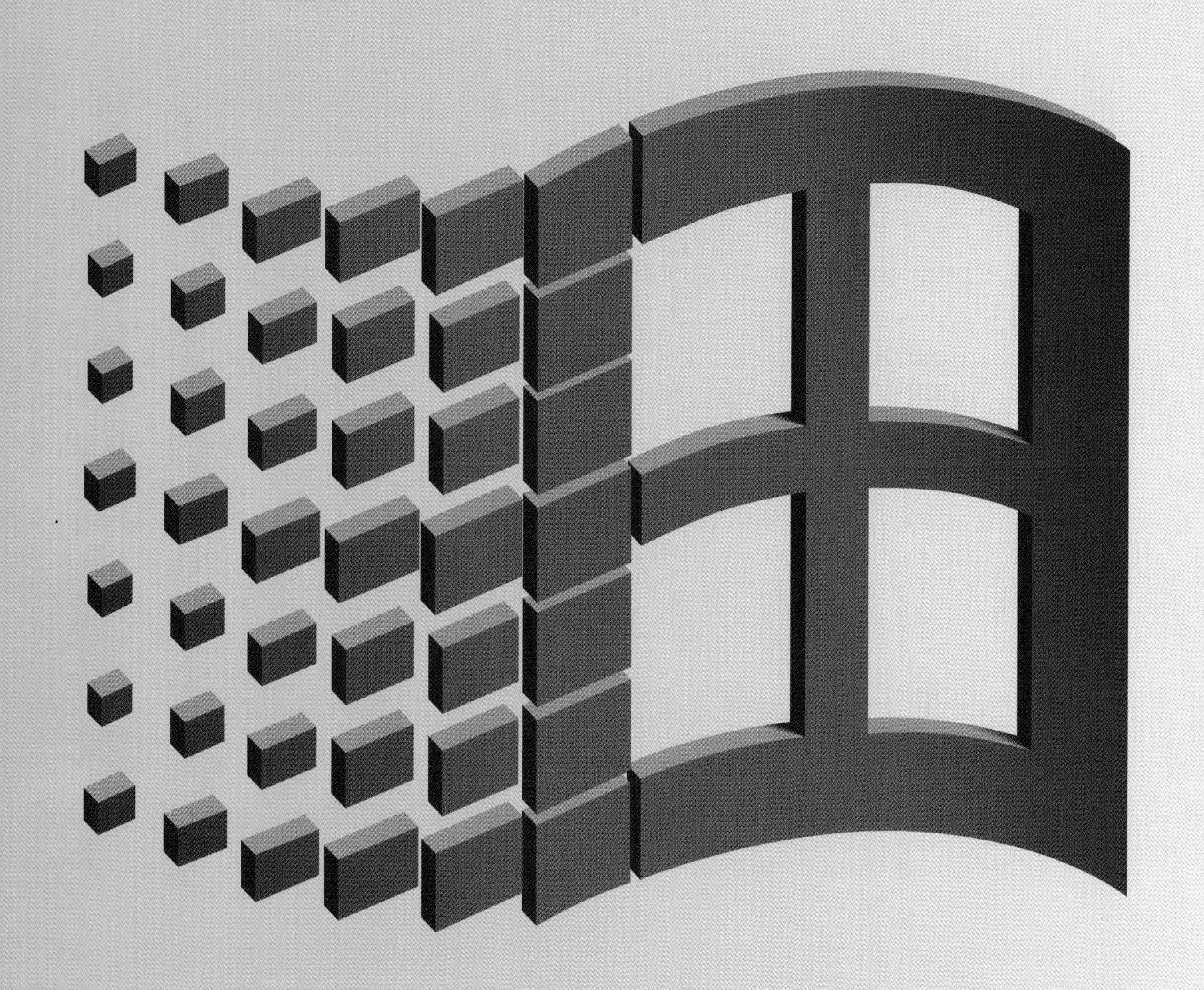

# CHAPTER 11

# Creating Artwork

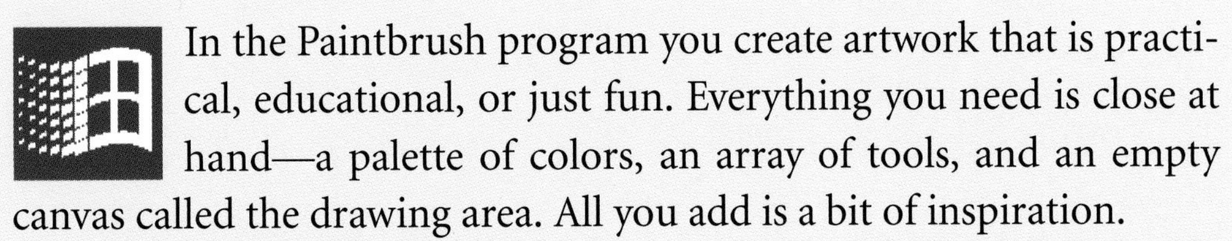

In the Paintbrush program you create artwork that is practical, educational, or just fun. Everything you need is close at hand—a palette of colors, an array of tools, and an empty canvas called the drawing area. All you add is a bit of inspiration.

To begin a Paintbrush picture, you select a tool and start drawing with the mouse. Some of the tools are for freehand sketching, while others are designed to help you create perfectly formed shapes such as lines, curves, boxes, circles, ovals, and multisided figures. With a special feature called a cutout you move shapes around the canvas or duplicate any part of your drawing. You can even add text to your work. If you make a mistake, you use an eraser to remove it—or you can clear the canvas in an instant to start all over again.

What you do with all these tools and colors is up to you. Whether you're drawing a map to your house, decorating a birthday invitation, or designing a corporate logo, Paintbrush provides an engaging medium for your creative efforts.

# How to Get Started in Paintbrush

The Paintbrush icon is in the Accessories group. When you start the application, you'll find an assortment of tools and color choices arranged conveniently around the perimeter of a large drawing area. You use the mouse for two main purposes in this program—first to select appropriate tools and then to draw pictures. When you click a drawing tool—the paint roller or the airbrush, for example—the mouse in effect *becomes* that tool in the drawing area.

The initial task ahead of you is to survey the features you'll use to create artwork in the Paintbrush program.

## TIP SHEET

- **Another way to clear the drawing area and start again is to double-click the eraser tool, located just above the brush. Again, Paintbrush asks if you want to save the current drawing before clearing the work area. Click Yes or No.**
- **Additional commands in the File menu are similar to those in other applications. For example, you choose the Save As command to save a drawing to disk for the first time. In the Save As dialog box, enter a name for the file and click OK. By default, Paintbrush supplies a .BMP extension. Once you've named and saved a file, you can simply choose the Save command from the File menu to update the file with the latest changes to your drawing.**
- **To open an existing .BMP file from disk, pull down the File menu and choose Open. Select a file name from the list and click OK.**

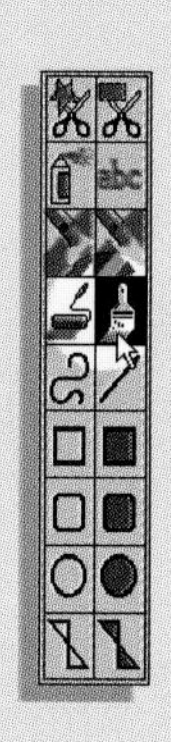

**2** Move the mouse pointer around the window and notice the different shapes the pointer assumes. First move to the *toolbox* at the left side of the window. The mouse pointer becomes an arrow. The toolbox contains the drawing tools you use to create artwork in Paintbrush. When you first start the program, the brush tool is selected.

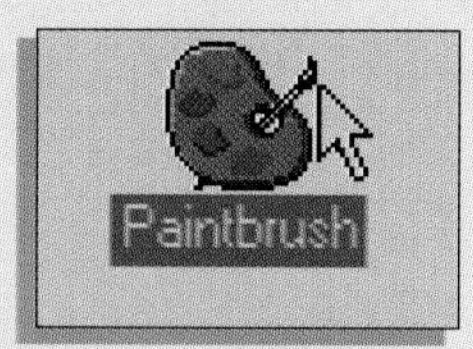


**1** If the Accessories group is not already open in the Program Manager, double-click the group icon. Then double-click the Paintbrush icon to start the program. When the application opens on the desktop, click the window's maximize button to give yourself as much room as possible.

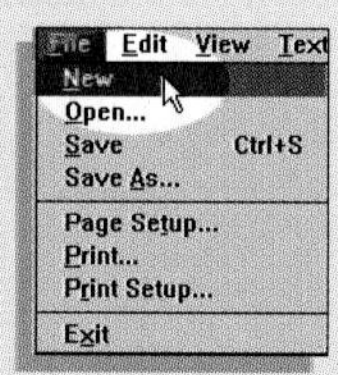


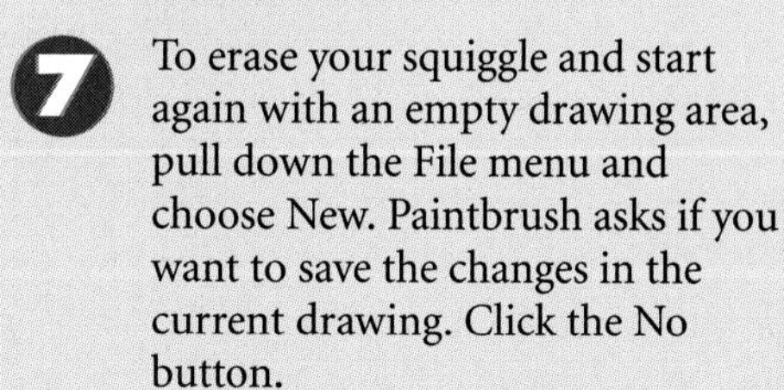

**7** To erase your squiggle and start again with an empty drawing area, pull down the File menu and choose New. Paintbrush asks if you want to save the changes in the current drawing. Click the No button.

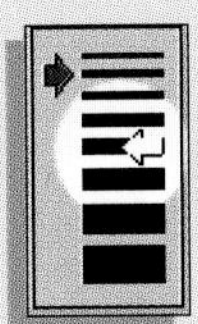

**3** Move down to the *linesize box*, at the lower-left corner of the application window. The mouse pointer turns into a left-pointing arrow. The black rectangles in this box represent drawing widths you can select for a given tool.

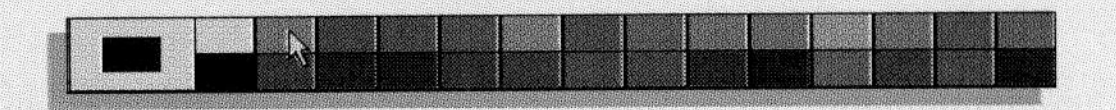

**4** Move over to the *palette*, the collection of colors you can use in your artwork. As you'll learn later, you can select foreground and background colors for your work. Some Paintbrush tools create enclosed areas that are filled with color; these tools use the foreground selection as the fill color and the background selection as the border color.

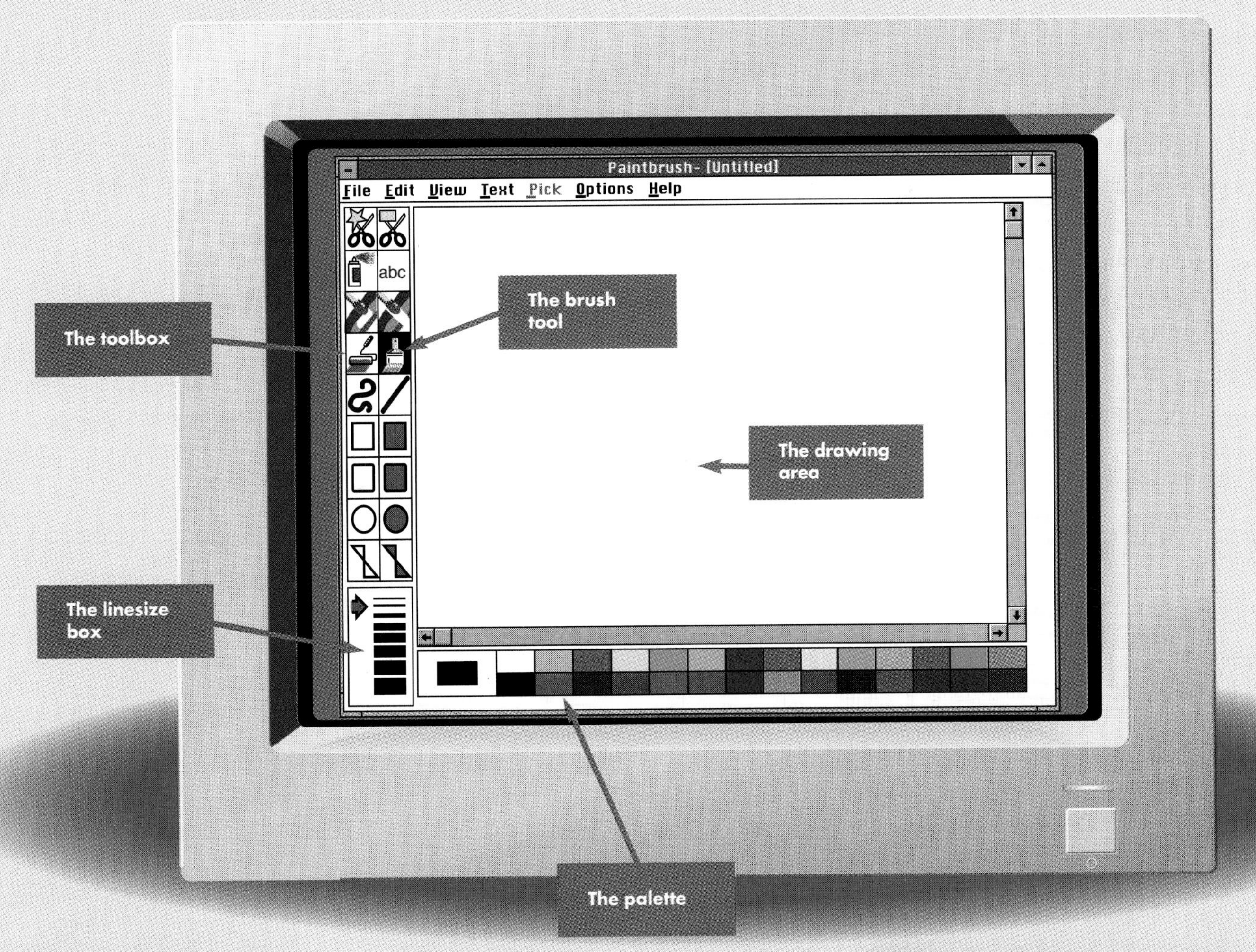


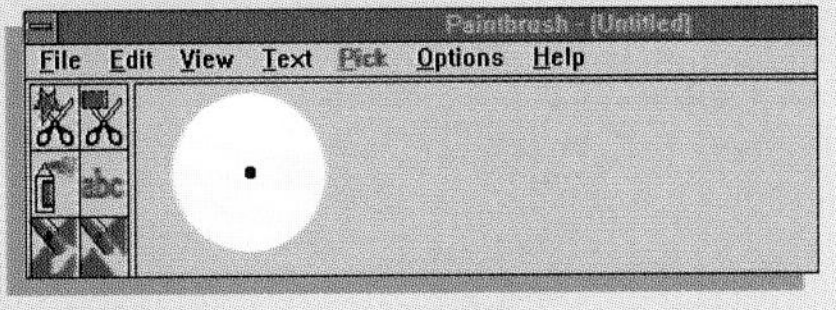


**5** Now move up to the *drawing area*, the large blank section of the Paintbrush window. Here the mouse pointer itself represents the current tool selection. With the brush tool selected, the pointer appears as a small black dot.

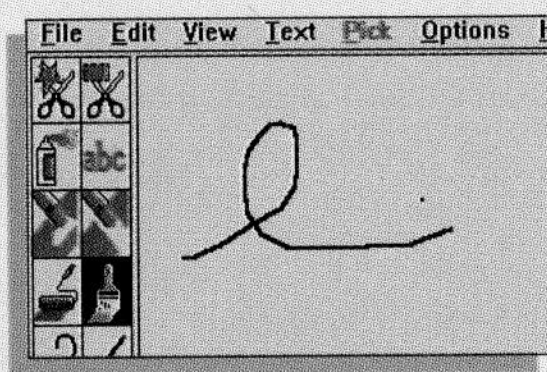


**6** Hold down the left mouse button and move the mouse to draw a first squiggle on the screen. (Release the mouse button when you're done.) As you can see, the brush is a freehand drawing tool that records the path of the mouse's motion. You'll try out other tools later in this chapter.

# How to Change Widths and Colors

To vary the effects of drawing tools in the Paintbrush program, you can change the line width and color settings. For example, suppose you are working with the brush, the tool that's active at the beginning of each program session. By clicking an option in the linesize box, you increase or decrease the thickness of subsequent brushstrokes. Likewise, by selecting a new foreground color in the palette, you change the brushstoke color. As you'll learn in the following steps, foreground and background color selections are made by clicking the left and right mouse buttons; the *selected color box* at the left side of the palette displays your current selections.

## TIP SHEET

- **If you want to create black-and-white drawings you can change the palette to a selection of grays and gray patterns. Pull down the Options menu and click the Image Attributes command. In the resulting dialog box, click the Black and White option button, and then click OK.**
- **In addition to width and color selections, you can change the shape used by the brush tool. To view the Brush Shapes dialog box, pull down the Options menu and click the Brush Shapes command, or simply double-click the brush tool in the toolbox. Six brush shapes are available; click the shape you want, then click OK.**
- **To quit the Paintbrush program, pull down the File menu and click the Exit command. (If there is an unsaved drawing on the screen, the program asks whether you want to save it.)**

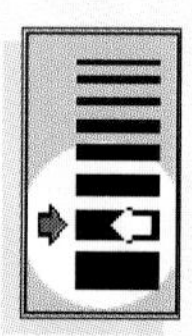

**1** Move the mouse pointer to the linesize box, and click any of the width settings. An arrow at the left side of the box marks the current selection.

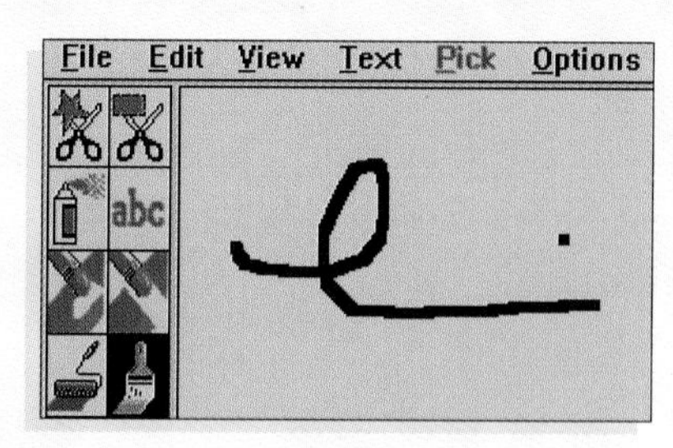


**2** To experiment with the new width, move the mouse pointer into the drawing area, hold down the left mouse button, and draw a squiggle of any shape. The brushstroke appears in the width you've selected.

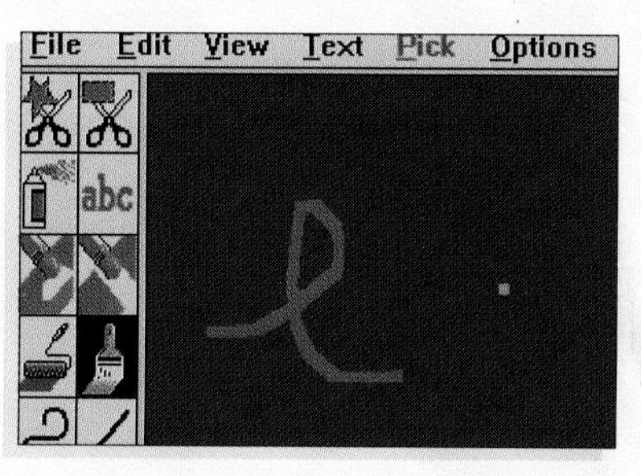


**6** Now try using the new colors. Begin by pulling down the File menu and clicking the New command. Click No to clear the drawing area. In response, Paintbrush fills the entire area with the background color you've chosen. Move the pointer into the drawing area and draw a squiggle. The brushstroke appears in the selected foreground color.

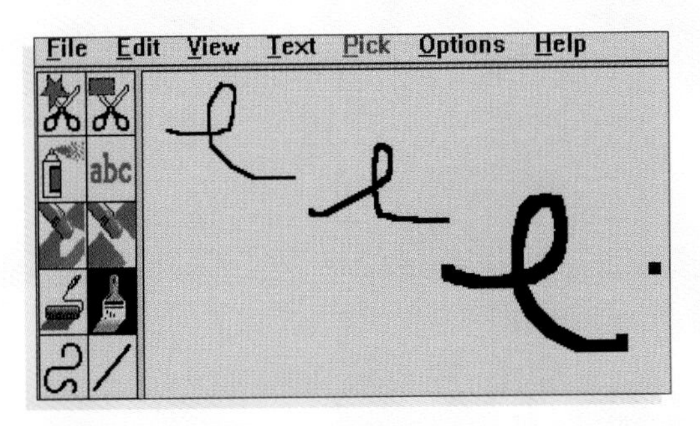


**3** Repeat steps 1 and 2 several times to try other widths. When you're finished experimenting, pull down the File menu and click the New command. In the resulting dialog box, click the No button to clear the drawing area.

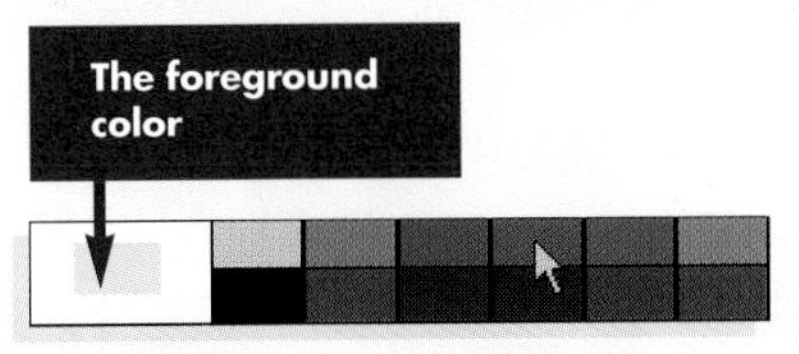


**4** Move the mouse pointer into the palette. To select the foreground color, position the pointer over a color of your choice and click the *left* mouse button. The new foreground color appears in the center rectangle of the selected colors box.

**5** To select the background color, move the pointer to a different color and click the *right* mouse button. The new background color appears in the perimeter of the selected colors box.

# How to Use the Drawing Tools

As you may have noticed by now, the brush is actually one of the most demanding of the Paintbrush drawing tools; it requires you to move the mouse pointer precisely and deliberately. Other tools require far less deftness and artistry for successful results. To use another tool, you position the mouse pointer over the tool's icon in the toolbox and click the left mouse button. Before you begin working with the tool, you can select a new drawing width and foreground color if you wish. (For the filled box and filled circle tools, you'll also want to select a background color to be used as the shape's border.) Move the mouse pointer into the drawing area and begin creating an image with the tool you've selected. Inside the drawing area, the mouse pointer appears in a variety of shapes representing the various tools.

**1** To draw a line, select the line tool and move the mouse pointer to a starting point in the drawing area. Hold down the left mouse button and drag the mouse through the length of the line you want to create. Then release the mouse button.

**2** To draw a curve, select the curve tool and use the mouse to draw a line across the area where you want the curve to appear. Then hold down the mouse button and drag the mouse in a direction perpendicular to the line; when the line forms the curve that you want, release the mouse button. Repeat this dragging action to produce a second curve in the line. When you release the mouse button for the third time, the curve is complete.

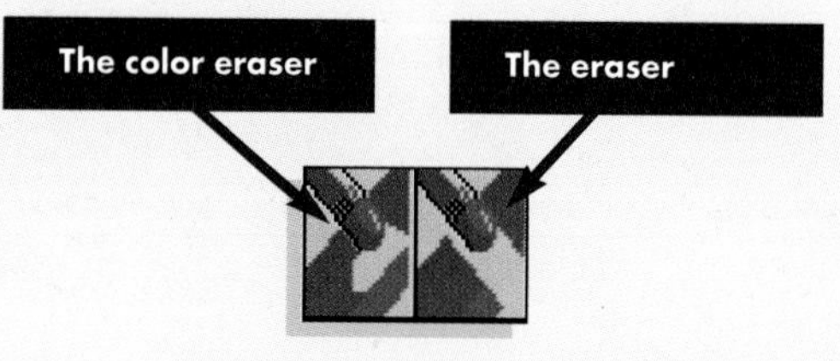


**3** To erase a portion of your drawing, select an eraser tool and drag the mouse over the area you want to erase. The color eraser tool replaces any instances of the selected foreground color with the background color. The eraser tool replaces everything in its path with the background color.

**TIP SHEET**

- **To draw a horizontal, vertical, or 45-degree diagonal line, select the line tool and hold down the Shift key while you drag the mouse.**
- **To select a font, style, and type size for a block of text, pull down the Text menu and click the Fonts command. Make selections in the resulting dialog box and click OK. Then select the text tool and type the text into the drawing area. Notice that the Text menu also contains several shortcut commands for various styles and effects. Text always appears in the selected foreground color. The background color is used for outlining and shadowing, which are two of the options available in the Text menu.**

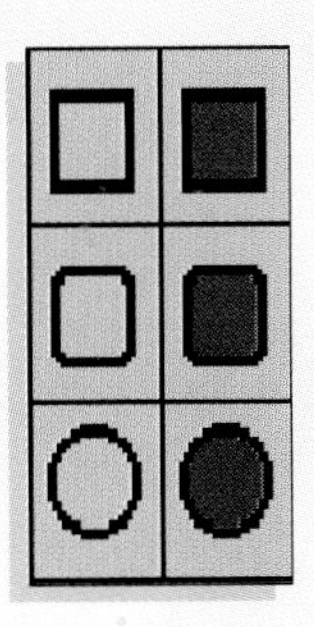

**3** To draw a box, a rounded box, or a circle, select the appropriate tool and move the mouse pointer to a starting point in the drawing area. Hold down the mouse button and drag the mouse to produce an outline of the shape you want; then release the mouse button to complete the process. For a filled shape, the border appears in the selected background color and the fill is the foreground color. The border of an unfilled shape appears in the foreground color.

To draw a polygon, select the filled or unfilled polygon tool and move the mouse pointer to a starting point in the drawing area. Hold down the left mouse button, drag the mouse to draw a line, and release the mouse button to complete this first line. Then click the mouse once at each corner of the polygon you want to create. To complete the shape, double-click the mouse at the final corner. The use of color is the same as it is for boxes and circles.

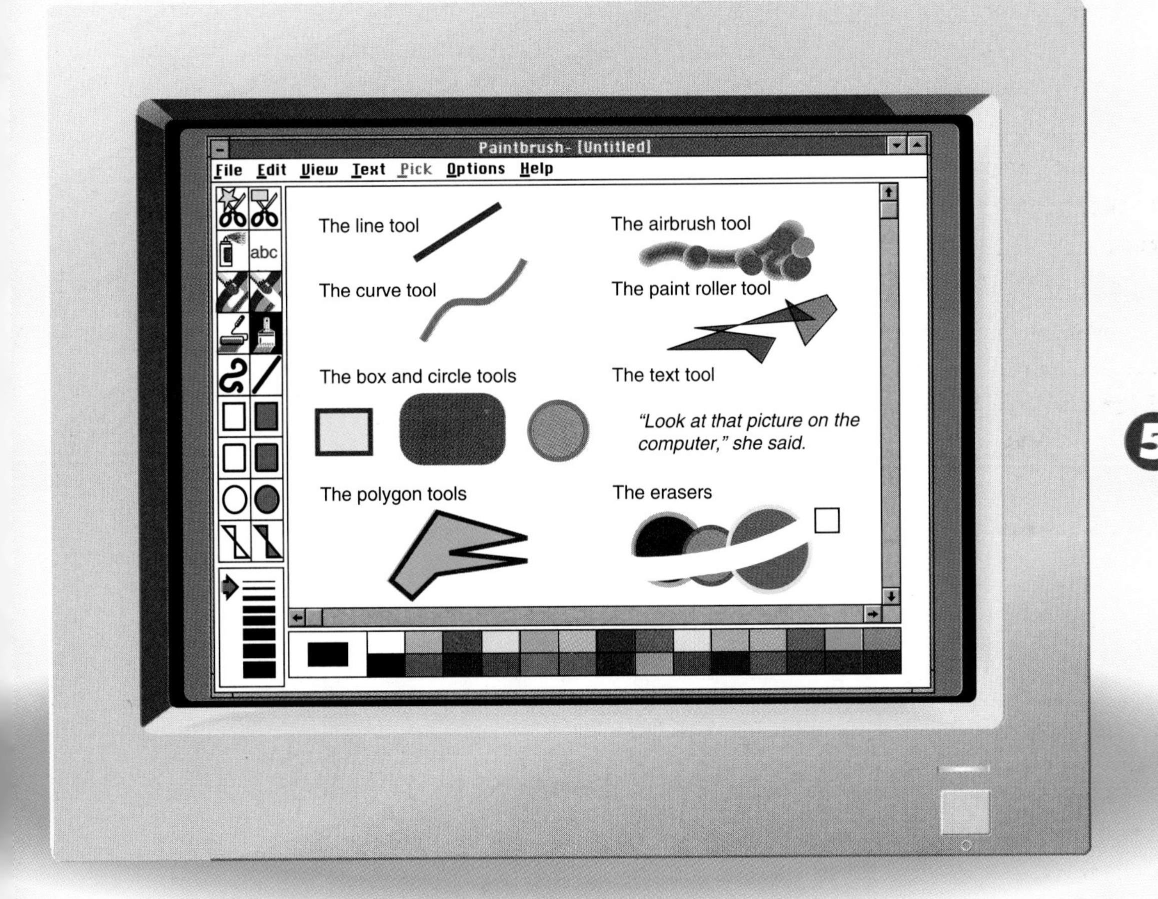

**5** To "spray" the airbrush, select the airbrush tool and move the mouse pointer to a starting point in the drawing area. Hold down the left mouse button and drag the mouse through the area you want to spray. Fast mouse movements produce a light spray, and slow movements produce a dark spray. Release the mouse button when you are finished spraying.

To add text to your drawing, select the text tool. Move the mouse pointer to the place where you want the text to begin, and click the left mouse button. Then begin typing the text on the keyboard. To start a new line, press Enter. Click elsewhere in the drawing area to complete the current text.

To fill an enclosed area with color, select the paint roller tool and move the mouse pointer to a spot inside the area you want to fill. Then click the left mouse button.

# How to Use a Cutout

A *cutout* is a portion of a drawing that you select for special actions. You can move a cutout, copy it, or *sweep* it to reproduce it many times along a path. A cutout is also the means of copying all or part of your drawing to the Clipboard; from there, the cutout can be pasted to another application, such as a Write document.

There are two cutout tools: the scissors and the pick tool. Both are located in the first row of the toolbox. With the scissors tool, you create a freehand cutout by dragging the mouse around the area you want to select. With the pick tool, you create a rectangular cutout by dragging the mouse from one corner to the opposite corner of an area. In either case, the cutout is marked by dotted lines around the perimeter of the selection. Once you have defined a cutout, you use mouse techniques to move, copy, or sweep the drawing it contains.

**TIP SHEET**

- **When you define a cutout, the Pick menu presents an assortment of commands you can use to further manipulate the selection. You can flip the cutout horizontally or vertically, invert its colors, make copies in different sizes, and create copies that are tilted at new angles.**
- **To sweep a cutout, you can hold down either the left or right mouse button while you drag the selection. The left button creates a *transparent* sweep, where each repetition of the image is completely visible (as in the example shown on these pages). The right button creates an *opaque* sweep, where part of one copy may be hidden behind another.**

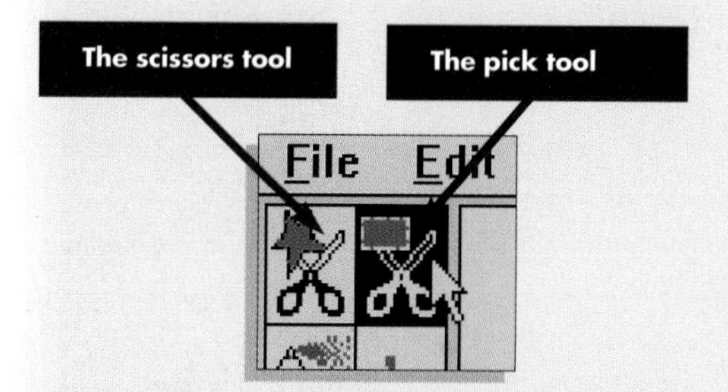


**1** If you haven't yet created a drawing, begin by drawing a shape to work with; then click one of the two cutout tools in the toolbox.

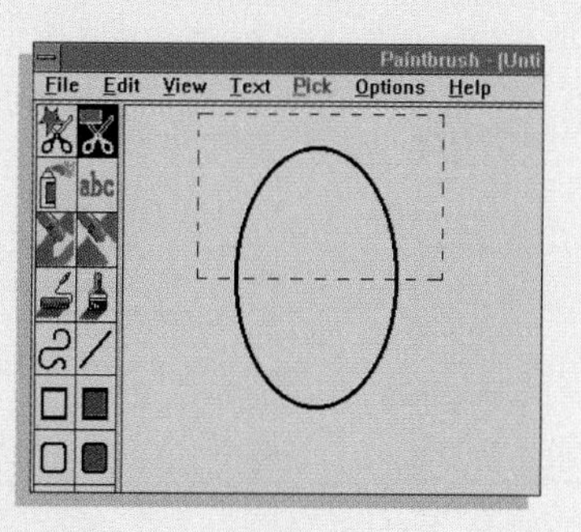


**2** Move the mouse pointer to a starting point in the drawing area. Hold down the mouse button and drag around the area you want to define as a cutout. When you release the mouse button, a border of dotted lines marks the cutout.

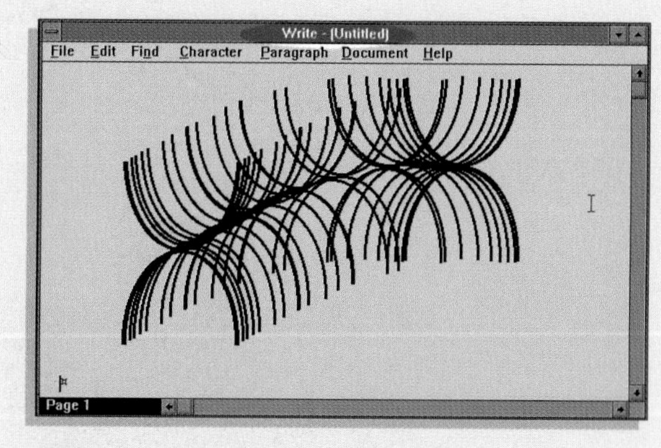


**6** To copy a selection from Paintbrush to another application, define a cutout and press Ctrl+C. Then start the other application and press Ctrl+V to paste the selection from the Clipboard.

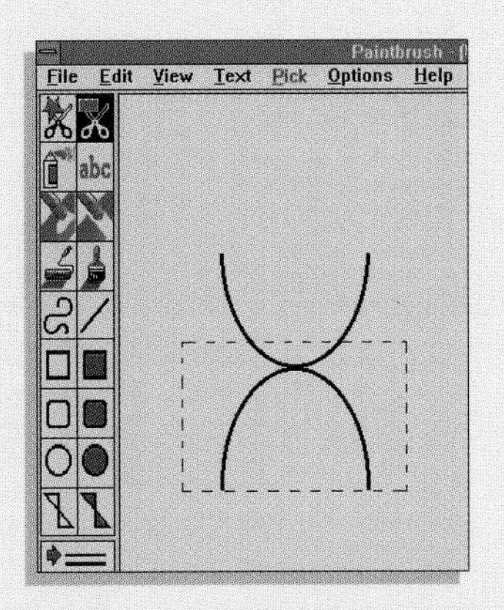


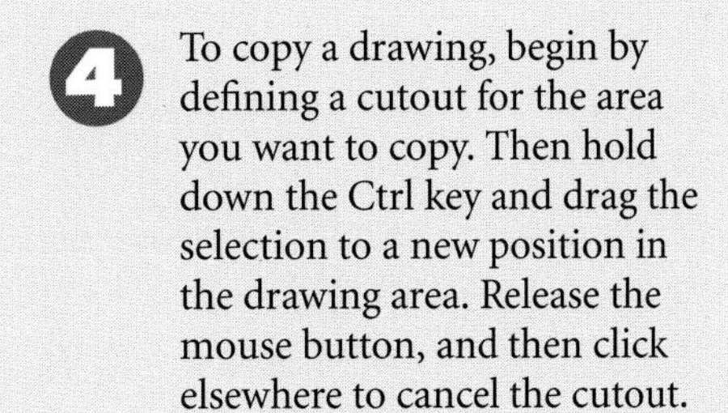

**4** To copy a drawing, begin by defining a cutout for the area you want to copy. Then hold down the Ctrl key and drag the selection to a new position in the drawing area. Release the mouse button, and then click elsewhere to cancel the cutout.

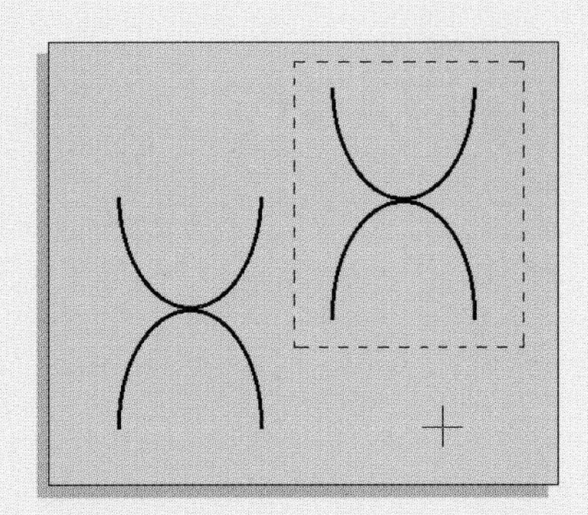

**3** To move the cutout, position the mouse pointer inside the selected area, hold down the mouse button, and drag the cutout to its new position. When you're done with the cutout, move the mouse pointer elsewhere in the drawing area and click the left mouse button to remove the dotted line.

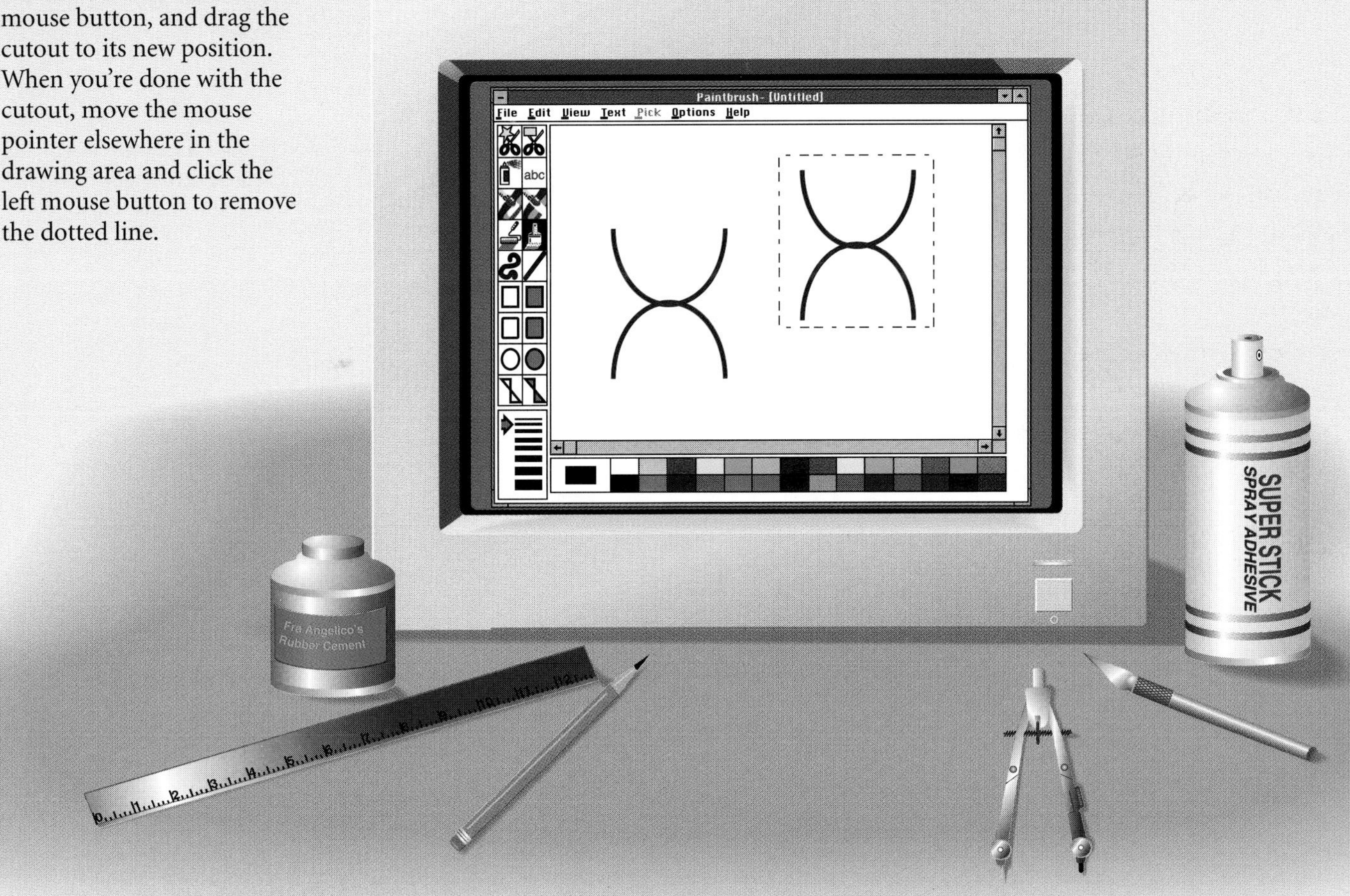


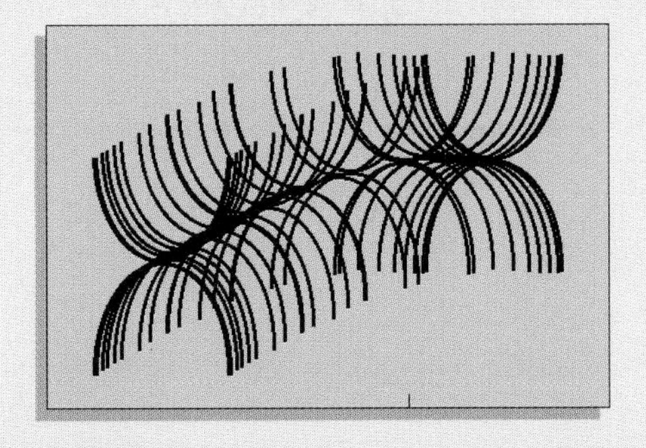

**5** To sweep a drawing, first define a cutout; then hold down the Shift key while you drag the selection through the sweep path. Release the mouse button and click elsewhere in the drawing area to cancel the cutout.

# TRY IT!

Is there a "serious" business use for an amusing program like Paintbrush? Here's an opportunity to find out. The owner of Hats 'n Ties, a specialty retail chain with several downtown locations, has asked you to come up with some ideas for her new logo and letterhead design. She wants a simple, snappy, whimsical logo that will instantly identify her business and fit in a variety of promotional materials. You've decided to use Paintbrush to develop some initial designs.

Open the Accessories group and double-click the Paintbrush icon to start the program. Maximize the application window.

**2**

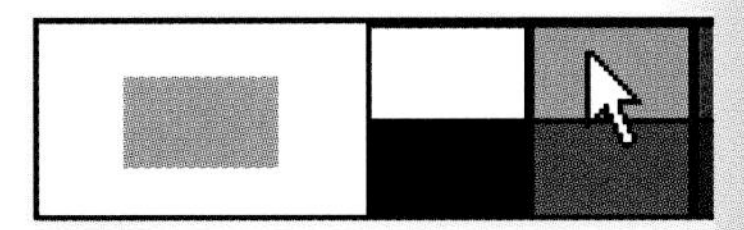

Using the left mouse button, click the light gray color selection in the palette (the second color in the top row). Then click the filled circle tool in the toolbox.

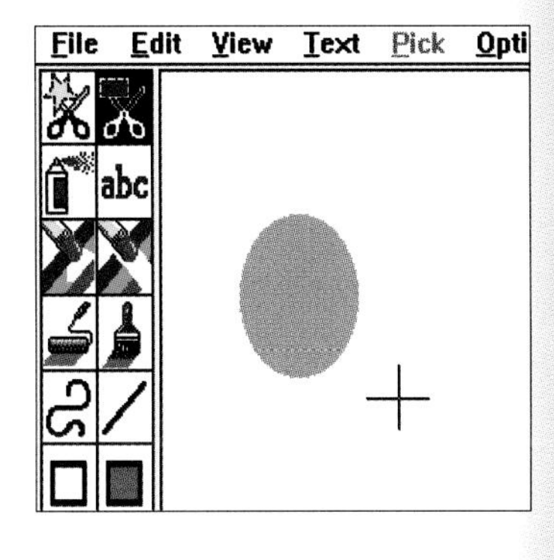


Move the pointer into the drawing area. Hold down the left mouse button and drag the mouse to draw an oval. Release the button. This light gray shape will become the face in the logo.

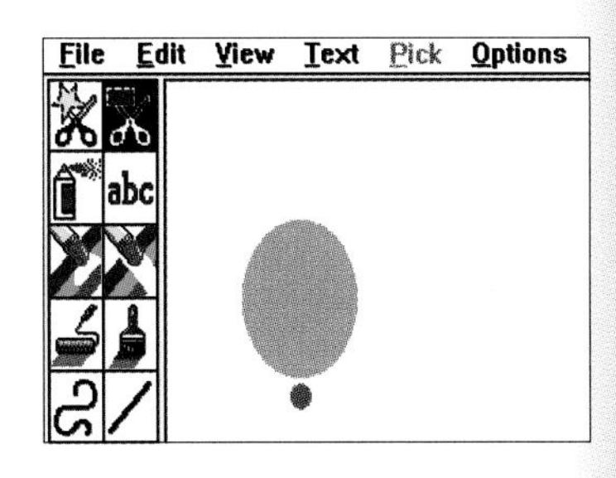


Use the left mouse button to select dark gray as the foreground color, and draw a small filled circle beneath the gray oval. This will be the knot of a tie.

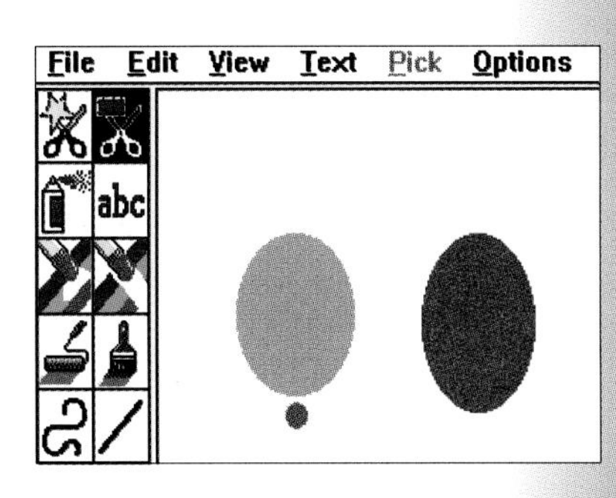


Select red as the foreground color, and then draw another oval next to the first one.

Click the filled box tool in the toolbox.

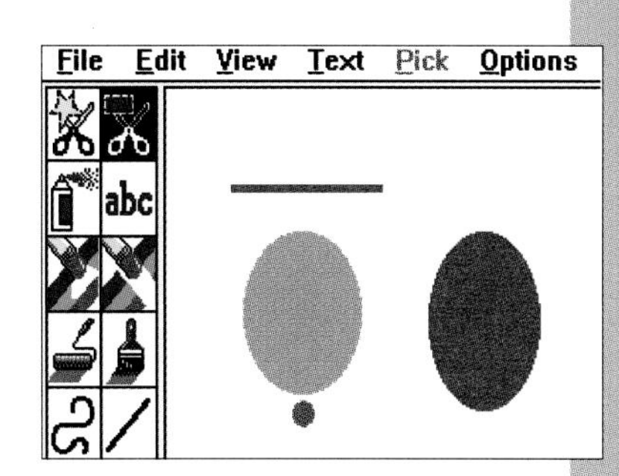


Move the pointer into the drawing area, and draw a thin horizontal rectangle to serve as the rim of the hat.

Click the scissors tool in the toolbox.

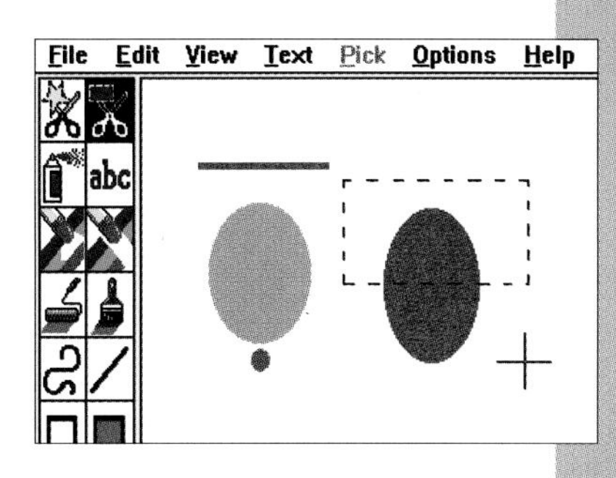


Move the pointer into the drawing area, and define a cutout around the upper half of the red oval.

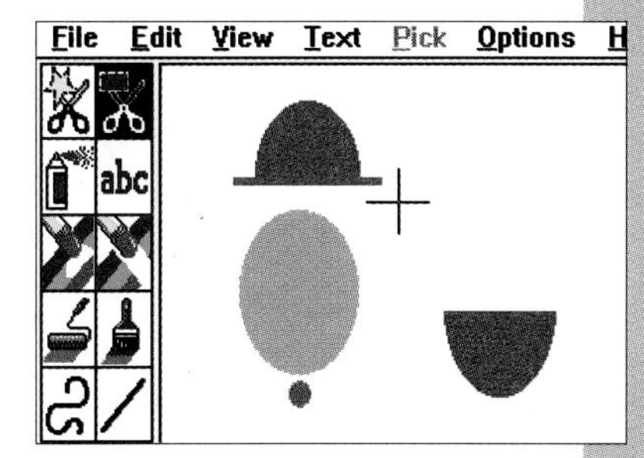


Move the mouse pointer into the cutout, and drag the shape to the top of the red rectangle. Together, the rectangle and the half-circle form a hat.

Continue to next page ▶

# TRY IT!

Continue below

Select the eraser tool and use it to erase the bottom half of the red oval.

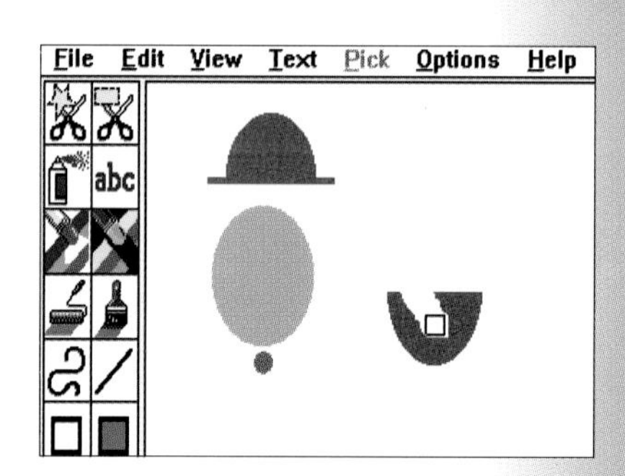

Click the scissor tool again, and define a cutout around the entire hat. Then drag the hat down into position on the head. Click elsewhere in the drawing area to cancel the cutout.

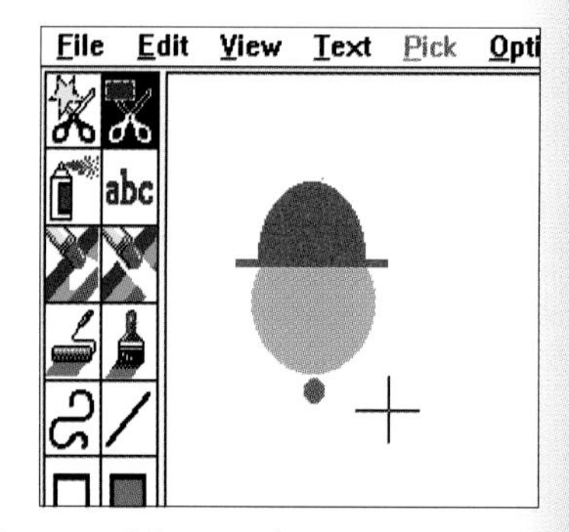

Define a cutout around the entire drawing. Hold down the Ctrl key and drag the cutout to the right to create a copy of the drawing.

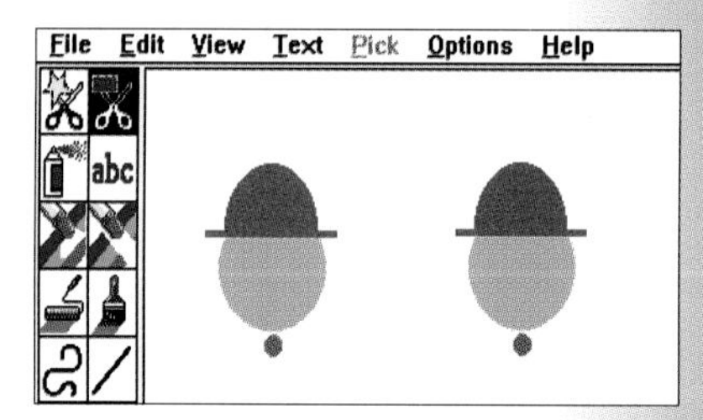

Select dark gray as the foreground color. Then select the filled polygon tool and use it to draw two multisided shapes that will serve as the long tie and the bow tie.

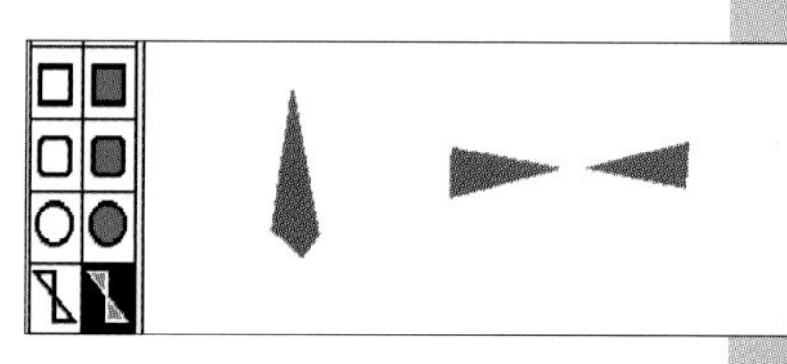

Click the scissors tool and use cutouts to drag both ties into place. Both versions of the logo are now complete.

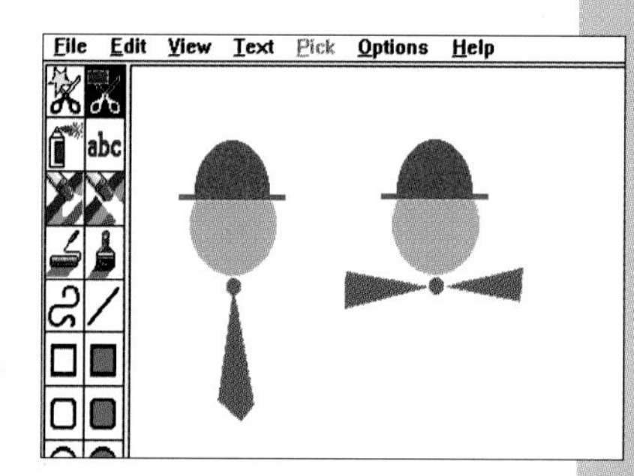

Select black as the foreground color. Then pull down the Text menu and click the Fonts command. The Font dialog box appears on the desktop.

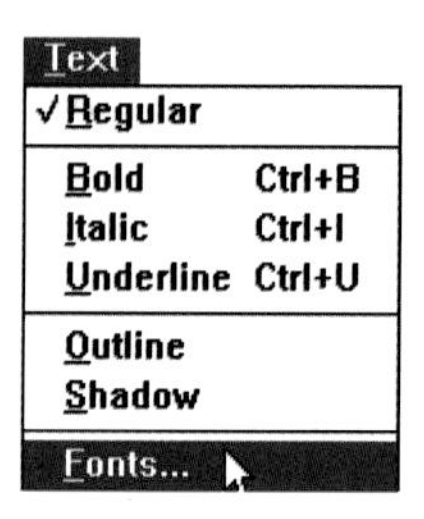

Select Arial on the Font list, Bold on the Font Style list, and 14 on the Size list. Then click OK.

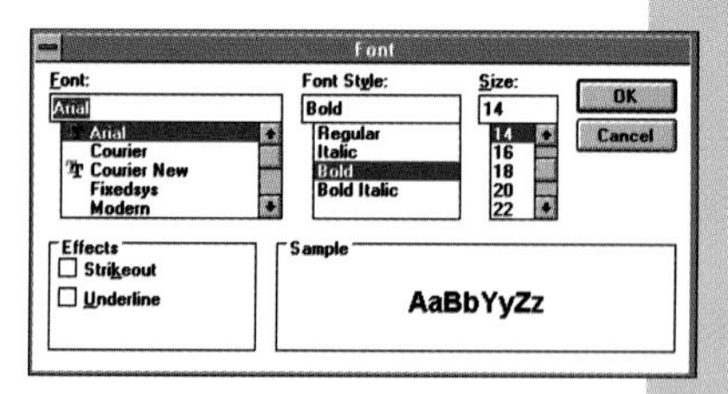

Select the text tool, move the mouse pointer to a blank space in the drawing area, and click the mouse button. Type **Hats 'n Ties.**

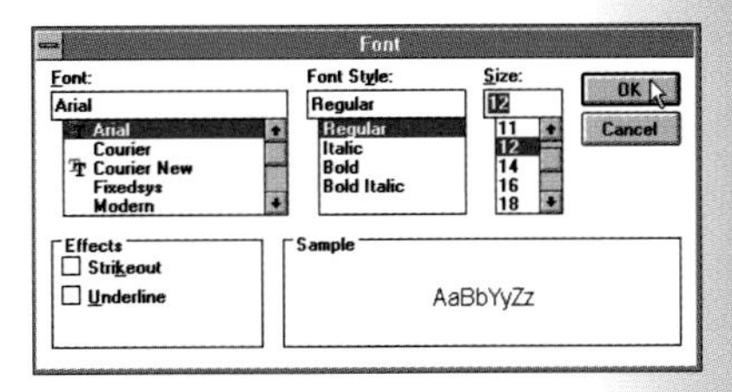


Click the mouse pointer just beneath the H in the first line of text. Then pull down the Type menu and click Fonts. Select Regular in the Font Style list and 12 in the Size list. Then click OK.

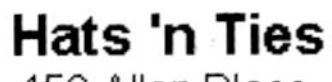


Type the first line of the address. Then press Enter and type the second line. Finally, press Enter twice and type the telephone number.

Use cutouts to create a copy of the address and rearrange the logos and addresses in the drawing area.

Define a cutout around one version of the logo and address, and press Ctrl+C to copy the cutout to the Clipboard.

Start the Write application, and press Ctrl+V to copy the logo and address to the top of the open document. Then print a copy of the document.

Go back to Paintbrush, and repeat steps 22 and 23 to copy, paste, and print the second logo.

# CHAPTER 12

# Keeping Appointments

A missed appointment is a lost opportunity. Staff meetings, business lunches, professional conferences, consultations, seminars, due dates, interviews, rendezvous, or mere tête-à-têtes—whatever your appointments and obligations are, you need effective ways to schedule them and remind yourself when it is time to keep them.

If you spend a lot of time in front of your computer, what better place to keep track of appointments than right on your screen? The Calendar application—like other programs that come with Windows—is simple enough to learn quickly, yet elaborate enough to meet all your requirements. When you first run Calendar, you create your own personal appointment file. You can then use this file to record the dates, times, and descriptions of future engagements, or even to keep brief notes about past events.

Calendar has several features designed to help you keep your appointments. An individual appointment sheet is available for every date from 1980 to 2099. You can record engagements for any hour of the day or night. Navigation from date to date within the calendar is easy. The program provides simple mouse and keyboard techniques for browsing through any sequence of dates or for jumping directly to a specific date. In addition, you can set alarms to remind you of your most important obligations. For help in planning your time, the program gives you two ways to view your calendar—the *day* view and the *month* view. You'll learn to use all these features in this chapter.

# How to Get Started in Calendar

When you start the Calendar application for the first time, you see a blank appointment sheet for today's date. You may want to begin by exploring the dimensions of this sheet and similar sheets for other days. Then you should create your own personal calendar file by customizing the appointment sheet so it meets the demands of your work schedule, and saving the file to disk. Over time, you'll keep all your appointments in this one calendar file.

1. Double-click the Accessories icon if the group window is not already open; then double-click the Calendar icon. The Calendar window opens onto the desktop and displays an hour-by-hour appointment sheet for today's date.

## TIP SHEET

- You can use this application to create any number of calendar files on disk, but you'll probably want to save all your own appointments in a single calendar, which you reopen at the beginning of each Windows session.
- To make sure your personal calendar file is available whenever you start Windows, add its icon to the Startup group. Open the Startup group window and choose New from the Program Manager's File menu. Program Item is selected in the New Program Object dialog box. Click OK to confirm, and enter the name of your personal .CAL file (for example, JSMITH.CAL) in the Command Line text box of the Program Item Properties dialog box; then click OK. (See Chapter 4 for further details.)
- To close the Calendar application, pull down its File menu and click the Exit command. If there are any unsaved changes in your calendar, the program asks whether you want to update the file.

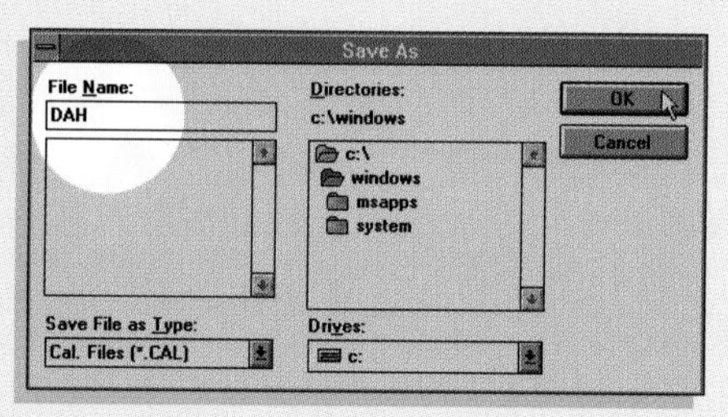


6. Pull down the File menu and click the Save As command. In the Save As dialog box, enter a name for your personal calendar file, and click OK.

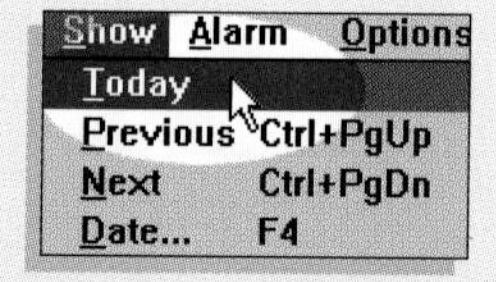


5. To return to today's appointment sheet, pull down the Show menu and click the Today command. Notice the other commands available in the Show menu: The Previous and Next commands move you forward and backward by one day; the Date command allows you to go directly to a date that you specify.

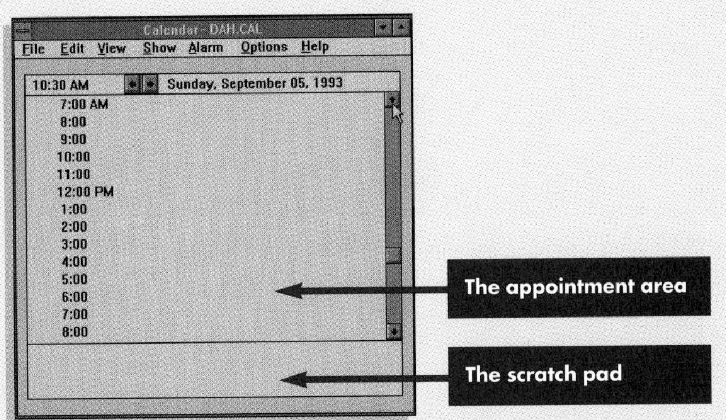


**2** Click the arrows at the top and bottom of the vertical scroll bar on the right side of the window to examine the entire length of the appointment area. You'll see that the calendar contains lines for hourly appointments from 12:00 a.m. to 11:00 p.m. Initially all the lines are blank. The space immediately below the appointment area is called the *scratch pad*; it is available for short notes that apply to the entire day.

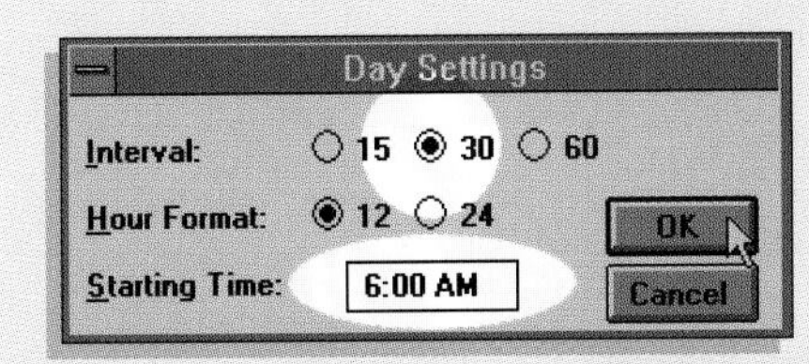


**3** Pull down the Options menu and click the Day Settings command. The resulting dialog box allows you to change three characteristics of the appointment sheet: the time interval between one appointment line and the next; the time representation (12-hour or 24-hour); and the time that initially appears at the top of the appointment area. Make changes in any these options if you wish, and then click OK.

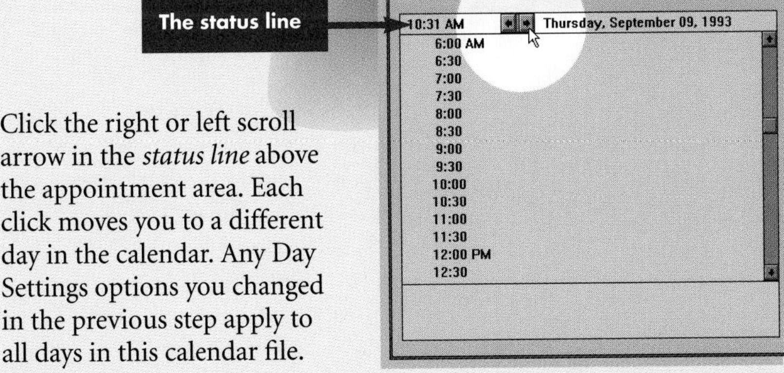


**4** Click the right or left scroll arrow in the *status line* above the appointment area. Each click moves you to a different day in the calendar. Any Day Settings options you changed in the previous step apply to all days in this calendar file.

# How to Record Appointments

Once you've created your personal calendar file, you can enter appointments for any future dates and times. (You may also want to use your calendar to record notes about events that took place in the past.) You can even create new time entries that don't appear in the intervals you've defined for your appointment sheet—for example, an entry for a 10:15 appointment on a sheet that normally displays only half-hour intervals. For an appointment that you absolutely must not miss, you can set an alarm; the Calendar program then alerts you at the appropriate moment by beeping and displaying a reminder on the desktop.

**TIP SHEET**

- **A day's appointment sheet can contain any number of alarms. You can set a particular alarm to go off 1 to 10 minutes *before* the appointment time. Select the appointment line for which the alarm is set; then pull down the Alarm menu and click the Controls command. In the resulting dialog box, enter a value from 1 to 10. (In this same dialog box, you can also disable the sound; click the Sound option to remove the X from the corresponding check box. When the alarm goes off, the reminder box will appear, but you won't hear any beeps.)**
- **To print a day's appointments, select the day, pull down the File menu, click Print, and then click OK in the Print dialog box. (If you want to print appointments for a range of days, enter a date in the To text box within the Print dialog box.)**
- **To save changes in your calendar file, pull down the File menu and click the Save command.**

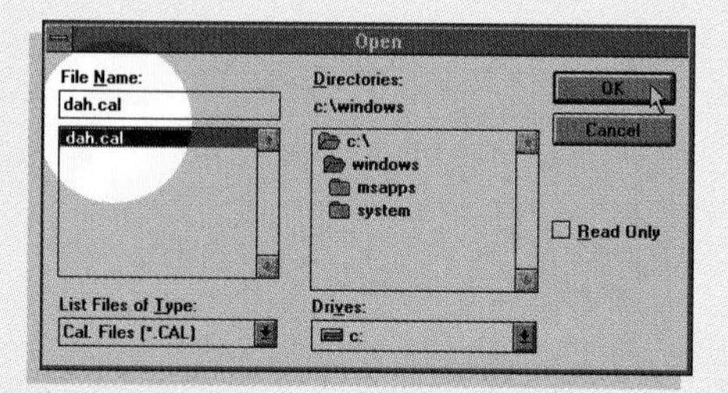


1. If the Calendar window is not yet open, double-click the Calendar icon in the Accessories group. Then pull down the application's File menu and click the Open command. Select the name of your personal calendar in the File Name list, and click OK to open the file.

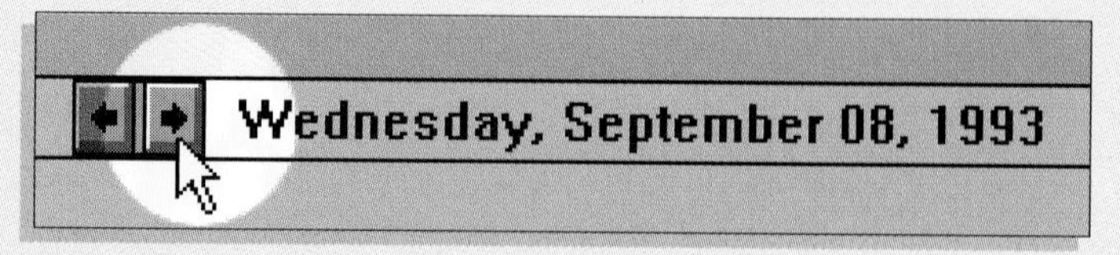


2. To record an appointment for a day in the future, click the right scroll arrow on the status line until the correct day is displayed.

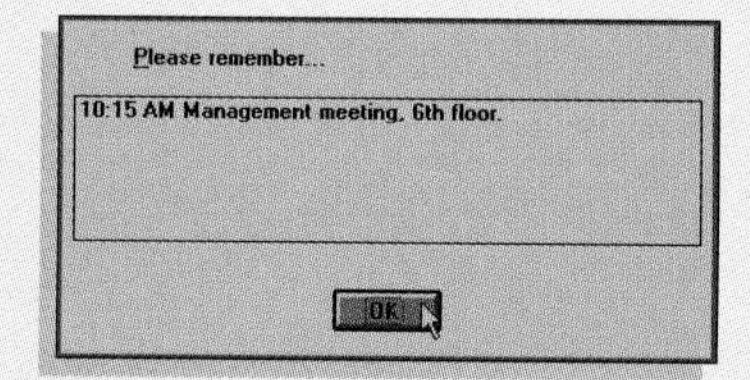


7. When an alarm goes off, you'll hear four beeps. If the Calendar window is open and active, a reminder box appears on the desktop, displaying the appointment entry for the current time. If Calendar is minimized, the program's icon flashes on and off; click the icon to view the reminder box.

**3** If necessary, scroll to the time of the appointment. To move the insertion point, click the time entry. Then type your appointment. An appointment line can hold up to 80 characters.

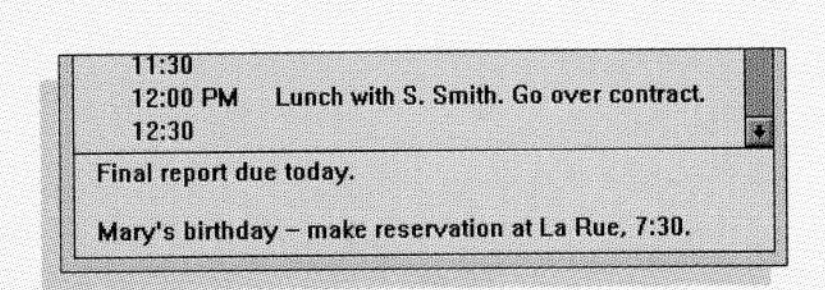


**4** To move the insertion point into the scratch pad for the current day, move the mouse pointer to the pad and click the mouse button or press Tab. You can type up to three lines of text in this area.

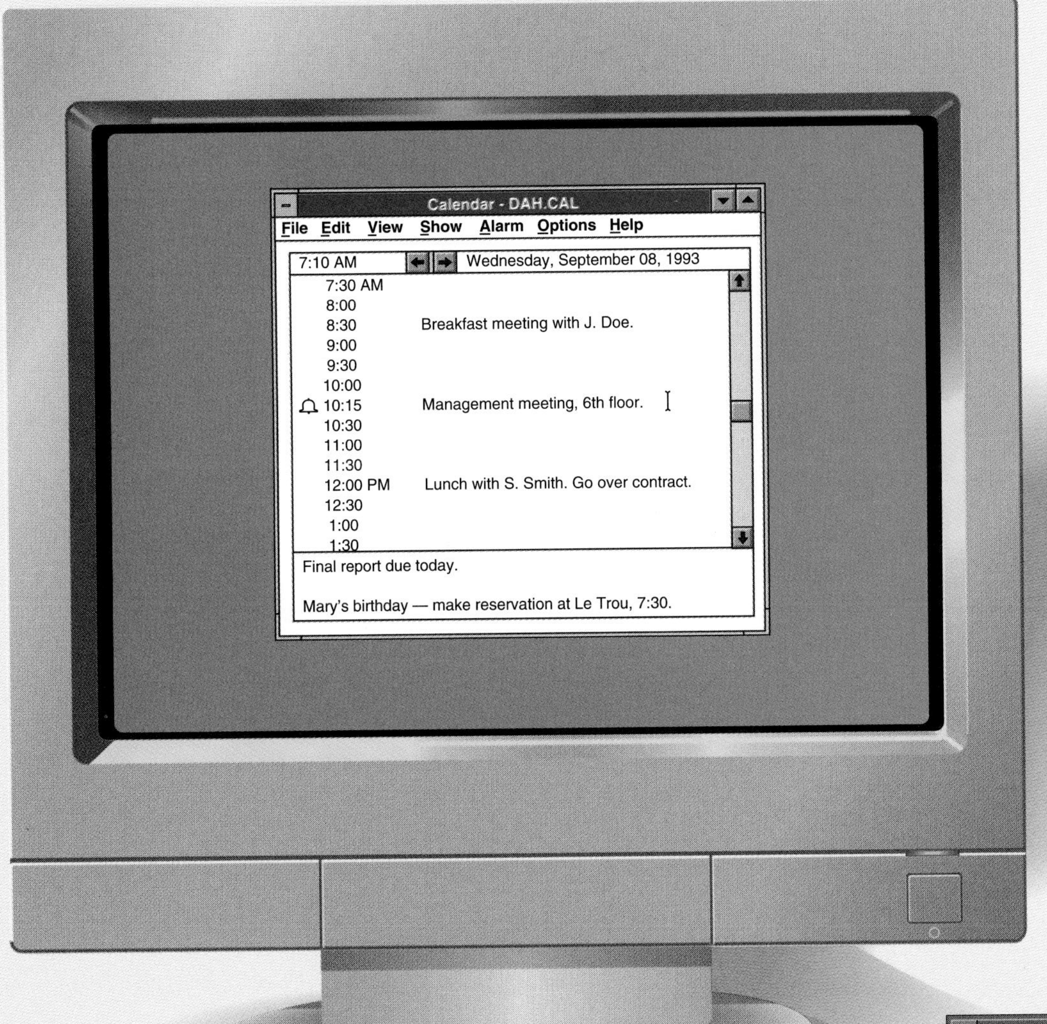

**6** To set an alarm, click the time when you want the alarm to sound. Then pull down the Alarm menu and click the Set command or press F5. A bell icon appears to the left of the time entry.

**5** To create a new appointment line for a special time (that is, for a time that is not in the regular intervals of your appointment sheet), pull down the Options menu and click the Special Time command or press F7. In the Special Time dialog box, enter the time and click the Insert button. Back on the appointment sheet, type a line of text for this new time entry.

# How to Use the Month View

The Calendar application gives you two ways to look at dates, the day view and the month view. As you've seen, the day view shows all your appointments for a given date. By contrast, the month view displays a rectangular grid of dates for an entire month at a time, just as a wall calendar does. In the month view you can scroll through the calendar month by month, which is an efficient way to locate a particular date. When you arrive at the date you want, you can quickly switch back to the day view to see that day's appointment sheet. In addition, you can mark important days with special symbols in month view. Like the notes you enter into the scratch pad, these symbols serve as reminders for dates, events, or activities.

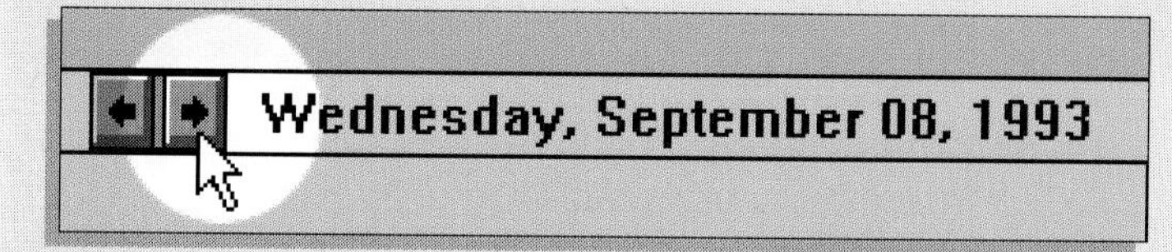


**2** To move forward or backward one month at a time, click the right or left scroll arrow or press the PgDn or PgUp key.

**1** To switch the Calendar program to the month view, pull down the View menu and click the Month command. (Alternatively, press F9 or double-click the date in the status line.) In month view, today's date is marked by angle brackets—for example, > 5 <.

**TIP SHEET**

- **You can display more than one mark in the box for a given day. The marks appear only in month view, not in day view.**
- **Use the available mark symbols consistently. For example, you might use one symbol for important business dates, one for personal or social events, and one for family activities. As you can see in the Day Markings dialog box, five symbols are available.**
- **Although you cannot set an alarm in month view, an existing alarm will alert you to an appointment regardless of the current view.**
- **The Print command in Calendar's File menu prints appointments from the day view, along with any notes you've entered into the scratch pad. You cannot print the month view.**

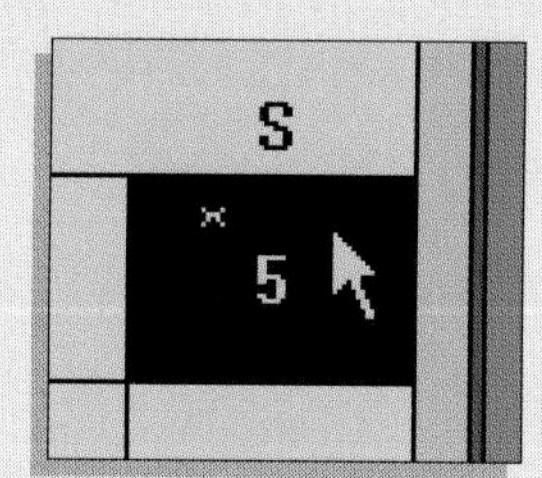


**6** To switch back to the day view for a particular date, double-click the day in month view. (Alternatively, select the day and choose the Day command from the View menu or press F8.)

**3** To display a special marker for a particular day in month view, click the day and then choose the Mark command from the Options menu.

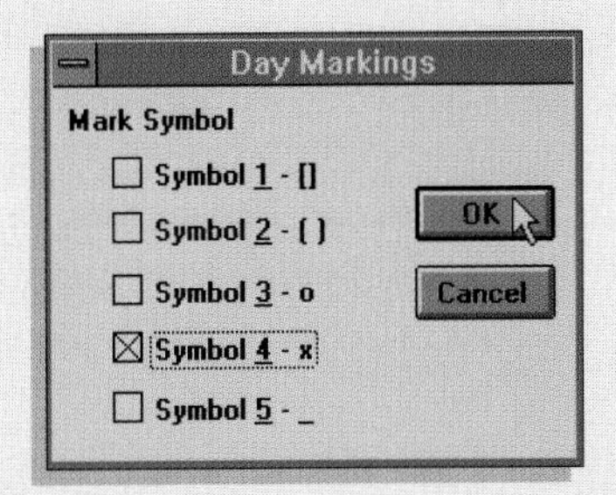


**4** In the Day Markings dialog box, select a symbol for the day and click OK.

**5** Optionally, enter a note in the scratch pad for any day of the month, especially as an explanation for a marked day. If a note already exists, it appears in the scratch pad just as it does in day view.

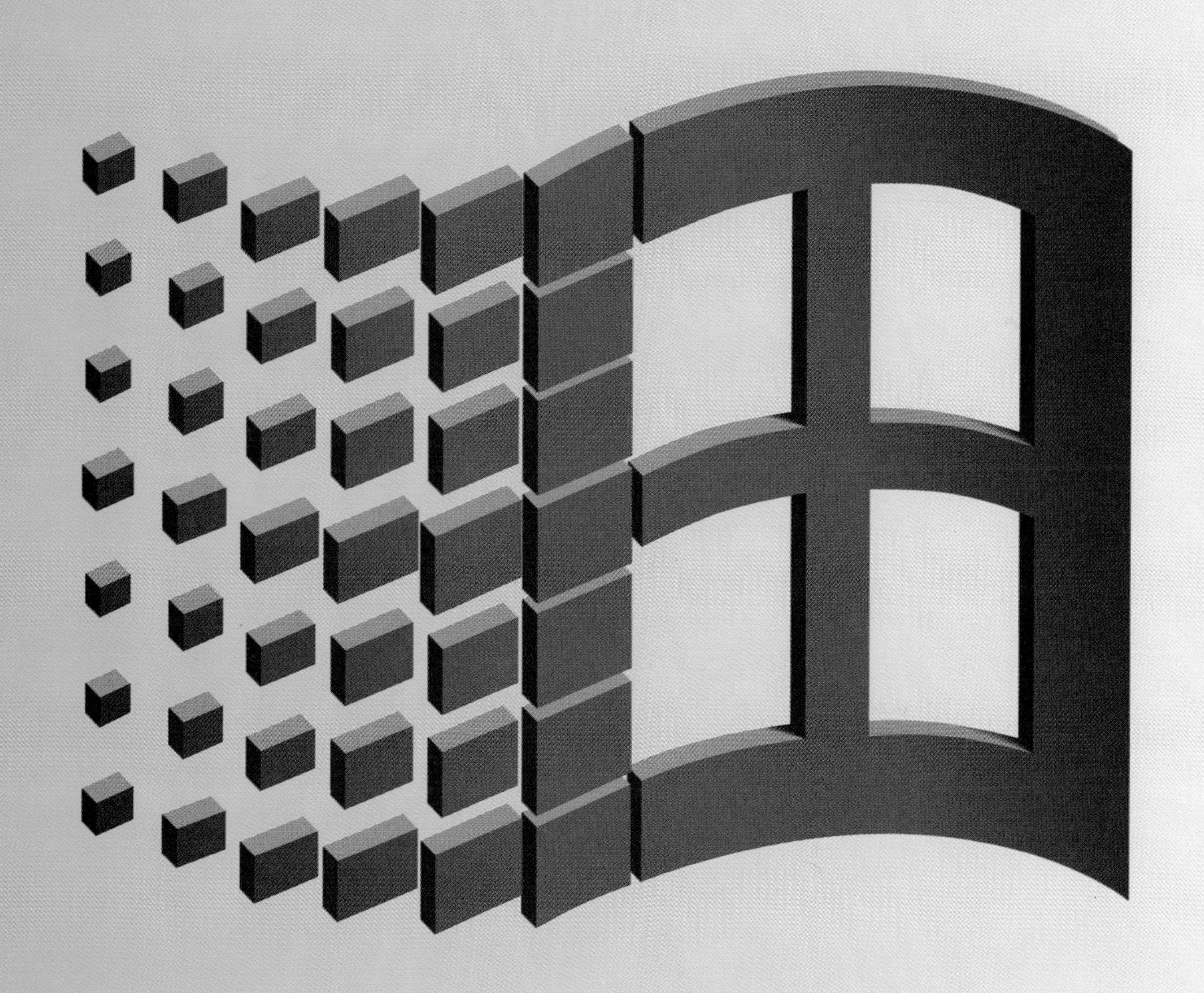

# CHAPTER 13

# More Applications

In previous chapters you learned to work with four of the most popular applications packaged with Windows: Write, Cardfile, Paintbrush, and Calendar. This chapter is a brief survey of several other programs you're likely to find useful.

Calculator gives you the equivalent of a multifunction hand-held calculator. You can use this program for quick calculations, and you can copy the results to other applications via the Clipboard.

Clock displays a digital or analog clock on the desktop. If you want to be able to read the time while you are running other programs, you can arrange the Clock window in a variety of convenient ways.

Notepad is a text editor, useful for creating and editing system files such as AUTOEXEC.BAT.

# How to Use Calculator

With the Calculator program open on your desktop, you can perform quick arithmetic operations or find the results of complex mathematical functions simply by clicking buttons with the mouse. For convenience, the application window appears in two versions; the one you choose depends on the complexity of the calculations you need to perform. A standard ten-key calculator provides the familiar arithmetic operations: addition, subtraction, multiplication, and division. A more elaborate scientific calculator has several columns of advanced mathematical functions.

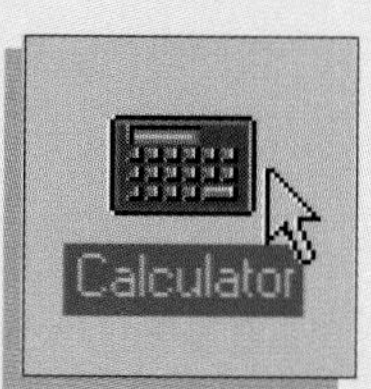


**1** To start the Calculator, double-click the program's icon in the Accessories group. The Calculator window appears on the desktop.

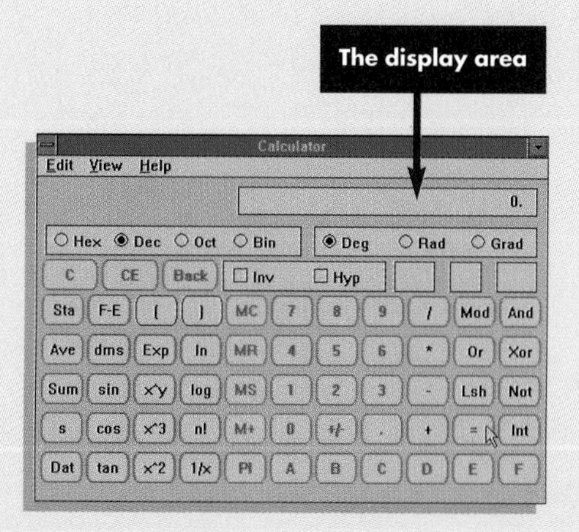


**6** To view the scientific calculator, pull down the View menu and click Scientific. Now the number buttons are in the middle columns of the window, and the various function keys are arranged on either side.

## TIP SHEET

- **The scientific calculator has an additional memory device called the Statistics Box, in which you can temporarily store a sequence of numeric values. To open this box, click Sta (just below the C button). Arrange your desktop so you can see the Calculator window and Statistics Box at the same time. To copy a number into the box, enter the value into the Calculator's display area, and then click the Dat button; repeat this process for additional values. To perform statistical operations on the values currently in the box, click Sum for the total of all the numbers, Ave for the average, or s for the standard deviation.**
- **The scientific calculator also gives you a quick way to find the hexidecimal, octal, or binary equivalent of a decimal number. Enter the value into the display area, and then click one of the number-base option buttons—Hex, Oct, or Bin.**
- **To close the Calculator program, double-click the window's control-menu box.**

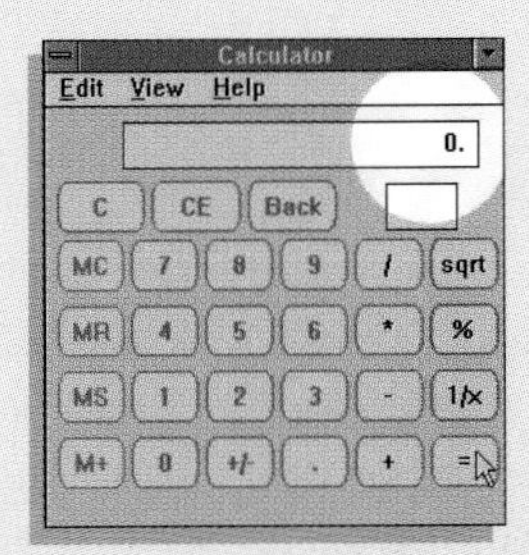


**2** Try performing an operation, just as you would on a hand-held calculator: Click a sequence of digits with the mouse, or type them from the keyboard. (To use the numeric keypad, activate the Num Lock key.) Select an operator (+, -, *, or /), and then enter a second number. Click the = button to calculate the result.

**3** Try another calculation, and experiment with the clear buttons. Click the Back button (or press Backspace) to erase the last digit you typed. Click the CE key (or press Delete) to clear the most recent number you've entered. Click the C key (or press Escape) to clear an entire calculation.

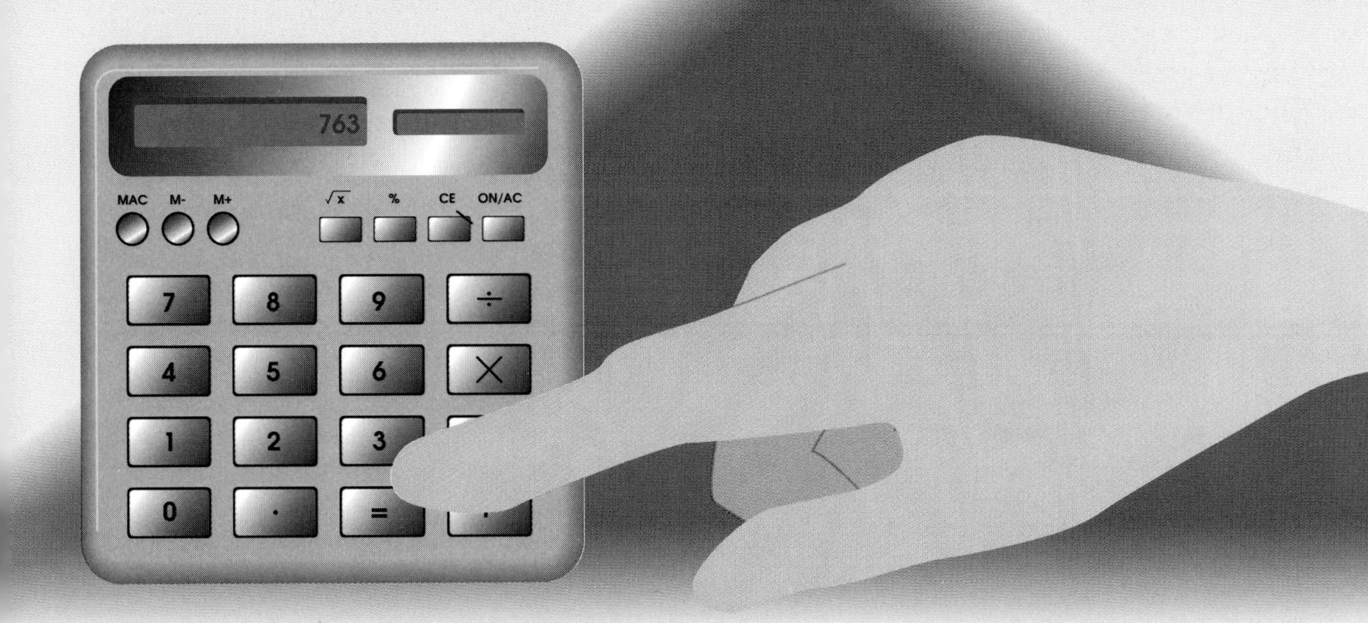


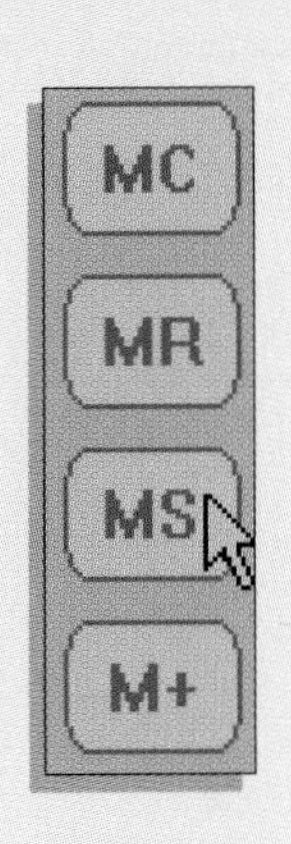


**4** The memory buttons allow you to store and reuse intermediate results in a multistep calculation. Click MS to store the current value in memory. Click MR to copy the contents of memory to the display area, where the value can be used in the current operation. Click M+ to add the currently displayed number to the value already in memory. Click MC to clear the memory. (Note that only one value can be stored in memory at a time. An M appears in the small box below the display area when there is a value in memory.)

**5** To copy the displayed value to the Clipboard, pull down the Edit menu and click Copy, or press Ctrl+C. You can then switch to another application and paste the result into a document. Switch back to Calculator when you're ready to resume work.

# How to Use Clock

Windows provides a clock for you to use alongside other applications on the desktop. There are two display modes for the clock. In *analog* mode the circular clock has hour, minute, and second hands; today's date appears in the title bar. In *digital* mode, the clock displays the time in formats like 4:42:12 AM, with the date just below the time. If you are working in an application that takes up the full screen, you can keep the clock visible on top of the desktop.

**1** To open the Clock window, double-click the program's icon in the Accessories group. The first time you start the program, the default display mode is analog.

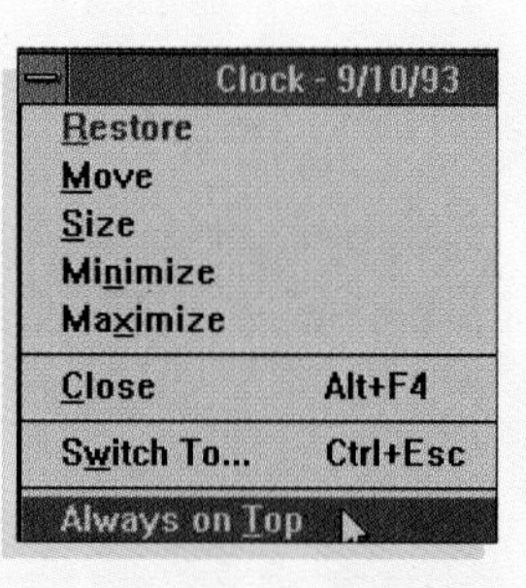


**5** Double-click the icon to restore the clock to its previous size. If you want the clock to be displayed on top of your other work on the desktop, click the control-menu box at the upper-left corner of the Clock window; then click the Always on Top command on the control menu. The clock now remains visible even when you are working in a full-screen program.

**TIP SHEET**

- **You can change the font in digital clock mode. To do so, pull down the Settings menu and click the Set Font command. Then select a font from the list and click OK.**
- **Other commands in the Settings menu allow you to display or hide the seconds and the date. You can also hide the application's title bar by clicking the No Title command. To restore the title bar, double-click inside the Clock window.**
- **To reset the time or date on the clock, open the Control Panel and double-click the Date/Time icon. Enter new settings for the date and time, and then click OK. (See "How to Change the Date and Time Settings" in Chapter 5 for more information.)**
- **To close the Clock window, double-click the program's control-menu box. The application has no Exit command.**

**2** Resize the clock window in the usual way: Position the mouse pointer over any side or corner of the application window, hold down the mouse button, and drag to reduce or increase the window's size. The clock display automatically adjusts to the new size. Drag the window by its title bar to move it to a convenient place on the desktop.

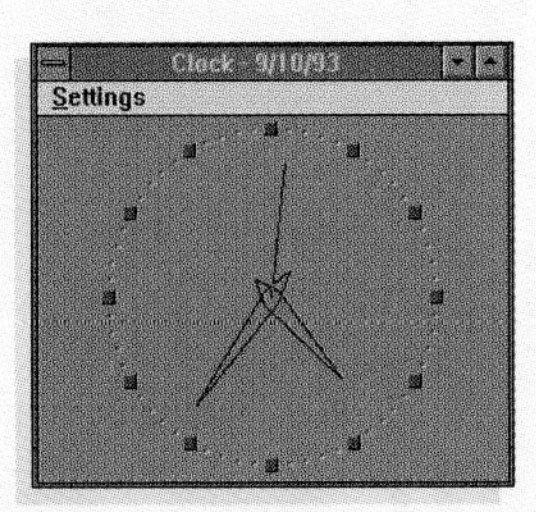


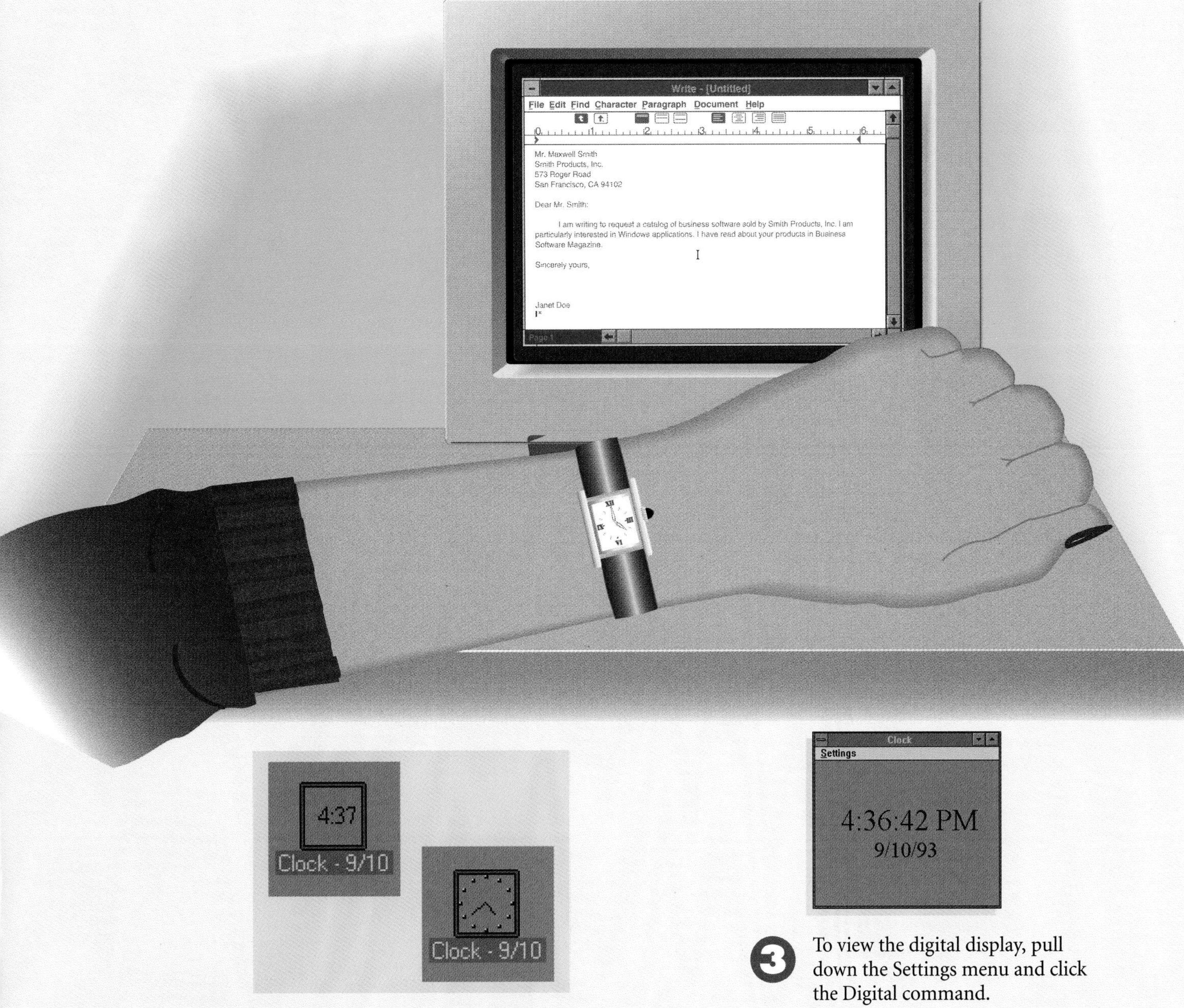


**3** To view the digital display, pull down the Settings menu and click the Digital command.

**4** Optionally, click the minimize button to reduce the clock to an icon on the desktop. In either display mode, the minimized clock still shows the time accurately.

# How to Use Notepad

In the Notepad application you can read, edit, or create files that consist solely of text. Here the word *text* generally refers to a sequence of characters that you type directly from the keyboard—uppercase and lowercase letters of the alphabet, digits from 0 to 9, punctuation, and other symbols such as #, @, and *. (Text files are sometimes called ASCII files, because each character is stored in memory as a number from the ASCII character code. A selection from this code appears in the main graphic on these pages.) Notepad files do *not* contain the formatting and typographical information typical of word processed files. This distinction is important: If you want to create a document that may include fonts, typographical effects, paragraph formats, and graphics, use Write or another word processing program. If you want to read or create a file that contains only lines of unformatted text, Notepad is the right choice.

Although the default extension for files you create in Notepad is .TXT, you may sometimes want to use the program to read files that have other extensions.

**TIP SHEET**

- **The end of each line in a text file is marked by a sequence of two ASCII characters, known as the carriage return (ASCII 13) and the line feed (ASCII 10). When you press Enter at the end of a line in Notepad, these two characters are added to the file.**
- **To enter the current time and date into a text file, pull down the Edit menu and click the Time/Date command, or press F5.**
- **The Search menu contains commands that allow you to find specific segments of text in an open Notepad file.**

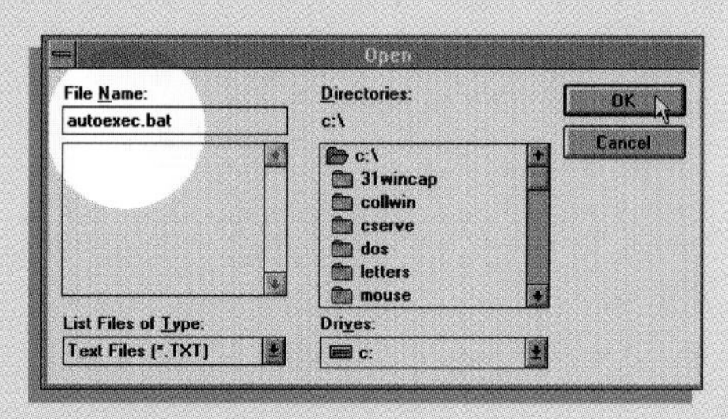


**2** To open an existing text file from disk, pull down the File menu and click the Open command. Then type the name of the file you want to open. (For a .TXT file, you do not need to type the extension name; for other files, include the full name and extension.) If necessary, use the Directories box to switch to a new directory; double-click the name of the directory that contains the file, and then click OK to open the file.

**1** To open the Notepad window, double-click the program's icon in the Accessories group. When the window first appears on the desktop, the application's work area is empty except for the flashing vertical insertion point.

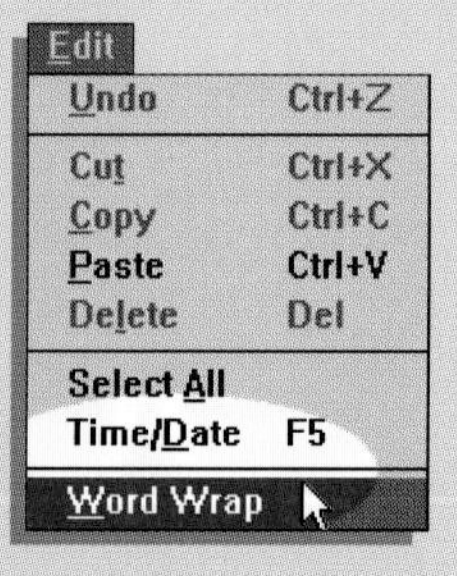


**6** If your text file contains long individual lines of text, pull down the Edit menu and click the Word Wrap command. Notepad then breaks the text into smaller lines that you can view within the dimensions of the application window. This option affects only the display of your text; no actual line break is added to your file unless you press the Enter key.

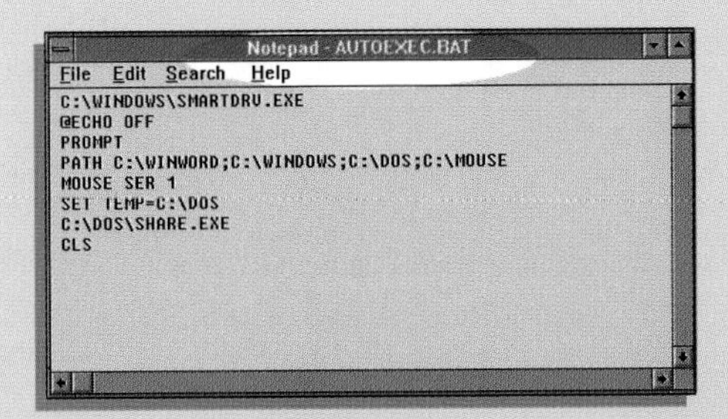


**3** The text of the file appears in the Notepad work area. You can now revise the text in any way. For example, you can delete characters by positioning the insertion point and pressing Backspace to delete characters before the insertion point, or Delete to remove characters after the insertion point. Insert new lines by moving the insertion point to the end of the preceding line and pressing Enter.

Notepad - TXT

File Edit Search Help

```
32      51 3    70 F    89 Y    108 l
33 !    52 4    71 G    90 Z    109 m
34 "    53 5    72 H    91 [    110 n
35 #    54 6    73 I    92 \    111 o
36 $    55 7    74 J    93 ]    112 p
37 %    56 8    75 K    94 ^    113 q
38 &    57 9    76 L    95 –    114 r
39 '    58 :    77 M    96 `    115 s
40 (    59 ;    78 N    97 a    116 t
41 )    60 <    79 0    89 b    117 u
42 *    61 =    80 P    99 c    118 v
43 +    62 >    81 Q    100 d   119 w
44 ,    63 ?    82 R    101 e   120 x
45 -    64 @    83 S    102 f   121 y
46 .    65 A    84 T    103 g   122 z
47 /    66 B    85 U    104 h   123 {
48 0    67 C    86 V    105 i   124 |
49 1    68 D    87 W    106 j   125 }
50 2    69 E    88 X    107 k   126 ~
```

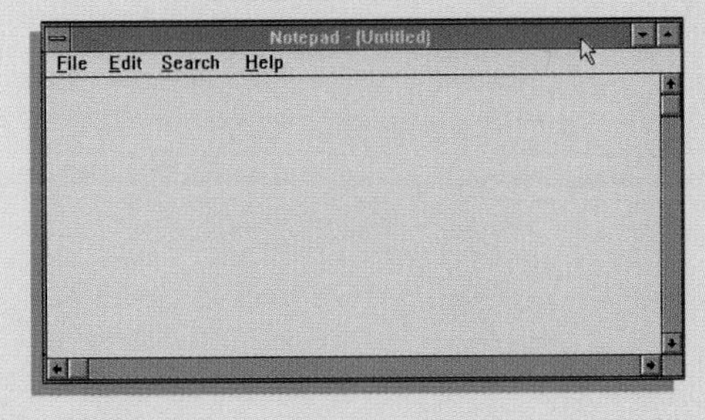

**4** To save the changes you've made, pull down the File menu and click Save. To print a copy of the current file, pull down the File menu and click Print. Printing begins immediately.

**5** To clear the current file from the Notepad window and start a new file, pull down the File menu and click New. You can then begin typing new lines of text. Press Enter at the end of each line.

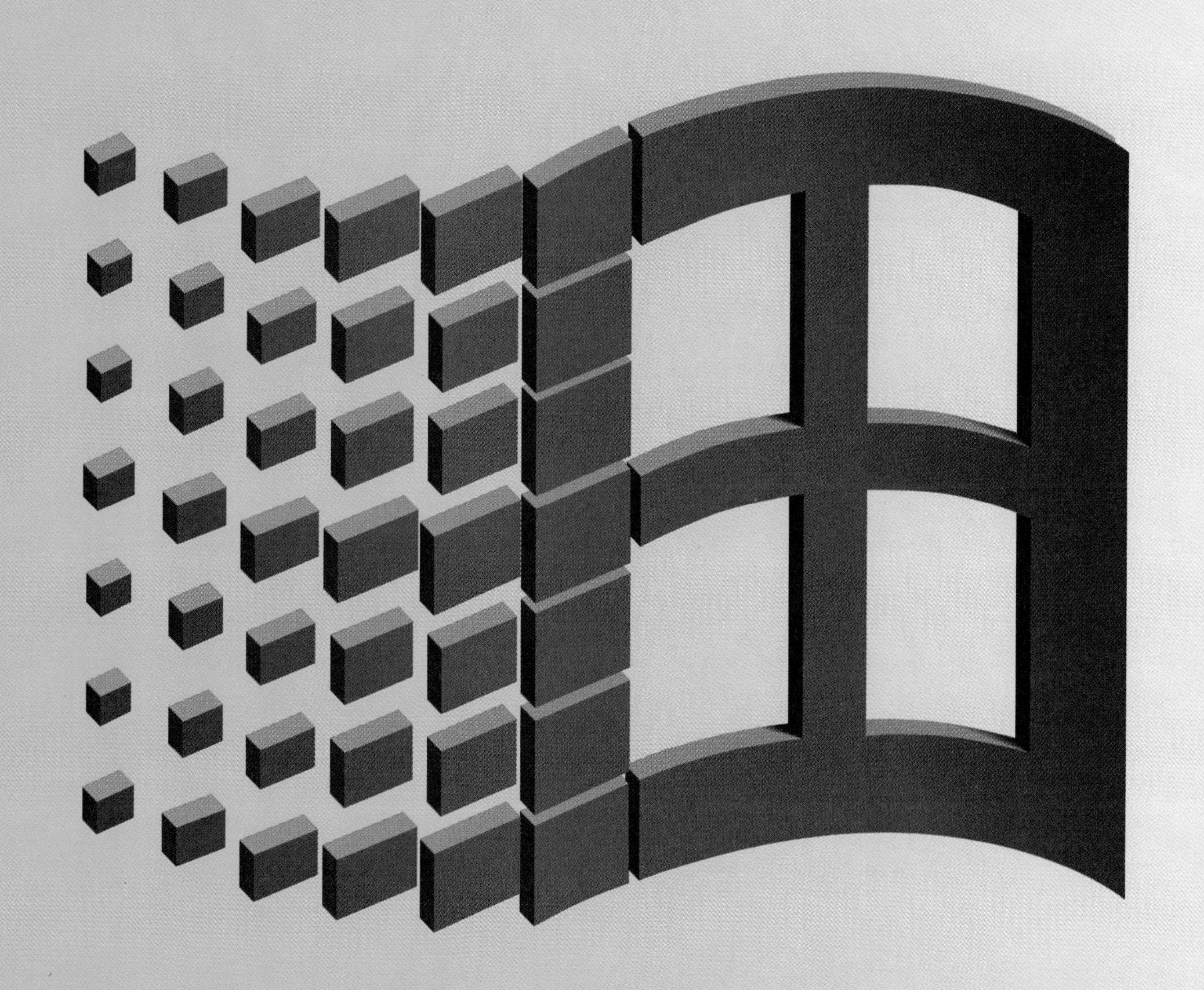

## CHAPTER 14

# MS-DOS Prompt

As personal computers continue to gain power and speed, the performance of Windows improves dramatically. Given a 486-based computer with sufficient RAM, a major Windows application can now operate as quickly and efficiently as its DOS equivalent. Accordingly, you may soon find yourself using Windows for nearly all the work you do on your computer.

Still, you probably have a few favorite DOS programs that you'll always return to from time to time. The MS-DOS Prompt icon in the Main group conveniently allows you to start a DOS session while Windows is running. During this session you can run a program or execute a sequence of commands such as DIR or COPY. You can also switch the session into a window of its own and use the Clipboard to copy information from DOS to Windows applications. When you exit from the session, the DOS window closes and you continue with your other work on the desktop.

In this final chapter you'll explore the MS-DOS Prompt facility and begin examining some of its uses.

# How to Run DOS Programs in Windows

The MS-DOS Prompt icon in the Main group allows you to return to the DOS prompt without leaving Windows. From DOS, you can view directory lists, copy files, run programs, or perform other DOS-based operations. If you use Windows in the 386 enhanced mode, you can even run MS-DOS Prompt in its own application window. This allows you to work with DOS operations and Windows applications side-by-side on the desktop. (See the Tip Sheet on this page for information about Windows modes.)

**1** To start a DOS session, double-click the MS-DOS Prompt icon in the Main group of the Program Manager window.

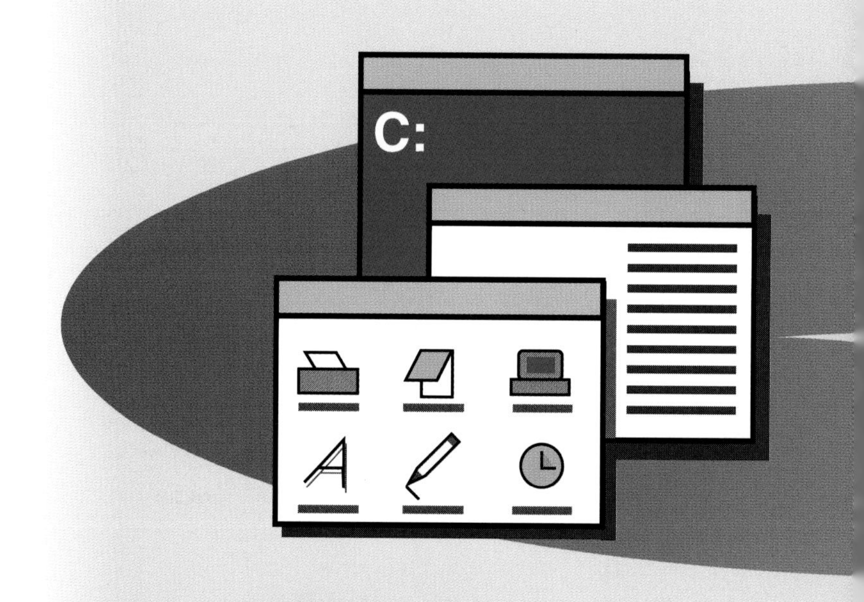

**7** To close MS-DOS Prompt, activate the window and type **exit** from the DOS prompt; press Enter to complete the command. The MS-DOS Prompt window disappears from the desktop.

## TIP SHEET

- **You can display MS-DOS Prompt in its own window only if you are running Windows in 386 enhanced mode. To find out which Windows mode you are in—386 enhanced or standard mode—pull down the Help menu in the Program Manager, and click About Program Manager. The mode is identified near the bottom of the resulting dialog box. If you are in standard mode, you can use MS-DOS Prompt only as a full-screen display.**
- **Don't use UNDELETE or CHKDSK /F from MS-DOS Prompt. These DOS commands can interfere with Windows.**
- **When you first installed Windows on your computer, icons for some DOS programs may have been placed in the Applications group. To start one of these programs, open the group and double-click the appropriate icon.**

**2** The Windows desktop temporarily disappears, and you see the DOS prompt on the screen. Read the box of instructions above the DOS prompt; they tell you how to return to Windows or switch to a Windows application. You can now enter DOS commands or run programs from the DOS prompt. For example, you might enter the DIR command to list a selection of files in the current directory. (There are some DOS commands that you should not try to use while Windows is running. See the Tip Sheet for details.)

**3** To display MS-DOS Prompt in its own application window, hold down the Alt key and press Enter. (This is possible only in 386 enhanced mode.) Windows reappears, and MS-DOS Prompt becomes a window on the desktop, which you can now view alongside your other work.

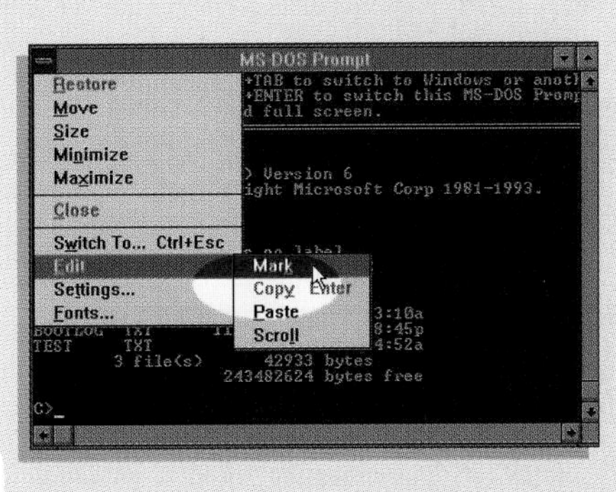


**4** To copy information from DOS to a Windows application, pull down the control menu in the MS-DOS Prompt window and click the Edit command. On the resulting cascading menu, click the Mark command.

**5** Use the mouse to highlight the DOS information you want to transfer; then click the right mouse button to copy the information to the Windows Clipboard.

**6** Now start the Windows application to which you want to transfer the information, and press Ctrl+V to paste from the Clipboard.

# INDEX

## A



## B



## C

# D

## E

## I



## J



## K



## L



## M

## X

*Cut Here*

*Cut Here*

## Ziff-Davis Press Survey of Readers

Please help us in our effort to produce the best books on personal computing. For your assistance, we would be pleased to send you a FREE catalog featuring the complete line of Ziff-Davis Press books.

1. How did you first learn about this book?

Recommended by a friend . . . . . . . . . . . . . . ☐ -1 (5)
Recommended by store personnel . . . . . . . . ☐ -2
Saw in Ziff-Davis Press catalog . . . . . . . . . . . ☐ -3
Received advertisement in the mail . . . . . . . ☐ -4
Saw the book on bookshelf at store . . . . . . . ☐ -5
Read book review in: ________________ ☐ -6
Saw an advertisement in: ______________ ☐ -7
Other (Please specify): ________________ ☐ -8

2. Which THREE of the following factors most influenced your decision to purchase this book? (Please check up to THREE.)

Front or back cover information on book . . . ☐ -1 (6)
Logo of magazine affiliated with book . . . . . ☐ -2
Special approach to the content . . . . . . . . . . ☐ -3
Completeness of content . . . . . . . . . . . . . . . . ☐ -4
Author's reputation. . . . . . . . . . . . . . . . . . . . ☐ -5
Publisher's reputation . . . . . . . . . . . . . . . . . ☐ -6
Book cover design or layout . . . . . . . . . . . . . ☐ -7
Index or table of contents of book . . . . . . . . ☐ -8
Price of book . . . . . . . . . . . . . . . . . . . . . . . . ☐ -9
Special effects, graphics, illustrations . . . . . . ☐ -0
Other (Please specify): ________________ ☐ -x

3. How many computer books have you purchased in the last six months? _____ (7-10)

4. On a scale of 1 to 5, where 5 is excellent, 4 is above average, 3 is average, 2 is below average, and 1 is poor, please rate each of the following aspects of this book below. (Please circle your answer.)

| | | | | | | |
|---|---|---|---|---|---|---|
| Depth/completeness of coverage | 5 | 4 | 3 | 2 | 1 | (11) |
| Organization of material | 5 | 4 | 3 | 2 | 1 | (12) |
| Ease of finding topic | 5 | 4 | 3 | 2 | 1 | (13) |
| Special features/time saving tips | 5 | 4 | 3 | 2 | 1 | (14) |
| Appropriate level of writing | 5 | 4 | 3 | 2 | 1 | (15) |
| Usefulness of table of contents | 5 | 4 | 3 | 2 | 1 | (16) |
| Usefulness of index | 5 | 4 | 3 | 2 | 1 | (17) |
| Usefulness of accompanying disk | 5 | 4 | 3 | 2 | 1 | (18) |
| Usefulness of illustrations/graphics | 5 | 4 | 3 | 2 | 1 | (19) |
| Cover design and attractiveness | 5 | 4 | 3 | 2 | 1 | (20) |
| Overall design and layout of book | 5 | 4 | 3 | 2 | 1 | (21) |
| Overall satisfaction with book | 5 | 4 | 3 | 2 | 1 | (22) |

5. Which of the following computer publications do you read regularly; that is, 3 out of 4 issues?

Byte . . . . . . . . . . . . . . . . . . . . . . . . . . . . . . . . ☐ -1 (23)
Computer Shopper . . . . . . . . . . . . . . . . . . . . ☐ -2
Corporate Computing . . . . . . . . . . . . . . . . . . ☐ -3
Dr. Dobb's Journal . . . . . . . . . . . . . . . . . . . . ☐ -4
LAN Magazine . . . . . . . . . . . . . . . . . . . . . . . ☐ -5
MacWEEK . . . . . . . . . . . . . . . . . . . . . . . . . . ☐ -6
MacUser . . . . . . . . . . . . . . . . . . . . . . . . . . . ☐ -7
PC Computing . . . . . . . . . . . . . . . . . . . . . . . ☐ -8
PC Magazine . . . . . . . . . . . . . . . . . . . . . . . . ☐ -9
PC WEEK . . . . . . . . . . . . . . . . . . . . . . . . . . ☐ -0
Windows Sources . . . . . . . . . . . . . . . . . . . . . ☐ -x
Other (Please specify): ________________ ☐ -y

**Please turn page.**

Cut Here

Cut Here

PLEASE TAPE HERE ONLY—DO NOT STAPLE

6. What is your level of experience with personal computers? With the subject of this book?

| | With PCs | | With subject of book | |
|---|---|---|---|---|
| Beginner | ☐ | -1 (24) | ☐ | -1 (25) |
| Intermediate | ☐ | -2 | ☐ | -2 |
| Advanced | ☐ | -3 | ☐ | -3 |

7. Which of the following best describes your job title?

| | | |
|---|---|---|
| Officer (CEO/President/VP/owner) | ☐ | -1 (26) |
| Director/head | ☐ | -2 |
| Manager/supervisor | ☐ | -3 |
| Administration/staff | ☐ | -4 |
| Teacher/educator/trainer | ☐ | -5 |
| Lawyer/doctor/medical professional | ☐ | -6 |
| Engineer/technician | ☐ | -7 |
| Consultant | ☐ | -8 |
| Not employed/student/retired | ☐ | -9 |
| Other (Please specify): ________________ | ☐ | -0 |

8. What is your age?

| | | |
|---|---|---|
| Under 20 | ☐ | -1 (27) |
| 21-29 | ☐ | -2 |
| 30-39 | ☐ | -3 |
| 40-49 | ☐ | -4 |
| 50-59 | ☐ | -5 |
| 60 or over | ☐ | -6 |

9. Are you:

| | | |
|---|---|---|
| Male | ☐ | -1 (28) |
| Female | ☐ | -2 |

Thank you for your assistance with this important information! Please write your address below to receive our free catalog.

Name: ______________________________

Address: ______________________________

City/State/Zip: ______________________________

**Fold here to mail.**

1900-13-08

NO POSTAGE NECESSARY IF MAILED IN THE UNITED STATES

**BUSINESS REPLY MAIL**

FIRST CLASS MAIL PERMIT NO. 1612 OAKLAND, CA

POSTAGE WILL BE PAID BY ADDRESSEE

**Ziff-Davis Press**
5903 Christie Avenue
Emeryville, CA 94608-1925
Attn: Marketing

ZIFF-DAVIS ZD PRESS